CLARENDON LAW SERIES

Edited by

PETER BIRKS

CLARENDON LAW SERIES

THE CONFLICT OF LAWS

ADRIAN BRIGGS

St Edmund Hall,
University of Oxford

OXFORD
UNIVERSITY PRESS

OXFORD
UNIVERSITY PRESS

Great Clarendon Street, Oxford OX2 6DP

Oxford University Press is a department of the University of Oxford.
It furthers the University's objective of excellence in research, scholarship,
and education by publishing worldwide in

Oxford New York

Athens Auckland Bangkok Bogotá Buenos Aires Cape Town
Chennai Dar es Salaam Delhi Florence Hong Kong Istanbul Karachi
Kolkata Kuala Lumpur Madrid Melbourne Mexico City Mumbai Nairobi
Paris São Paulo Shanghai Taipei Tokyo Toronto Warsaw

with associated companies in Berlin Ibadan

Oxford is a registered trade mark of Oxford University Press
in the UK and in certain other countries

Published in the United States
by Oxford University Press Inc., New York

British Library Cataloguing in Publication Data

Data available

Library of Congress Cataloging in Publication Data

Data available

ISBN 0–19–925115–0 (hbk)
ISBN 0–19–876333–6 (pbk)

1 3 5 7 9 10 8 6 4 2

Typeset in Ehrhardt
by RefineCatch Limited, Bungay, Suffolk
Printed in Great Britain by
Biddles Ltd.,
Guildford and King's Lynn

Preface

The challenging aim of this modest book is to describe English private international law at the beginning of a new century, and to do so in a way which may make this rewarding discipline accessible, maybe even enticing, to those who have not been here before. More experienced hands may find the occasional sideways (but, I hope, not cross-eyed) look at some old orthodoxies, but the book is not written with them first in mind. Within the tight word limit imposed on this series, this is quite a task.

Two-fifths of the space is claimed by the law on civil jurisdiction and the recognition of foreign judgments. Anyone who thinks that this is too much is free to blame the courts. Choice of law is not dead, but one could hardly claim that it is vibrant: the House of Lords produces judgments on choice of law only once in a blue moon. When the world loses its fascination with jurisdictional issues—something it shows no sign of doing anyday soon—it will be time to write a different book; but the broad issue of jurisdiction is where today's litigators focus their attention. Today's conflict of laws must look very odd to those who introduced me to it. One can debate whether its new look is progress or regression, but it is reality. Much the same may be said of the manner in which the institutions of the European Union have finally worn down those who cannot see why the completion of the single market requires a uniform conflict of laws. Ten years after the Rome Convention, there is little evidence of French shoppers piling onto Eurostar every Saturday to buy their televisions in Tottenham Court Road, fortified as they are by uniform choice of law rules for contractual claims. Yet Brussels believes nothing if it does not believe that one size fits all; and the concreting over of the common law conflict of laws is the one activity which never seems to require an environmental impact assessment.

The pleasure of thanking those who have helped the writing process is a sweet one. Within Oxford, my enduring debt to Ed Peel (fellow combatant in the struggle to keep the conflicts flag flying in Oxford, and who read the manuscript) and to Derrick Wyatt (the colleague without whose patient enthusiasm I would have been utterly swamped by the waves of new Council Regulations), is happy and is gratefully acknowledged. And though he will tell me not to, I add my thanks to the General Editor of this series, Peter Birks, whose selflessness in the encouragement of others knows no charted bounds. In the outside world, Oliver Parker, of the Lord Chancellor's Department, was always and patiently willing to help with news of impending legislation. Further afield, friends and fellow travellers in Brisbane, Sydney, and Singapore sustained me with aid and comfort of every kind. They know who they are, but in this modern world are entitled to respect for their privacy. Their support is, and was at all material times, invaluable.

But much the greatest debt of gratitude is owed to the past and present Deans of the Faculty of Law of the National University of Singapore, Chin Tet Yung and Tan Cheng Han, and to the youthful academic community of the Faculty, for providing so welcoming an environment (and air-conditioning of a ferocity which would put the average refrigerated container to shame) in the spring of 2001. Their open-handedness to a self-inflicting visitor, courteous efficiency in all things, and cheerful conversation and lively company meant that the Faculty was a stimulating and rejuvenating place to work and to be. This made happily achievable what would have otherwise remained a hopeless impossibility. The first draft of this account was started and completed during all too short a sojourn at NUS, and the finishing touches were applied during a brief return visit; and if this book has any virtue my temporary, and much missed, colleagues in Singapore have joint tenure of it.

The law is described as it appeared to me on 28 August 2001, except that the material on jurisdiction and foreign judgments is written as though all the jurisdictional legislation which takes effect on 1 March 2002 were already in force. Though the serial number of the Civil Jurisdiction and Judgments Order 2001 is, at the date of writing, not yet assigned, it will be possible to fill in this blank by visiting http://www.legislation.hmso.gov.uk/stat.htm. Or by alternative means.

ADRIAN BRIGGS

Singapore, 28 August 2001

Contents

Decisions of National Courts

Decisions of the European Court of Justice

United Kingdom Legislation

EU Legislation

Directives

International Agreements and Conventions

I

The Structure of the Subject

THE NATURE OF THE SUBJECT

The cover of this book states that it is concerned with the conflict of laws. As an illustration of the proposition that a book should never be judged by its cover, this can hardly be bettered. For our subject has nothing to do with conflict, legal or otherwise. In the chapters which follow, our fields of inquiry will be three in number. First, we will examine the rules which define whether an English court has jurisdiction to hear a claim where one or more of the parties, or some other aspect of the story, may be foreign to England or to English law.[1] Secondly, we will see to what extent a foreign judgment may have an effect in the English legal order.[2] And thirdly, we will consider those rules, 'choice of law rules', which tell an English court, hearing a case with a foreign element, whether to apply English or a foreign law or a combination of laws to resolve the dispute.[3]

The traditional name for this collection of material is the conflict of laws, because in the third category just mentioned there may be a conflict between the answers which would be given by the various potentially applicable systems of law: a conflict of laws. Whether this name was ever apt is debatable,[4] but it can only ever have made sense when the subject was predominantly concerned with the question of choice of law: whether a claim for damages for breach of contract was governed by English or French law; whether an alleged tort was governed by English or German law; whether the succession to an estate was governed by English or Spanish law; whether the validity of a marriage or effectiveness of a divorce was governed by English or Mexican law, and so on. These were the questions which dominated the subject in the period of its classical development, from the middle of the nineteenth to the middle

---

[1] Chap. 3.   [2] Chap. 4.   [3] Chaps. 5–10.

[4] Dr Morris considered that it was not: Dicey's *Conflict of Laws* (6th edn., Stevens, London, 1949), at p. 7, a view endorsed by the majority of the High Court of Australia in *John Pfeiffer Pty. Ltd.* v. *Rogerson* (2000) 172 ALR 625, [2000] HCA 36, at para. [43].

of the twentieth centuries. But in recent years this emphasis has been lost. For one thing, there has been substantial legislation, which has diminished the domain of the conflict of laws as traditionally understood. But much more important has become the question whether the English courts have and will exercise jurisdiction in a given case, at least if a count of reported cases is any guide. This has cast the science of choice of law into deep, and possibly permanent, shade. The principal reason for the former development is the harmonization of European law, and the perception, more apparent to some than to others, that the rich diversity of national choice of laws rules is an impediment to the completion of the single market. The principal reason for the latter is the realization that the question where a trial takes place is of critical importance to the outcome of litigation; that once parties have skirmished on the question of jurisdiction the case may well settle; and a consequential development and refinement of the law on jurisdiction.

One can improve on the nomenclature of the conflict of laws. The traditional secondary title, private international law, takes a step in the right direction, for the subject matter is almost entirely private law, and its concern is with international elements and points of contact. And it is under the label of *droit international privé* that French lawyers think about our subject. But this title may suggest that there is a relationship with public international law, which describes or regulates relations between states; and this would be misleading. Very little public international law infiltrates the subject. For example, when dealing with the confiscation or nationalization of private property by states, there may well be rules of public international law which specify whether the property of a foreign citizen may be seized, whether compensation has to be paid, and so forth. But the conflict of laws has no concern with this: as long as the property was within the territory of the seizing state, the title acquired by seizure will usually be effective in private international law, whatever public international law may say about the steps taken. Nor is there a private international law of crime, an archetypal matter of public law: the international aspect of criminal law is dealt with by specific local legislation, or by extradition.

But 'international private law' is accurate and, it is thought, helpful; it is also reflected in the German conception of the subject, as *internazionales Privatrecht*. It concerns private law—the law of contracts, torts, property, status—in those contexts when a foreign element may be present within the factual matrix. One day a writer in the English language will publish a book under this title and, when this happens, the label will, once again, describe the contents of the box. But this has not happened yet.

The body of the conflict of laws is made up of statute and case law. In two respects the source material is, however, distinctively different. First, much of the common law conflict of laws has been overlaid with legislation; and of this by far the largest part is legislation attributable to the United Kingdom's membership of the European Union. Secondly, the influence of two textbooks is peculiarly and distinctively noticeable: Dicey and Morris's *The Conflict of Laws*[5] and, to a lesser extent, Cheshire and North's *Private International Law*,[6] tend to be treated by the judiciary as authoritative to a degree still unusual in England.

THE APPLICATION OF FOREIGN LAW BY AN ENGLISH JUDGE

The principal characteristic of the conflict of laws is that it will some-times lead to a judge being asked to apply foreign law to the dispute.[7] In the ordinary course, an English judge will apply English domestic law: common law, equity, and statute. He will apply only English law, and cannot and will not apply a foreign law, to a question unless four condi-tions are satisfied. First, the choice of law rules of English law must tell him that a foreign law is in principle applicable to the issue in question; secondly, he is not prohibited from doing so by English legislation; thirdly, the party who relies on foreign law must plead and establish its applicability; and, fourthly, the party relying on foreign law must adduce evidence which proves its content to the satisfaction of the court. Meeting these four conditions means that the judge will be enabled and obliged to apply a rule of foreign law.

As regards the first point, we will consider in Chapters 4 to 9 the rules of choice of law which may lead a judge to the point where he may be required to apply a foreign law: he may deduce that the law which gov-erns a contract is French law, or that the law applicable to an alleged tort is German law. As regards the second point, however, in certain cases the rules of choice of law may be overridden by English legislation which supervenes to prevent the application of a foreign law. So, for example, a contract admittedly governed by French law may contain a provision limiting or excluding the liability of the defendant in circumstances

---

[5] Currently the 13th edn. (Sweet & Maxwell, London, 2000).
[6] Currently the 13th edn. (Butterworths, London, 1999).
[7] See generally R. Fentiman, *Foreign Law in English Courts* (OUP, Oxford, 1998).

where this would not be permitted were the contract governed by English law. In such a case, English legislation may stipulate that the rules of English law on exemption clauses are to be applied even though English law is not otherwise the governing law.[8] This being so, the judge will, to that extent, be precluded from applying foreign law.

As regards the third point, the party or parties seeking to rely on foreign law must plead its applicability. The consequence of this is that if neither party does, the judge will be obliged to apply English domestic law to the issues in dispute. The judge has neither right nor power to apply foreign law *ex officio*. So in the example of personal injury or damage to property taking place overseas, the claimant may consider that the law of the place where he was injured affords him a cause of action, whereas English domestic law would not: he will be well advised to plead the applicability of foreign law to the claim.[9] Again, the defendant may consider that the law of the place where the alleged tort happened furnishes him with a defence which would not be available to him as a matter of English law: he will be well advised to plead the applicability of foreign law to the claim so as to rely on foreign law in his defence. But neither party is obliged to do this, and a judge will therefore be obliged to apply English domestic law when the parties do not invoke foreign law. According to the English way of thinking, this is so even when an international convention stipulates that an issue *shall* be governed by a particular law.[10] As a matter of observable fact, the great majority of overseas tort cases will be decided by reference to English law. This may reflect the truism that the principles of the law of obligations are all pretty similar, meaning that there is little point in proving foreign law; and it may also be driven by the practical problems of actually establishing the rules and effect of foreign law, as will be seen below. However, it results in English private international law taking a pragmatic, rather than dogmatic, view of the role of the courts: the parties are entitled to establish a common position on the applicability or not of foreign law, and once they have done that, it is not for a judge to take a contrary view. Now in so far as the court is called on to adjudicate a matter in the law of obligations, this is perfectly justified: the question whether a contract was valid or broken, or whether

---

[8] e.g., Unfair Contract Terms Act 1977, s. 27(2).

[9] Private International Law (Miscellaneous Provisions) Act 1995, s. 11(2)(a).

[10] One might say that the foreign law *is* in fact being applied, on the footing that it is taken to be the same as English law until the court finds differently. But this conspicuous sleight of hand is not convincing; and there is an argument, occasionally heard from the continent, that the English approach is in formal conflict with the particular conventions.

a defendant was the victim of negligence or *volens* to the risk, is a matter of interest to the two parties alone,[11] and if they agree to the application of English domestic law to their dispute, there is no third party interest to disagree with this. But in cases where the court is called on to decide an issue with an effect *in rem*, such as whether V conferred good title to a car on P, or whether H and W were validly married, this stance is less attractive, for a ruling on status may well be relevant to non-parties, such as a subsequent purchaser or an intending spouse. In this context the decision of the original parties to have an adjudication by reference only to English domestic law affects other interested persons who were not privy to the agreement. Yet English law has never taken the view that in questions of status the court is obliged to apply foreign law in defiance of the wishes of the litigants.

As regards the fourth point, the content and effect of an applicable foreign law are a matter of fact, to be proved by the parties as a question of fact.[12] Every pleaded proposition of fact requires to be proved; and as foreign law is a question of fact, evidence will have to be given by experts, usually one for each side and evaluated by the judge.[13] Expertise in foreign law is, however, easier to describe than to define. There is no fixed category of individuals who are qualified, still less authorized, to give such evidence to an English court; there is no reliable way to evaluate the expert or his evidence; it may not be clear whether an expert's knowledge is practical and up to date. Nor is it always clear whether the content of a foreign law as derived from statute and code is in every respect consistent with the result which would result from its application by a foreign judge: and anyway, does Ruritanian law mean the law as derived from the written sources of Ruritanian law or the outcome which would be reached by a Ruritanian judge in his application of it? The answer appears to be that the expert is required to testify to what the law means, if this is distinct from what the legislative text appears to say. The fact that an expert has written books may still mean that he has little or no practical experience of how the law he has described would be applied in a court; the fact that

---

[11] And their insurers. But for the view that the court is not invariably obliged to accept that foreign law is the same as local law, see *Damberg* v *Damberg* [2001] NSWCA 87, 25 May 2001, not yet reported.

[12] It might be thought to follow that a finding on the state of foreign law is not subject to reversal on appeal, unless the primary judge's conclusion was so unreasonable that no judge could properly have reached the conclusion he did. But it is said that foreign law is a fact of a rather peculiar kind, and that, as a result, appeals are more frequent, and the substitution of an appellate court's own conclusion more common, than its formal status as a question of fact might suggest.

[13] See generally *Glencore International AG* v. *Metro Trading Inc.* [2001] 1 Lloyd's Rep. 283.

an expert is a lawyer in private practice or judicial office may nevertheless leave him wholly unsuitable to give evidence of an area of law of which he has no direct experience. An English judge may be more impressed by the reported decisions of a foreign court than a local court would be; it may be less persuaded by the writings of scholars than a foreign court would be. These are not trivial points, for as English private international law has committed itself to this particular view, it is legitimate to question whether the approach is suitable for the ends it is designed to serve. There are several cases in which the judge has had to pick his way through subtly conflicting bodies of evidence of foreign law, with the result that one may applaud the effort yet still lack confidence in the outcome; and the financial cost to the parties can be quite disproportionate to the substance of the claim.

If the party seeking to prove the content of foreign law fails to satisfy the judge, it is sometimes said that the judge will apply the foreign law, but will do so in the sense that foreign law is taken to be the same as English law as the contrary was not proved. It is high time that such nonsense was eliminated from the discourse of the law. No-one in his right mind actually believes that this presumption is a statement of a reliable truth. In default of proof of the content of foreign law, an English judge still has to adjudicate; and his default position is that he will apply English law, *faute de mieux*. That is more than sufficient to explain why the rule or rules of English law will be applied. To purport to justify this with the presumption that the relevant foreign law just happens to be identical to English domestic law only goes to weaken the sensible answer already sufficiently justified.

The proposition that the judge may go off on a frolic of his own and inquire into foreign law for himself has no place in an English court. The same principle should serve to prevent a judge from founding on his own personal recollection of a particular foreign law,[14] even if he was trained and qualified in that system, for the law may have changed, memories are notorious for being fallible, even when bewigged, and, in any event, to arrogate to himself the privilege of the parties would be for a judge to ignore the limits on judicial power: the principle that *curia novit jus*, that the court knows the law, begins and ends with English law.

It may be thought that the practical difficulties in the English system reveal so many shortcomings that the model of other countries, in which the judge will investigate and apply foreign law as well as his own, is to be

---

[14] Examples exist, but are best left unidentified.

preferred. But this proposition does not stand up at all well to closer inspection. A national judge manifestly does not know foreign law; a report on it must be commissioned. Whether it will be possible for a court to find a competent expert from whom to obtain a report must be doubt-ful, at least where the law in question is exotic; and where the reporter will require close and detailed knowledge of the entire dispute, in order to be sure that he has seen all the issues which bear on the legal analysis, it is improbable that a court-commissioned expert will be able to do this. And even if the report is signed by an authoritative figure, the chances will be that it was researched and written by someone rather more junior. So despite the claims sometimes heard, that the continental system of prov-ing and applying foreign law is superior to the English one, the truth probably is that the application of foreign law by a judge is fraught with difficulty of a general complexity which cannot be made to go away unless the trial is made to go away. This in turn may point to the real truth, that a court should have the power to decline to hear certain cases in which it feels that a court elsewhere would be better placed to give the parties a reliable adjudication.

A final question, to which we return when examining the doctrine of *renvoi*, is what it means to apply foreign law: that is, what exactly is the judge asked to do? The common law understanding is that if a judge is called upon to apply French or Ruritanian domestic law, he should apply it as a French or Ruritanian judge would interpret it were he trying the case (or the issue, if there is more than one issue to be dealt with). In other words, 'French law' means 'French domestic law as a local judge would apply it'. If he would apply this rule to this particular contract, or would not apply that rule to that claim or claimant, then an English judge, in applying foreign law, should do likewise, for this is the truest sense in which foreign law is applied. This technique is of particular value when a court is asked to apply foreign statute law. In deciding whether and how the statute applies, the relevant question is whether, and if so to what effect, a judge in the foreign court would apply the particular statutory provision were he hearing the case. If he would not apply it to the case in question, it is, for present purposes, not part of the foreign law which an English judge may be invited to apply. So if an Australian judge would not apply a provision of the Trade Practices Act 1974 to conduct taking place outside Australia, an English court, if applying Australian law as *lex causae*, should not apply it either. If a New Zealand judge would interpret and apply the Accident Rehabilitation and Compensation Insurance Act 1992 as precluding a civil claim for damages resulting from an industrial injury, an English court, applying New Zealand law as *lex causae*, should hold that there is no civil liability under the law of New Zealand,[15] and should not be tempted to hold that whilst a New Zealand judge might be required to apply the Act, there is reason why a foreign judge need not do so. The other side of the coin is that where a statute is intended by its legislator to apply, but this is not the *lex causae*, it will be ignored by an English court. So if an English borrower and a Victorian lender enter into a contract of loan governed by English law, Victorian legislation reducing interest rates will be irrelevant to an English court, even if it was designed by the Victorian legislator to apply to the contract,[16] and even though a Victorian judge would be required by his own law to apply the Act.[17] The simple point is that where a statute is part of the *lex causae*, it should[18] be applied by the English judge, along with all other substantive provisions of the *lex causae*, in the way the foreign judge would have applied it; and if it is not part of the *lex causae* it is to be ignored.

A significant point of principle arises if the foreign judge would not have applied his own domestic law at all, but would instead have used his choice of law rules to point to a different substantive law which he would then have applied. Whether the parties are entitled to invite an English judge to go down that path depends on the impact of the doctrine of *renvoi*, which is examined below.

BASIC CHOICE OF LAW REASONING: THE FOUR ANALYTICAL TOOLS

We have seen that a judge may be asked and required to apply a foreign law in the determination of a dispute. But in any case in which he has to do so, there is a framework for the analysis, which keeps the exercise under reasonably manageable or reviewable control. We have also seen, and will frequently observe, that the grammar of the conflict of laws is assembled from propositions which connect issues to a particular law. So we say that the material validity of a contract is governed by its applicable law; liability in tort may be governed by the law of the place where the

---

[15] *James Hardie & Co. Pty. Ltd.* v. *Hall* (1998) 43 NSWLR 554 (CA); *James Hardie Industries Pty. Ltd.* v. *Grigor* (1998) 45 NSWLR 20 (CA).
[16] Cf *Mount Albert Borough Council* v. *Australasian Temperance and General Mutual Life Assurance Society* [1938] AC 224 (PC) (where the borrower was a New Zealander).
[17] *Akai Pty. Ltd.* v. *People's Insurance Co. Ltd.* (1997) 188 CLR 418.
[18] Unless there is some rule of English law which overrides and instructs the English judge to do differently.

person was when injured; the validity of a transfer of movable property is governed by the law of the place where the thing was when transferred; the capacity of an individual to marry another is governed by the law of his or her domicile at the time of the marriage; the ranking of claims and distribution of assets in an insolvency is governed by the law of the court hearing the case; and so on.

The simplicity of these propositions is deceptive, for they contain three legal ideas, and suggest a fourth. The first is the concept of an 'issue': how do we know whether to frame a question in terms of the material validity of a contract as opposed to its formal validity, or just its validity? How do we know whether to frame a question in terms of the capacity of persons to marry as opposed to the validity of the marriage? The answer is that we *characterize* an issue, or issues, as being presented for decision. The second is the concept of a law: how do we know whether the applicable law means the domestic law of the relevant country, or (if this is different) the law which would be applied by a judge in that country were he hearing the case himself? How do we know whether the law of the domicile means the domestic law of the country in which the person is domiciled or (if this is different) the law which would be applied by a judge in that country were he hearing the case himself? The answer is that the principles of *renvoi* tell us whether our rule of decision is one pointing to a domestic law only or includes a reference to the private international law rules of that country. The third is this: suppose the facts are characterized as giving rise to two issues, each having a choice of law rule, and for each of which English law and the foreign law would pre-scribe different solutions. Do we approach them independently, and try to combine the answers at the end, or does one play a dominant role, applying its rules to the determination of the other issue? The answer is that this raises the *incidental question*, to which a solution must be found. Fourth and last is the identification of the point of connection: what actually is the applicable law, or the domicile, or the relevant place for the purpose of one of these 'law of the . . .' rules? The answer is that these are the *connecting factors*, and the principles which determine their nature will answer the question for us. These four elements of the choice of law process now need to be examined.

CHARACTERIZATION OF ISSUES

As a choice of law rule is formulated by reference to connecting factors, this requires that the facts be accommodated within one, or perhaps more, legal categories to which a choice of law rule may be applied. The definition of these categories, and the location of facts within them, comprises the process of characterization.[19]

Both aspects of the process of characterization are undertaken by reference to English law: the available categories are those created by English private international law; and the placing of the facts within one or more of them is done according to English private international law: for those who find analogies helpful, English law designs the pigeonholes, and an English sorter decides which facts belong in which pigeonhole. This exercise has to be undertaken by reference to English law, for at this stage we are far from having explained why, still less which, foreign law is going to be relevant.

As regards the definitional list of the available categories or characterizations, these are established in part by authority, and in part by principle.[20] As we look at different substantive areas of law we will identify them: the capacity to contract, the proprietary effect of a transfer, the formal validity of marriage, the capacity of a corporation to do an act, and so on. Though the categories are established, there is no reason in principle why the law may not develop a new one, and every reason why it should. So, for example, it has been proposed that the category of essential validity of marriage should be broken down into capacity to marry and the quintessential validity of marriage, for which separate choice of laws rules would be prescribed;[21] it has been proposed that the category of capacity to marry should be broken down into the capacity to contract a polygamous marriage and the remainder of capacity to marry.[22] And again, the choice of law rules for the transfer of intangible moveables may yet divide so that certain complex cases, as arise in the system for indirect holding of financial instruments, are dealt with separately from other intangibles. It is to be expected that the process of change in this context will be slow and measured: the certainty of the law will be damaged if new categories are created more or less at will. Moreover, the need which this process addresses could also be met by making exceptions in individual cases, rather than by the creation of new categories of general application. For all that, it is clear that the creation of new characterization categories is not impossible, but is sometimes overdue. For example, there may still be a characterization category for equitable claims, for which the choice

---

[19] Dicey & Morris, above n. 5, chap. 2.
[20] *Raiffeisen Zentralbank Österreich AG* v. *Five Star Trading LLC* [2001] CA Civ. 68, [2001] 2 WLR 1344.
[21] *Vervaeke* v. *Smith* [1983] 1 AC 145.
[22] *Radwan* v. *Radwan (No 2)* [1973] Fam. 35.

of law rule is the *lex fori*, the law of the court hearing the claim. Quite apart from the point, considered below,[23] that this may not be a desirable choice of law rule, it is doubtful that 'equitable claims' represents a coherent characterization category in the first place. Similar doubts have been expressed whether there should be a characterization category for 'receipt-based restitutionary claims'.[24] Though these divisions may[25] make perfect sense as a matter of domestic English law, it does not follow that they are useful tools in the conflict of laws.

As regards whether a particular issue raised for decision in a case should be fitted into one or another of these categories, the usual explanation is that this is done by using English law as the point of departure, and treating an issue as one would treat its nearest English equivalent: the exercise is undertaken 'in a broad internationalist spirit in accordance with the principles of the conflict of laws of the forum'.[26] So, for example, an argument that a contract was unenforceable because not notarized will raise the formal validity of contracts, even though English law does not require contracts to be notarized; an argument that a promise is enforceable as a contract even though not given for consideration will raise a question of the material validity of a contract, even though English law would not see a gratuitous promise as a contract at all;[27] an action claiming damages for insult will be treated as tortious even though English domestic law knows no such tort; and a polygamous marriage will be treated as a marriage, even though English domestic law does not allow for polygamy. Occasionally this has led to a result which appears unsatisfactory. In the case[28] of a marriage celebrated in England between English and French persons, it was alleged that the marriage was invalid by reason of the lack of consent from the French parents. One[29] analysis adopted by the court was that the need for third party consent raised a question of the formal validity of a marriage, which was governed by the law of the place (England) of celebration, and under which the lack of consent was immaterial. It is argued by some that the issue should instead have been treated as one of capacity to marry and governed by the domestic law of

---

[23] Chap. 7.

[24] *Macmillan Inc* v. *Bishopsgate Investment Trust plc (No 3)* [1996] 1 WLR 387 (CA).

[25] But which is not admitted.

[26] *Raiffeisen Zentralbank Österreich AG* v. *Five Star Trading LLC* [2001] CA Civ. 68, [2001] 2 WLR 1344, at para. [27].

[27] *Re Bonacina* [1912] 2 Ch. 394.   [28] *Ogden* v. *Ogden* [1908] P 46 (CA).

[29] The other was that if the facts raised an issue of capacity, it was still governed by English law, under the principle in *Sottomayor* v. *De Barros (No 2)* (1879) 5 PD 94.

the person (French) alleged to lack marital capacity.[30] There is some
force in the alternative view, especially if the approach of the court did
reason that as third party consent is a matter of formal validity in
domestic English law it must be the same in the conflict of laws. Quite
apart from the fact that the categories of the two (domestic law, private
international law) systems have no need to be strictly congruent, it is
sensible that the allocation of an issue to one or another of the characterization categories is done with a degree of flexibility. Even so, there is
difficulty in seeing why the capacity solution is intrinsically better than
the alternative; and the truth may be that some cases are inescapably
hard ones. More novel cases can be expected in the future, as domestic
laws are refashioned and reshaped to meet changing social conditions.
In the context of family law, foreign[31] legislative provision for marriage
between persons of the same sex,[32] and the creation of legal regimes for
the registration of a civil partnership between persons whether of
opposite or the same sex,[33] will mean that the courts have to decide
whether these unions are to be characterized as marriage, or as contract,
or as founding an entirely new characterization category, in order to
provide a framework for litigation about their international validity and
effects.

As for what represents the object of characterization, the 'thing' characterized, the usual understanding is that issues, rather than rules of law,
are characterized.[34] The initial justification for this is that the language of
the subject is written in terms which connect categories of legal issue
with a choice of law. It also has the immense practical advantage that a
single law is identified as the source of the solution to the single issue. If,
by sharp contrast, one were to adopt the approach of characterizing rules
of law found in the legal systems having some connection to the dispute,
applying the one which was framed so as to apply in the given context,
one could end up with two contradictory solutions or none at all. Take
the case of marriage without parental consent, discussed above. Suppose
it had been held that the English rule that parental consent was not
required was a rule about the formal validity of marriage, and hence

[30] Though under the rule in *Sottomayor* v. *De Barros (No 2)*, above n. 29, this would not
in fact have been the outcome.
[31] Danish and Dutch, e.g.
[32] Under Danish and Dutch laws this is now provided for.
[33] As under French and German law.
[34] However, as will be seen in Chap. 2 below, the rule of private international law that an
English court will not enforce a foreign penal or revenue law will require characterization of
the particular law, and not of an issue.

applicable to a marriage taking place in England; and the French rule requiring parental consent was held to be a rule about capacity to marry, and hence applicable to the marriage of a French domiciliary. Both rules would have been 'characterized' as applicable; the results of their combined application is an impossible contradiction. Or, taking the opposite possibility in each case, each rule might have been characterized as being inapplicable. This does not seem sensible. Accordingly the judge is required to identify an issue and apply the law which governs that issue. In the only case to have confronted the issue directly,[35] a mother and daughter, both domiciled in Germany, had died in an air raid. The court was asked to decide who succeeded to the estate of the mother. It being unknown which victim died first, both English law and German law would apply a presumption: English law presuming that the older died before the younger, German law, that they died simultaneously. The judge held that he had to decide an issue of inheritance or succession, which was governed by German law and not a question of evidence governed by English law. He therefore applied the German rule. But whether he was right or wrong about this, his technique of identifying *an* issue raised by the facts is the critical point to notice. Had he simply characterized the competing rules of German and English law, he might have found that both applied or neither applied: this would have been so self-defeating that, whatever else may be said in its defence, the solution cannot be acceptable.[36]

A final question concerns exactly what happens after characterization has pointed the court to a particular law from which to find the answer. Suppose a marriage has taken place in France, without the parental consent required by the French domiciliary law of one of the parties. An English court will characterize the issue as one of formal validity, and look to French law for an answer. But an answer to what question? If the question is 'is this marriage formally valid as a matter of French law despite the absence of parental consent?', the answer may be a rather puzzled 'yes': puzzled because, in the eye of the French expert, this is the wrong question to be asking. If, by contrast, the question is 'is this marriage valid as a matter of French law despite the lack of parental consent?', the reasoning may be more complex, but the answer will be 'no': the French expert will explain that this issue is seen by French law as raising an issue of capacity, governed by the national (French) law of the

---

[35] *Re Cohn* [1945] Ch. 5.
[36] For a different view, see C. Forsyth, 'Characterisation Revisited: an Essay in the Theory and Practice of the English Conflict of Laws' (1998) 114 *LQR* 141.

allegedly incapable party, and according to which the marriage is invalid. To take another example, suppose that the requirement of consideration or a seal is regarded by English law as a matter going to the material validity of the contract, but that Italian law would regard it as relevant to the formal validity of the contract. If the law applicable to the contract is Italian, is the expert required to state his view on the material validity of the contract, or is he allowed to address the issue of seals in the very way an Italian judge would? It will be seen that the outcome of the case may well depend on the manner in which the question is formulated: put shortly, is the question as formulated for the expert to answer one expressed in and bounded by the precise terms of the characterization which led there in the first place, or is the process of characterization defunct and forgotten once it has served to make a connection to a law? The answer may well require an understanding of the principles of *renvoi*, and the suggested solution will be found at the end of the next section.

THE MEANING OF LAW: *RENVOI*

If an issue is governed by the *law* of a particular country, what is the meaning to be given to the word *law*? Does it mean the rules of domestic law, as these would apply to a wholly internal case, or does it refer to law in a wider sense, including, perhaps, the private international law rules of that legal system? This question can be formulated another way: is the issue to be resolved by applying the domestic law, or by permitting a reference on—a *renvoi*—from that law to another? The short answer is that there is no short answer: sometimes it will be the former, sometimes the latter. Which is which is in large part a matter of authority; why this represents the considered view of English private international law is more controversial.[37]

We can illustrate the operation of the principle of renvoi by taking an example. Suppose a person has died without leaving a will, and the question arises concerning succession to his estate.[38] Suppose he died domiciled in Spain, but still a British citizen. As a matter of English private international law, succession to his moveable estate would be governed by Spanish law as the law of his domicile. Suppose that according to Spanish domestic law, X would succeed to the estate, but that according to Spanish private international law, succession would be governed by the law of

[37] Dicey & Morris, above n. 5, chap. 4.
[38] For the rules on intestate succession, see Chap. 8, below.

the nationality, which would be taken to be English; and as a matter of English domestic law, Y would succeed. What is the judge to do?

He faces three possibilities, at least in principle. First, he may interpret his choice of law rule as pointing him to Spanish domestic law, and hold in favour of X. Or he may interpret his choice of law rule as pointing to Spanish law as including its rules of private international law, follow the path by which this points to English law, interpret this as meaning English domestic law, and find for Y. Or he may interpret his choice of law rule as pointing to Spanish law, follow the path by which this points to English law, interpret this as meaning English law including its conflicts rules, which point back to Spain, ask what the Spanish judge would do when informed that English law would look back to Spanish law, and accept whatever answer the Spanish judge would then give. As a matter of authority, the English judge will not take the second of these three possibilities. Sometimes he will take the first, and interpret the 'law' as meaning the domestic rules of the chosen law; but on other occasions, which include issues of succession, he will take the third, and interpret the 'law' as meaning what the foreign judge, hearing the case in the court whose law has been chosen, would do.[39] In other words, he will, so far as the evidence on the content of foreign law allows him to do so, ask what a Spanish judge would do if he were deciding the case himself, and adopt that answer as his own, whatever it may be. For this reason the English approach to *renvoi* is sometimes called the 'foreign court theory' of *renvoi*; sometimes 'total *renvoi*'; and sometimes as involving the 'impersonation' of the foreign judge. Is this not all very difficult? Should the judge not simply have applied Spanish domestic law, *malgré lui*, and left it at that?

Judges and writers have suggested so. But before looking at the authority and the arguments, it is well to be reminded that *renvoi* applies only in certain areas of private international law; and that, as the proof of foreign law lies primarily in the hands of the parties, a court will have neither need nor opportunity to examine the principles of *renvoi* unless the parties choose to raise them on the pleadings. One criticism of *renvoi*, that it makes life very difficult for the parties and for the judge, is therefore susceptible to overstatement. Another, that choice of law rules were inherently formulated, without any thought for *renvoi*, as pointers to a domestic system of law, is simply a rejection of the principle without

---

[39] *Re Annesley* [1926] Ch. 692; *Re Ross* [1930] 1 Ch. 377; *Re Askew* [1930] 2 Ch. 259; *Re Duke of Wellington* [1947] Ch. 506.

separate justification. Another, which is that *renvoi* involves the subordination of English choice of law rules to those of a foreign system, is
misconceived, particularly if English law has for its own reasons seen fit
to choose to follow a foreign court's pattern of reasoning. Yet another is
that the English 'impersonation' approach works only if the judge who is
being impersonated is not himself trying at the same time to do the very
thing which the English judge would do, which just goes to show that the
very idea is flawed.[40] But this creation of the febrile academic imagination
has never surfaced in a reported case, and would be perfectly capable of
practical solution if the need arose, by applying the principle that where
the content of foreign law has not been proved to the satisfaction of the
court, English law will be applied by default.

The arguments in favour of *renvoi* are considerably stronger. Rules of
private international law in general, and of *renvoi* in particular, are rules
of a foreign legal system: if this foreign law is selected for application, it is
odd that parts of that law are sheared off and ignored when it comes to be
applied. It may be convenient to imagine the rules of private international
law as separate and distinct, but this is a pedagogic device which may
damage the coherence and integrity of the law. If one is to apply foreign
law, it seems right to apply all of it; and equally right to apply it in the
same way, and to the same effect (so far as this is possible) as the foreign
judge would: realism teaches that the law is what a judge will say it is.
Moreover, although it may not matter very much whether X or Y succeeds to the moveable estate in our example, it would seem very strange
that an English court could consider and declare that one person is
entitled to foreign land when, as a matter of that foreign law, the register
of title will not be amended in conformity with this view. If[41] it is ever
right for an English court to make a judgment about title to foreign land,
it should surely do so in conformity with what it understands to be the
law which the local courts would themselves apply; and if this subjugates
English choice of law rules to those of another system, that is what reality
demands.

There is another justification for the general operation of the principle
of *renvoi*.[42] When applied by an English court, the aim of *renvoi* is to

---

[40] It being said that it is hardly a recommendation that the English doctrine of *renvoi*
works only if other states reject it. This is nonsense: one may as well say that one should
never hold a door open for another to pass through, for if the other person is equally polite
neither will make any progress at all.

[41] See further below, Chap. 8.

[42] See further A. Briggs, 'In Praise and Defence of Renvoi' (1998) 47 *ICLQ* 877.

ensure that the case is decided as it would be if the action were brought in the courts which are probably the closest to the facts of the dispute. Consider a case in which a claimant is injured in a traffic accident in Malta, under the domestic law of which state he would have no claim for damages for pain and suffering, but only for pecuniary losses.[43] Suppose he sues in England, hoping to rely on English law which would not so limit his claim. An English court might well consider this to be a case where the claimant is forum-shopping—suing in a court in which he has no legitimate expectation of being allowed to proceed, so as to avoid a hard judgment from the courts at the place where the action really did belong. In order to prevent this, an English court may decide to apply Maltese law, as the law of the place where the tort occurred; but to accomplish what it sets out to achieve, it will have to interpret 'Maltese law' as meaning that law—all of it, including its conflicts rules—which a Maltese court would have brought to bear on the adjudication, and all of it, including its conflicts rules. The doctrine of *renvoi* would, on this view of the matter, have a supporting role to play in the prevention of forum-shopping.[44]

As for the proposition that there is an unacceptable subordination of English conflicts rules if these are allowed to incorporate *renvoi*, this appears to be mere rhetoric, and of a rather unedifying kind. The truth is that our choice of laws rules are designed in two patterns. In one, the choice of law rule can be expressed as the choice of a domestic law to determine the issue. So the material validity of a contract is governed by the domestic law chosen and expressed by the parties or, in default of such expression, by that domestic law with which it is most closely connected. The rule is formulated as the choice of a domestic law, and *renvoi* is irrelevant. In the other, the choice of law rule is not expressed directly, but formulaically: as the choice of that law which would be applied by a judge holding court at the relevant place. So a question of title to land is governed by that law which would be applied by a judge sitting at the place where the land is; the succession to moveable property is governed by that law which would be applied by a judge sitting in the place where the defendant died domiciled. Expressed in those terms the principle of *renvoi* does not lead to the upsetting of choice of law, but reflects the intellectual diversity of English choice of law rules.

[43] Cf *Boys* v. *Chaplin* [1971] AC 356.
[44] If it is said that this need is now met by the doctrine of *forum conveniens* (discussed in Chap. 3), the reply is that modern reform of the rules on civil jurisdiction removes the possibility from courts in a large number of cases.

It is necessary to admit, however, that *renvoi* is viewed with a peculiar hostility in many quarters, and is often legislated against, though without much thought usually being given to the disruption which this may bring about. Statute now provides that it has no application to the choice of law for contract[45] and tort,[46] and this was probably the view of the common law which has now been largely superseded. It does, in principle and if pleaded and proved by the parties, apply to questions of title to property, whether by *inter vivos* transaction or on death, and whether moveable or immoveable.[47] It also applies to the validity of marriage,[48] and therefore applies to the invalidity of marriage; it does not apply to divorce for the reason that choice of law rule for granting and recognizing divorces is for the law of the forum.[49] Though some have questioned whether it still does apply in these cases, the answer must be that it does, though the failure of the parties to plead or prove it will lead to its absence from the analysis. In other words, when the court is being asked to give a judgment which will have its effect only on the litigants themselves, *renvoi* does not apply. But when it is asked to give a judgment on status, either the ownership of a thing or the marriageability of an individual, which will have a potential impact on third parties it will, if invited to do so, interpret the law in the *renvoi* sense. If this increases the chance that the view reached by an English court will align with that which might be reached by a potentially-involved other law so much the better.

Finally, it is necessary to return to the question left unanswered at the end of the examination of characterization: how to formulate the question which is to be referred to and answered by the expert on foreign law. The answer should be along the following lines. In a context where the principle of *renvoi* has no application, there is no compelling need to reach the same answer as would be given by the foreign judge. The question may therefore be asked in terms of the English characterization: 'was the contract formally valid?', etc. But in a case where the principle of *renvoi* does apply, and where the aim is to reach the same conclusion as would be stated by a judge in the local court, it will impair the chances of success if the law is not interpreted in a *renvoi* sense: only by allowing the expert to start with the characterization and choice of law rules of his own system

---

[45] Contracts (Applicable Law) Act 1990, Sch. 1, art. 15.
[46] Private International Law (Miscellaneous Provisions) Act 1995, s. 9(5).
[47] See below, Chap. 8.
[48] *Taczanowska* v. *Taczanowski* [1957] P 301 (CA); *R.* v. *Brentwood Superintendent Registrar of Marriages, ex p. Arias* [1968] 2 QB 956.
[49] See below, Chap. 9.

will it be possible for him and for the court to produce an answer of the quality sought. So in the case of the absence of parental consent, the question put should be whether the absence of parental consent makes the marriage invalid, without regard to the way that the issue was earlier characterized by the English judge; but in the case of the absence of consideration or a seal, the question should be whether this affects the material validity of the contact, even though the foreign law would have regarded the absence of a seal as a question of formal validity.

INTERLOCKING ISSUES AND THE INCIDENTAL QUESTION

We have seen how the machinery for isolating the law to be applied to determine an issue identifies an issue and applies a law to it. But a set of facts may contain more issues than one, and characterization may refer these to separate laws. So, for example, a claim for damages for an alleged tort may be defended by pointing to a contractual promise not to sue; a claim for the delivery up of goods over which a seller has reserved his title may be met by a defence that they were sold to the defendant who bought them in good faith and thereby destroyed the title of the claimant; the validity of a marriage may be impugned by the alleged incapacity of one of the parties, the factual basis for this lying in a disputed prior divorce. The problem arises if there is a conflict between the laws which English private international law chooses for the two issues. To take the first example, English law will apply the *lex delicti* to a claim in tort, but the *lex contractus* to the contractual defence; how it combines them can be left for later.[50] But it may happen that the private international law of the *lex delicti* has its own view, which differs from that of English private international law, of what the *lex contractus* is. On any view the intrinsic validity of the contractual defence depends on first identifying the *lex contractus*: so is this done by the rules of English private international law or by the conflicts rules of the *lex delicti*? Or do the conflicts rules of the law which governs the earlier-made contract identify the *lex delicti*? Again, the capacity of a person to marry will be affected by the recognition or otherwise of the anterior divorce: is the law which governs the validity of the divorce chosen by the conflicts rules of English law or by those of the law which governs capacity? Or is the capacity of the party to marry determined by the conflicts rules of the law which governs the validity of the earlier divorce?

Though it may seem complicated, the law reports suggest that it rarely

[50] Below, Chap. 6.

arises for application and decision in practice. In the end, the considerations which underpin the doctrines of characterization and *renvoi* probably allow a coherent result to be reached. The starting point is that the prevailing view of the common law is to regard one of the issues, if possible, as the main one. The conflicts rules of the law chosen to govern that main question will then choose the law which governs the incidental question, so that the overall result is generated by the law (including its conflicts rules) which governs the main question. This assumes that a question can be identified as the main one; in many cases this will be the question which arises or occurs later in time, because in the end this is the decision which counts. Accordingly, the effectiveness of the ultimate sale of the goods is the main question, the incidental one being that of the validity and effect of the prior reservation of title; the law governing the later sale will be the *lex causae* whose conflicts rules identify the law which governs the earlier reservation of title. Again, personal capacity to (re)marry is the main question, the incidental one being that of the validity and effect of the prior divorce;[51] the law governing capacity to marry will be the *lex causae* whose conflicts rules identify the law which governs the earlier divorce. In neither case does English private international law take a simple chronological approach, applying its choice of law rules to the issues individually and sequentially and then seeking to combine the results.

But title to property and personal status are two areas in which the principles of *renvoi* apply, and where the court aims to replicate the result which would be reached by the foreign judge if he were trying the case; the focus is immediately on the final or main question, and therefore any prior or incidental questions should be dealt with as if by the judge in the final court. It follows that a different analysis is needed to deal with a case where the principles of *renvoi* have no acknowledged part to play in the choice of law, and where the dominance of the final judge's perspective is absent. So in the case of a contractual defence to a tort claim, the *lex delicti* will determine whether there is a claim in tort. But if a contractual defence is pleaded, the first step is to decide whether the conflicts rules of the *lex delicti* or of English law identify the *lex contractus*. There being no necessity to decide the overall question as a judge of the *lex delicti* would, there is no reason to prefer the conflicts rules of the *lex delicti* to those of English law. Accordingly the law which governs the contract, and assesses

---

[51] *Schwebel* v. *Ungar* (1964) 48 DLR (2d) 644 (Ont. CA), but only to the extent that statute has not provided otherwise.

the intrinsic validity of the defence, is determined by applying English conflicts rules. If according to the law thus identified the defence is intrinsically valid, whether it works to defeat the claimant is a matter for the *lex delicti*, but the *lex delicti* has to take the validity of the contract as given, and does not make that judgment for itself.

In this way it can be seen that the incidental question is a rational and integrated aspect of the common law methodology for choice of law. But it can be overridden by statute, for Parliament may have enacted a law in such a way that it precludes the possibility of assessing, say, the validity of a divorce by anything other than English law. To that extent, the solution given above will be displaced, and the validity of the divorce conclusively determined, in accordance with Parliamentary intention, by English law.[52]

CONNECTING FACTORS

The identifier which forms the end of the 'law of the . . .' expression is traditionally known as a 'connecting factor', on the ground that these points of contact are what connect an individual or an event to a system of the law which will, in principle, then be applied to determine the issue. They are almost all defined by exclusive reference to English, and not foreign, law: this is inevitable, for until the choice of law machinery has identified a foreign law to apply to a dispute, there is no rational basis for using any law other than English for definitional purposes. For example, if as a matter of English law X is domiciled in France, this attribution of domicile is unaffected by the possibility that French law may not agree, and would, if it were relevant to know it, regard him as being domiciled in England instead.[53] If English law considers the law applicable to a contract to be Swiss law, it is irrelevant that a Swiss court would have taken a different view, or that, as a matter of Swiss private international law, the contract would be governed by some other law.

For it to be functional, the connecting factor will need to point to a territory having *a* system of law, as opposed to indicating a larger political unit which may have many systems of law or have none. For example, an individual may be found to be domiciled in England, but not in the United Kingdom: there is English law on his capacity to marry, but no 'United Kingdom law' on the point; and a statute which has been enacted to apply in England, Scotland, and Northern Ireland, and may in some

---

[52] *Lawrence* v. *Lawrence* [1985] Fam. 106; Family Law Act 1986, s. 50.

[53] *Re Annesley* [1926] Ch. 692. But if choice of law rules refer to French law in a *renvoi* sense, and as a matter of French law he is domiciled in England, this detail will form part of the overall decision, and will not be contradicted.

sense be considered as the law of the United Kingdom, will apply because it is part of English law, not for any other reason. An individual may be domiciled in Florida, but not in the United States, with the result that the law of Florida, as distinct from the law of the United States, will be applied; though where the relevant law of Florida is in fact a federal rule of the United States, the federal rule will be applied as part of the law in the state of Florida. But by contrast, in true cases where a federal state has defined itself as a single legal unit for certain purposes, the connecting factor may point to that law. So a person may be regarded as domiciled in Australia for the purpose of capacity to marry, for Australia is constituted by its own legislation a single law district so far as concerns the law of marriage,[54] but in Queensland for the purpose of making a will, for the law of testamentary succession is a matter on which state jurisdiction is sovereign, and state laws are several. An occasional form of expression for the special sense of a country in which a person can be domiciled is a 'law district'.[55]

Connecting factors fall into two broad categories: those which define the law in terms of a personal connection, and those which define the law in terms of a state of affairs. For ease of exposition they need to be examined separately.

Personal connecting factors

The personal connecting factors are domicile, habitual (or ordinary or usual) residence, (simple) residence, and nationality. As a matter of English law, domicile is the most significant, and it is the law of the domicile which, to a greater or lesser extent, determines the status and capacities of an individual.

Domicile

At common law, the fundamental personal connecting factor is domicile.[56] As a matter of legal definition, every person has a domicile and, subject to what appears below,[57] no person can have more than one domicile at any time. The domiciliary law—the *lex domicilii*—has a dominating role in

---

[54] And, according to *John Pfeiffer Pty. Ltd.* v. *Rogerson* (2000) 172 ALR 625, [2000] HCA 36, for all matters which fall within the federal jurisdiction.

[55] In *John Pfeiffer*, above n. 54, referred to as a 'law area'.

[56] Dicey & Morris, above n. 5, chap. 7.

[57] The persistence of the domicile of origin constitutes a general half-exception to the rule; the jurisdictional domicile which forms the backbone of the Civil Jurisdiction and Judgments Act 1982, and Civil Jurisdiction and Judgments Order 2001, is a completely separate concept, irrelevant to the common law of domicile.

family and in property law, but it may also define the capacity of persons, especially companies,[58] to make contracts; and it plays a part in the law of taxation. From this very general introduction two points may emerge: the concept of domicile regulates a wide but diverse range of matters, and it may be that its meaning should adjust from one context to another. It is also essential that it represent a rational connection to a particular law. In these two respects the English law of domicile scores very badly indeed. On the first, though it has been suggested from time to time that domicile should adjust its definition to its context, there is no trace in English law of its having done so. So a case in which it was held that a taxpayer had not, despite nearly forty years' residence in England, acquired an English domicile[59] will be authoritative on whether and how a person may acquire an English domicile for the purpose of his or her capacity to marry or make a will, as also will be the decision on whether a member of a German terrorist group has acquired a domicile in England.[60] It seems reasonable to suppose that the policies which underpin the individual decisions in the various contexts will not be identical and may even be contradictory, but this fact, if it is a fact, cannot be formally reflected in the definition of domicile, for there is only one domicile and only one definition of it.

A particular difficulty, on which authority is surprisingly sparse, is how to determine the domicile of a person who, in some sense, belongs to a territory whose borders have moved. A person domiciled in Czechoslovakia will now face the impossibility of being domiciled in a non-country, in something which has no law and is no longer a law district, since the country split into two. At a guess, he will be held to have acquired a domicile of choice in the part in which he was resident on the date on which the country split, but this will be more difficult to defend as a conclusion if the person had not, on that date, made up his mind whether to remain, and hence to reside, in the part-country. A person who was domiciled in the USSR or Yugoslavia, both of which disappeared by disintegration, is in much the same position; likewise one who was domiciled in East Germany, which country disappeared by absorption. In all these cases there are practical problems in defining domicile in terms which look backward to an earlier set of facts, but there is no transparent solution to the problem created by the fact that, not only do people change their domiciles, but domiciles change their people.[61]

---

[58] Where it means the law of the place of incorporation: see below, p. 247.

[59] *IRC* v. *Bullock* [1976] 1 WLR 1178 (CA).

[60] *Puttick* v. *Att.-Gen.* [1980] Fam. 1: she did not.　　　[61] *Re O'Keefe* [1940] Ch. 124.

On the question whether the concept of domicile yields rational responses to the need for a personal connecting factor, it is necessary to distinguish three *genera* of the single domiciliary *species*.

The *domicile of origin* is the domicile of one's father (or mother, for one who is born out of wedlock or after the death of the father) at the date of one's birth. The domicile of origin will therefore be the first domicile of a child. It will prevail as the actual domicile until superseded by the acquisition of another, either a domicile of choice or a domicile of dependency. But it is only ever superseded. This has the result that when a later-acquired domicile is lost, then unless at the same moment a new domicile is acquired, the domicile of origin reasserts itself as the person's actual domicile. It is therefore a characteristic of the domicile of origin that is can never be shaken off; and if it revives at a point late in a person's life it has the potential to connect him to a legal system which may be far and remote from the circumstances of his present life.[62] It is sometimes said that this potential to reassert itself goes to illustrate why the domicile of origin should be abolished by legislation, but the truth is less clear-cut. After all, if a refugee flees from the country in which he has had a domicile of choice, it may be more offensive to hold that he remains domiciled in a country which may now be practising genocide against his ethnic group than to revive his domicile of origin until he is able to establish a new domicile of choice somewhere less awful.

A *domicile of choice* is acquired by taking up residence in a particular country and intending to reside there permanently or indefinitely. Both conditions must be satisfied in relation to the law district in which the domicile is to be established before acquisition is complete. The *intention* must be geographically specific, unconditional, and deliberate in order to meet the restrictive conditions of the law. As regards the first of these, if a person emigrates to the United States and has an intention to remain there, but has not yet settled on which state he will, permanently or indefinitely, reside in, he will not have established a domicile of choice in any American state;[63] by parity of reasoning, if he intends to reside in Texas but has not yet taken up residence there he will not have established a domicile in Texas. As regards the second, the intention must be one of permanent or indefinite residence. So an intention to reside for a term certain, or until the occurrence of a certain specific event, such as

---

[62] *Udny* v. *Udny* (1869) LR 1 Sc. & Div. 441. See also *Re O'Keefe* [1940] Ch. 124.
[63] *Bell* v. *Kennedy* (1868) LR 1 Sc. & Div. 307 (England and Scotland).

retirement or the death of a spouse, does not suffice either,[64] though if the condition upon which the residence would be determined is vague and unspecific it may be disregarded.[65] It can follow from this that residence even of several decades will not necessarily establish a domicile of choice.[66] As regards the third, a number of cases have regarded a person's intention as insufficient because the residence was, in a sense, unintended. A fugitive from justice who intends to remain only until the passing of time has prescribed his offence will not acquire a domicile of choice,[67] but this has been extended to a terrorist who fled to England but whose intention to remain was apparently unconditional.[68] A wastrel who came to England to sponge off his relatives was held to be too indolent to have an intention to establish an English domicile;[69] and an American citizen who was advised on medical grounds to remain in England, but who spent his time planning the destruction of the British maritime empire by various lunatic schemes, was held not to have the requisite intention either.[70] It is difficult to regard these colourful authorities as cases of conditional intention, but what they add to the requirements for the acquisition of a domicile of choice is difficult to define with specificity. What constitutes *residence* is hard to say; and the definition of 'present as a resident' hardly advances matters very much. It has been held that residence originating in unlawful entry into a country is insufficient, but this may be seen as a rule of English public policy applicable only to residence in England.[71] A person can be resident in a country though absent from it, but it is unclear whether he can be a resident upon the instant of his arrival.[72] In principle one can be resident in two countries at once, but to avoid the inadmissible result of this leading to there being two domiciles of choice, it is probable that the residence requirement identifies the principal residence if there is more than one.[73]

The domicile of choice can be lost by being abandoned, by the person ceasing to reside and to intend to reside indefinitely—both elements, not one, must be brought to an end—or lost on the acquisition of a new domicile of choice on the basis of the rules set out above. But if the

---

[64] *IRC* v. *Bullock* [1976] 1 WLR 1178 (CA) (unless wife died first).
[65] *Re Fuld's Estate (No 3)* [1968] P 675; *Re Furse* [1980] 3 All ER 838.
[66] *IRC* v. *Bullock* [1976] 1 WLR 1178 (CA).
[67] *Re Martin* [1900] P 211.   [68] *Puttick* v. *A.-G.* [1980] Fam. 1.
[69] *Ramsay* v. *Liverpool Royal Infirmary* [1930] AC 588.
[70] *Winans* v. *A.-G.* [1904] AC 287.   [71] *Puttick* v. *A.-G.* [1980] Fam. 1.
[72] In the case of habitual residence, this will not suffice: *Re J (a Minor)(Abduction: Custody Rights)* [1990] 2 AC 562.
[73] *Plummer* v. *IRC* [1988] 1 WLR 292.

abandonment is not contemporaneous with the acquisition of a new domicile of choice, the domicile of origin will reassert itself to prevent any domiciliary hiatus.[74]

A child's *domicile of dependency* is that, from time to time, of the parent upon whom, until the age of 16 or lawful marriage under this age, the child is dependent.[75] In principle, therefore, a child may supplant its domicile of origin with a domicile of dependency as soon as the cord is cut. When the age of independence is reached, it is debatable whether the domicile of dependency is lost by operation of law, so that the domicile of origin, if different, revives unless a domicile of choice is immediately acquired, or whether instead the domicile had from dependency continues as a 'deemed' domicile of choice. Statute suggests that the latter is possible,[76] but principle, and the balance of authority, suggests that it is not, and that the domicile of dependence ceases and is defunct on the attaining of majority.[77] The domicile of dependency of married women was abolished in 1974.[78]

It will have become apparent that the rules of domicile, comprising as they do some implausible rules and peculiar authorities, are capable of producing a capricious answer in a given case, and all the more so in Europe as political states and boundaries move and change.[79] But repeated proposals for reform have been ignored or rejected,[80] and the cause of reform is now lost. The reasons for this probably lie in the substantial fiscal (and potentially adverse) consequences of having a domicile in England and the political clout of those who would stand to lose out if domicile were aligned more closely to simple residence. One particular consequence of this inability to rationalize the common law of domicile was that it was manifestly unsuitable to identify a court in which a person should be liable to be sued in a civil or commercial action. For this reason the term 'domicile' in the Civil Jurisdiction and Judgments Act 1982 and Civil Jurisdiction and Judgments Order 2001 is statutorily defined to make it separate and distinct from its common law homonym; it is examined in Chapter 2.

Residence (habitual, ordinary, usual, simple)
Habitual residence, for which expression ordinary residence and usual

---

[74] *Udny* v. *Udny* (1869) LR 1 Sc. & Div. 441.
[75] Domicile and Matrimonial Proceedings Act 1973, s. 3.   [76] Ibid., s. 1.
[77] See J. A. Wade, 'Domicile: a Re-evaluation of Certain Rules' (1983) 32 *ICLQ* 1.
[78] Domicile and Matrimonial Proceedings Act 1973, s. 1.
[79] Cf *Re O'Keefe* [1940] Ch. 124.
[80] Most recently in Law Commission Report No 168, *The Law of Domicile* (HMSO, London, 1987).

residence are probably synonymous, is more usually employed as a personal connecting factor in laws which derive from international conventions; but its use will increase each time the cause of reform of the law of domicile is defeated. At one time it would indicate a person's usual residence, but with few of the technical complications of the common law of domicile. But its use in areas liable to generate high emotional stress—child abduction being the most notable[81]—has increasingly meant that courts have to be increasingly precise about its meaning. It is probable that it indicates only one place, though regular absence will not by itself deprive a residence of its habitual or usual character.[82] It is also probable that it is not significantly affected by a party's intention, though where it is contended that a new habitual residence has been acquired, there will need to be evidence of a settled intention to remain there on a long-term basis.[83] By contrast, (simple) *residence* may be found to exist in more than one place. It and the concept of presence play a significant part in the rules of the common law dealing with jurisdiction and the recognition of judgments, though the relationship between residence and presence in these contexts can sometimes be obscure. Because its relevance is so closely related to these jurisdictional questions, it is examined in Chapter 3.

Nationality

As a connecting factor, nationality features only rarely in the English conflict of laws, by contrast with civilian jurisdictions where it is the dominant personal connecting factor. The reasons for its non-use in English private international law are pragmatic but compelling. To begin with, a person's status as a national of a particular country is defined by the law of the proposed state: no rule of English law can determine whether someone is or is not a national of Russia. Nationality is therefore immune to the judicial refinement and control which can be brought to bear on other connecting factors. Although it plays a significant part in the law of the European Union, it may be supposed that the Member States are content for this purpose to accept each other's ascription of nationality; it does not follow that it would be a useful tool outside that context. Moreover, a person may retain a nationality long after he has

---

[81] Below, Chap. 9.

[82] *R. v. London Borough of Barnet, ex p. Shah* [1983] 2 AC 309. But one cannot become habitually resident in a single day: *Re J (a Minor)(Abduction: Custody Rights)* [1990] 2 AC 562; *Nessa v. Chief Immigration Officer* [1998] 2 All ER 728.

[83] *Re J (a Minor)(Abduction: Custody Rights)* [1990] 2 AC 562; *Re S (a Minor) (Abduction: European Convention)* [1998] AC 750.

ceased to have any practical connection to the state in question, retaining it, perhaps, for emotional or other idiosyncratic reasons: in such a case it may not be the most appropriate law to serve as the person's personal law. Most tellingly, though, instances of dual nationality, or of nationality in a federal or complex state, such as the United States or the United Kingdom, or statelessness, would cause formidable difficulties for any person for whom nationality was a personal connecting factor; it is unclear how those jurisdictions which employ nationality deal with these practical objections, and convenient that English law rarely has to.

Causal connecting factors

Those terms which describe a connection between a fact or an event and a law are also defined by reference to English law; where the meaning is not obvious it will be explained in the particular area of the law where it is utilized. Those which will be encountered in the conflict of laws are summarized here. Even though recourse to latinate expression is considered by some to add to the obscurity of the law, with the result that the usage is less frequent than before, the definitional concepts of the conflict of laws are still rendered in classical forms. Up to this point in this chapter the attempt has been made to express connecting factors in an English language paraphrase, but it is undeniable, by all but the most fanatical *faux*-modernizers and other enemies of learning, that these lack the elegance and the economy of the traditional usages. From this point on, therefore, these connecting factors will generally be referred to in the form in which they appear in the authorities and as they are used internationally in the discourse of the conflict of laws. In addition to the *lex domicilii*, the law of the domicile, they include the *lex fori*, the law of the court in which the trial is taking place; the *lex contractus*, the law which governs a contract, whether determined under the rules of the common law (in contracts made before 2 April 1991, the 'proper law') or the Rome Convention (contracts made after 1 April 1991, the 'governing law'); the *lex loci contractus*, the law of the place where the contract was made; the *lex delicti*, the law which governs liability in tort, whether determined under the rules of the common law or statute; the *lex loci delicti commissi*, the law of the place of the tort, which is a component of the *lex delicti* under the rules of the common law; the *lex situs*, the law of the place where land, or other thing, is; the *lex loci actus*, the law of the place where a transaction was carried out; the *lex loci celebrationis*, the law of the place of celebration of marriage; the *lex incorporationis*, the law of the place of incorporation; the *lex protectionis*, the law under which legal protection of an intellectual property right is conferred; and the *lex causae*, which is used to refer generically to the law applicable to the dispute.

ALTERNATIVES TO THE TRADITIONAL APPROACH

It is accurate to describe the traditional approach as jurisdiction-selecting: the choice of law process selects a legal system whose rule will govern the issue, and this legal system, more or less automatically, provides the answer. Though it has proved remarkably durable in England and much of the common law world, and though it appears to be found in most civilian systems as well, the approach is certainly open to criticism. Several points may be suggested. First, the creation of characterization categories is to some extent an artificial process, an attempt to impose a spurious order on a market of conflicting legal rules and tending, unless vigilance is exercised, to be rigid and blinkered.[84] Secondly, the idea that within each of these categories—material validity of contract, personal capacity to marry—there is an intellectual unity which justifies grouping all the sub-issues within the single category is implausible: should the one law really determine the age at which a person may marry, whether a blood or other relative may be married, whether polygamy or same-sex union is permitted, and the effect of inability or refusal to consummate the marriage? Is this a single and coherent group of issues? Thirdly, and tellingly, little attempt is made to discover whether the rule of law actually chosen for application was developed or enacted with the intention that it be applied to the instant case. Fourthly, little or no attempt is made to compare and evaluate the result which would be produced by the rules of law from the various systems which connect to the facts, still less to choose between them. For these among other reasons, American jurists[85] and some others drawing their inspiration from these have proposed a variety of alternative approaches. These are varied in their content; have received some, but not substantial, judicial support; are more prominent in inter-state torts than elsewhere; and are more complex than the more mechanical traditional approach. Take for example the case of an inter-state traffic accident, involving cars registered in and drivers and passengers resident in, different states; supposing that the laws of some, but not

---

[84] Cf *Raiffeisen Zentralbank Österreich AG v. Five Star Trading LLC* [2001] CA Civ. 68, [2001] 2 WLR 1344.

[85] Especially D. F. Cavers, *The Choice of Law Process* (University of Michigan Press, Ann Arbor, Mich., 1965), and (1970) III *Hague Recueil*, 143; B. Currie, *Selected Essays on the Conflict of Laws* (Duke University Press, Durham, NC, 1963); American Law Institute, *Restatement Second of the Conflict of Laws* (American Law Institute, St. Paul, Minn., 1971).

all, of these states restrict the type and extent of damages which can be recovered. The mechanical application of a *lex delicti*, probably the law of the place where the tort occurred, may appear too unconcerned for the actual and personal facts of the case.[86] One alternative solution would propose that the law having the closest and most real connection to the particular claim be applied. Another would be to ask whether each of the various rules contained in the competing systems were intended by their legislators to be applied to a case with this combination of international elements: a 'rule-selecting' approach. It may be that only one can, in fact, be shown to be designed to apply; if so, there will have been a false or illusory conflict of laws, and the one concerned law will apply. It may be that more than one was intended to apply to the given facts, at which point the court may settle the conflict of laws by applying its own domestic law or the 'better' law. The scientific analysis of these alternatives to traditional choice of law is too uncertain to be susceptible to concise analysis, but if and in so far as the approach involves construing conflicting statutes to discern what they really mean, it taps into an ancient and respectable tradition. But it also works better in a system where the majority of actual rules from which the selection must be made are contained in codes or statutes, for the common law has no legislator and his purpose is, therefore, unknown and unknowable. This contrasts with a statute where *travaux préparatoires* and constitutional theory may shine light on the actual or deemed legislative intention by a process called, if rather oddly, governmental interest analysis. Whether this could ever be made to work in England is open to doubt;[87] and as choice of law for tort and for contract is now mostly contained in legislation, there is relatively little scope for an English judge to follow whatever he may take to be the American way ahead.

NEW TECHNOLOGIES AND THE CONFLICT OF LAWS

If English private international law is to continue to use connecting factors which select a law to be applied, the greater challenge may yet come from those new technologies which make the operation of a 'law of the place where . . .' rule seem inappropriate. The growth of the Internet as a medium for communication, publicity, trade, and defamation has yet to be properly examined in the context of the conflict of laws. Opinions vary.

[86] Cf *Babcock* v. *Jackson*, 191 NE 2d 279 (1963).
[87] O. Kahn-Freund (1974) III *Hague Recueil* 147; J. Fawcett, 'Is American Governmental Interest Analysis the Solution to English Tort Choice of Law Problems?' (1982) 31 *ICLQ* 189.

At one extreme, there are those who consider that these new media mean that a rethinking of jurisdiction and choice of law cannot be avoided; at the other, it is suggested that just as the conflict of laws came to terms with the telephone, telex, and fax, it will simply adapt its basic ideas to the factual challenges of this electronic technology. It is too early to announce the death of the traditional conflict of laws.

If the past is any guide to the future, specific choice of law rules which have reached the end of their shelf life may be superseded by more flexible ones. A couple of examples may illustrate the point. In the private international law of restitution, there is authority for the view that certain claims will be governed by the law of the place of the enrichment.[88] But in the context of electronic transfer—except that nothing is transferred—of funds by banks, the place of enrichment may be fortuitous or artificial, and the choice of law rule may become a more flexible proper law of the obligation to make restitution.[89] In the private international law of intangible property, dealings with negotiable instruments are traditionally governed by the law of the place where the document is. But widely-used, international electronic dealing or settlement systems, and the custodianship of securities, would risk being defeated by the rigid application of this choice of law rule to these new methods of dealing, and it may be anticipated that new choice of law rules will evolve so as to apply the most appropriate law to the issues raised by this new technology.[90]

It may well be that something similar will be required for general electronic commerce and communication. When contracts are made over the Internet, it may be necessary to decide where a contract was made or was broken,[91] or whether a supplier directed his professional or commercial activities to the place of a consumer's domicile.[92] It seems unlikely that a technical analysis of the locations of the customer's computer, his Internet server, the server which hosts the supplier's website, the supplier's computer, and of the various ways in which this information is read or downloaded, and so forth, can offer a solution which is scientifically respectable, sensible to the people involved, and jurisprudentially rational. Where it is alleged that a claimant has been defamed by a statement displayed on a web page accessible by computer users from China to Peru, it may be necessary to ask where the tort occurred, or where the

[88] Dicey & Morris, above n. 5, Rule 200(2)(c).
[89] Ibid., para. 34–036; cf *El Ajou* v. *Dollar Land Holdings plc* [1993] 3 All ER 717 (reversed on other grounds [1994] 2 All ER 685 (CA)).
[90] Dicey & Morris, above n. 5, para. 24–064.   [91] See CPR r. 6.20(5), (6).
[92] Council Reg. 44/2001 [2001] OJ L12/1, Art. 15.

damage occurred or where was the event which gave rise to the damage;[93] and the points of contact listed above are now multiplied by the number of people who may have had access to the information. For the purpose of jurisdiction[94] or the recognition of foreign judgments,[95] it may be necessary to ask whether the defendant was present (or carrying on business) in or at a particular place; and the same basic facts of electronic exchange of information may make this a difficult question to answer. For the purposes of regulation of deposit takers and investment businesses, it may be necessary to determine whether an individual carried on business in the United Kingdom.[96] How will the conflict of laws adapt itself to this brave new world?

A tentative guess may be that the place where the individuals, or their office premises,[97] are will prove to be more significant than where the hardware is located, and that both will be more significant than the notional places where links in the chain of communication may be found. After all, domestic law and the conflict of laws deal with communication and contracts made by telephone, and it appears to be assumed that the place of the telephone subscriber is decisive. It appears not to matter that the offeree left a message on an answering machine on the premises, or in a voicemail box maintained by a telephone company; or that either caller used a mobile phone. Rough and ready locations are ascribed to the persons who communicate, and the legal analysis proceeds from there. For defamation, it should be the eye of the reader which is significant, and not the place where or from which his computer 'reads' the information in question.[98] For presence or the carrying on of business, it seems probable that this can indicate only where living, breathing, individuals do what they do, rather than a notional place where information is transferred. This is not to say coming to terms with conflicts issues presented by the new technology will be plain sailing, or that no legislation will be required. But calm creativity from commercial judges may well be all that is required to reach rational solutions.

---

[93] Council Reg. 44/2001 [2001] L12/1, Art. 5(3). Cf *Gutnick* v. *Dow Jones & Co. Inc.* [2001] VSC 305, 28 Aug. 2001 (Vic. SC).
[94] CPR r. 6.5(6).
[95] *Adams* v. *Cape Industries plc* [1990] Ch. 433 (CA).
[96] Financial Services and Markets Act 2000, s. 418.
[97] Ibid.
[98] But computers do not read.

The Role of the *Lex Fori*

It has been indicated, and will be seen, that the rules for choice of law will sometimes select the *lex fori* to govern the issue in question. The choice of law for divorce,[1] for the distribution of assets in an insolvency,[2] and until recently (and it has not been wholly eliminated even today) for liability in tort[3] was to apply the *lex fori*: these will be examined in the chapters dealing with these subjects. Moreover, questions of trial procedure are governed by the *lex fori*, and the scope of this principle is examined immediately below. It is sometimes said that the application of English domestic law to these substantial areas results in English private international law making less recourse to the doctrine of public policy than it otherwise would. This seems plausible. But by contrast with these instances where the *lex causae* is the *lex fori*, there are others in which the *lex fori* supervenes to contradict and negate a choice of law rule pointing to a foreign law which would otherwise have been applicable. A partial summary of the role of the *lex fori* is now given: it examines the role of the *lex fori* in relation to procedural issues, and two areas in which English law will simply apply the *lex fori* in contradiction of any conflicting choice of law.

PROCEDURAL MATTERS

Issues characterized as procedural are governed by English law, and a rule of the *lex causae* which conflicts with it will not be applied, for the *lex causae* governs issues of substance, but not those of procedure. This is the first level of characterization in any case: is the issue one of substance or one of procedure?[4] So the question whether an intending litigant has such personality and other competence as to allow him to sue in an English court is a matter of procedure and governed by English law. That said, though, English law will be applied with a measure of flexibility. For

---

[1] Chap. 9 below.   [2] Chap. 10 below.   [3] Chap. 6 below.
[4] Dicey & Morris, *The Conflict of Laws* (13th edn., Sweet & Maxwell, London, 2000), chap. 8.

example, it does not necessarily follow that juristic persons unfamiliar or unknown to English law may not litigate: although the curator, appointed by a court, of a disappeared person has been denied *locus standi*,[5] a Hindu temple, which enjoyed legal personality under Indian law, has been recognized as competent to sue.[6] But the trial process is governed by English law. So its nature and form will be as provided by English law and, in principle at least, the question whether, or upon what matters, witnesses may, or may be compelled to, give evidence is a matter for English law. It has been held that where English law requires evidence to be in writing, this applies equally in cases where the *lex causae* would not have imposed a similar requirement; but this may be due for reconsideration.[7] More flexibility may apply to the acquisition of evidence for use at trial. There is no rule which prevents the acquisition of evidence by lawful means not known to English law, so the product of depositions taken under United States federal procedure is admissible at trial,[8] as will be documents obtained by disclosure under rules which are more liberal than those of English law. If it is objected that this distorts the balance which each system of civil procedure establishes between the parties to litigation, the answer is that in an extreme case the court may use its inherent power to regulate the trial to prevent it.

If the admissibility of evidence is a procedural issue, it may also be argued that the location and content of the burden of proof must be also; and that if this is so, the operation of presumptions must also be included within the category. This is, however, less clear. Though the meagre balance of authority holds that the burden of proof is a matter for English law as *lex fori*,[9] insistence on this as a matter of principle may distort or denature the substantive right to which it relates. If the *lex contractus* provides that a particular loss will be taken to have been caused by the breach unless the defendant proves that it was not, or the *lex delicti* that the impairment will be presumed to be attributable to the tortfeasor's breach of duty unless it is proved that it was not, it will appreciably alter the rights of the parties if an English court applies its rules on the burden of proof and disregards the alien presumption. The present state of the

[5] *Kamouh* v. *Associated Electrical Industries International Ltd*. [1980] QB 199.

[6] *Bumper Development Corp.* v. *Commissioner of Police of the Metropolis* [1991] 1 WLR 1362 (CA).

[7] *Leroux* v. *Brown* (1852) 12 CB 801.

[8] *South Carolina Insurance Co.* v. *Assurantie Maatschappij De Zeven Provincien NV* [1987] 1 AC 24.

[9] *Re Fuld's Estate (No 3)* [1968] P 675.

law is uncertain,[10] but its future direction should be to the contraction of the category of procedure where this would enhance the effect of the *lex causae* and can be accomplished without significant adverse effect on the management of the trial process. In this regard, recent decisions of the High Court of Australia are instructive. That court had held that limitation of actions was in general a procedural matter, governed by the *lex fori*, and also that rules of law which fixed a statutory cap on the amount of recoverable damages were procedural, both decisions[11] being in line with traditional common law conflict of laws. It followed that in a tort case, therefore, the impact of these two critical factors would be determined by the accident of where the claimant succeeded in bringing the defendant to court. That this was impossible to defend as a matter of principle was also clear: there was no reason why the local court should be bound or entitled to apply its rule on these issues to the exclusion of the corresponding rules of the *lex delicti*; and seeing the point the High Court overruled its earlier decisions.[12] There had been a theoretical justification for the earlier decisions, but if the rules needed to produce a justifiable result before one tenable theory was preferred to another, the earlier cases simply failed the test.

A similar reductivist argument may apply to the quantification of damages. Although the matters in respect of which damages may be recovered are seen as a substantive issue for the *lex causae*,[13] the procedural quantification of the sums due under each of those heads is done in accordance with English law.[14] Accordingly, whether a tortfeasor is liable to pay damages for loss of earnings, loss of earning capacity, medical expenses, pain and suffering, and loss of amenity, and so on, is a heads of damage question determined by the *lex delicti*, but for those which are available under the *lex delicti*, the calculation—both its basis and the arithmetic—is a matter for English law methods. It is obvious that while this may

[10] In the case of contracts, though, see the Contracts (Applicable Law) Act 1990, Sch. 1, art. 14(1).
[11] *McKain* v. *R. W. Miller & Co. (SA) Pty. Ltd.* (1991) 174 CLR 1 (limitation); *Stevens* v. *Head* (1993) 176 CLR 433 (cap on damages).
[12] *John Pfeiffer Pty. Ltd.* v. *Rogerson* (2000) 172 ALR 625, [2000] HCA 36 at paras. [97]–[103] (at least on this point and in relation to torts committed within Australia).
[13] *Boys* v. *Chaplin* [1971] AC 356; the same is true for the question of remoteness of damage: *D'Almeida Araujo Lda* v. *Becker & Co. Ltd.* [1953] 2 QB 329.
[14] Ibid; also *D'Almeida Araujo Lda* v. *Becker & Co. Ltd.* [1953] 2 QB 329; *Edmunds* v. *Simmonds* [2001] 1 WLR 1003. But in the case of contract claims, the Rome Convention (given effect by the Contracts (Applicable Law) Act 1990), provides by Art. 10(1)(c) that the *lex contractus* should be applied so far as the assessment of damages is governed by rules of law.

guard an English court from finding itself having to award damages at astronomic[15] or miserly levels, there is a dislocation which is not always easy to justify. It also follows that a line of division has to be drawn which is itself not always straightforward. For example, French law allows the victim of a tort to return to court for a further assessment of damages if the original injury turns out to be more severe than was predicted and compensated at trial. If he brings such a claim before an English court, it may be necessary to ask whether this is to be regarded as a substantive or a procedural issue; but it might be better if the question did not need to be asked at all. For an English court ought to be able and willing to quantify according to the principles of the *lex causae* where evidence of foreign law allows it to, and subject to its ability to disapply foreign law and apply its own, on the ground of public policy, wherever this appears to be a necessary corrective. Likewise with other remedies: it is sometimes said that an English court will grant remedies only when English law, *qua* procedural *lex fori*, considers them to be available, but will not do so if the English remedy does not dovetail with the particular right under the *lex causae* for which it is claimed, nor if the remedy, though notionally existing in the *lex causae* and the *lex fori* would not in the particular case be granted as a matter of English law. Thus an English court dismissed a claim brought by a Greek daughter for an order that her father constitute a dowry for her, as no English remedy corresponded to the right;[16] and at common law, an English court would not order specific performance of a foreign contract in circumstances where English law would not grant it for an English one, even though no such objection were found in the *lex causae*. On the other hand, the statutory choice of law rule for contracts now encourages the court to allow the *lex contractus* to govern the grant of remedies to the maximum extent possible;[17] and the constructive approach taken by the Court of Appeal to litigation by entities not known to English law[18] may also be prayed in aid of a constructive and flexible application of English remedies beyond the bounds of their usual limits.

INTERLOCUTORY PROCEDURE

An important sub-category of procedure is that of interim and interlocutory relief: this is awarded by an English court according to English law

---

[15] *Mitchell* v. *McCulloch* 1976 SC 1.   [16] *Phrantzes* v. *Argenti* [1960] 2 QB 19 (CA).
[17] Contracts (Applicable Law) Act 1990, Sch. 1, art. 10(1)(c).
[18] *Bumper Development Corp.* v. *Commissioner of Police of the Metropolis* [1991] 1 WLR 1362 (CA).

and represents one of the main prizes at stake when issues of jurisdiction are fought.[19] An English court has no power to make orders unknown to English civil procedural law; but equally, it will not withhold relief even if the only connection to England is that the trial is taking place there. Certain specific limitations on the power of the court may be imposed by international agreement or by the principles of comity. For example, an order freezing a defendant's assets worldwide, the making of which is within the power of an English court, should probably not be made in relation to assets within the territorial jurisdiction of another Member State bound by Council Regulation (EC) 44/2001[20] unless the English court is seised of the substantive proceedings.[21] And an injunction ordering a respondent to discontinue an action in a foreign court, which is no more than an instance of the power of an English court to make procedural orders against someone within its personal jurisdiction, will be made with a measure of restraint which reflects the competing interest of the foreign court in the matter.[22] But in all cases the relief is governed wholly by English procedural law.

THE CURRENCY OF JUDGMENT AND LIMITATION OF ACTIONS

Because of their potential to apply a disproportionately English gloss to a case not substantively governed by English law, certain issues which were once regarded as procedural are now characterized as substantive. The first results from a judge-made alteration to the common law. Until 1976 an English court had no power to award damages in foreign currency, even if the loss was sustained in that currency: the rule of English law, regarded as procedural, was that the claim was quantified in sterling as at the date of the claim and judgment, years afterwards, would be for that sterling sum.[23] This began to imperil the role of England as a centre for commercial litigation once the currency began to devalue. Consequently, in two cases in the 1970s, it was held that if, in effect, the loss was sustained in a foreign currency, an English court should be able to give judgment in that foreign currency or in its sterling equivalent as at the

---

[19] See generally L. A. Collins, *Essays in International Litigation and the Conflict of Laws* (OUP, Oxford, 1994), chap. 1.

[20] See Chap. 3, below.

[21] Case C–391/95, *Van Uden Maritime BV* v. *Deco-Line* [1998] ECR I–7091.

[22] *Airbus Industrie GIE* v. *Patel* [1999] 1 AC 119.

[23] Though the judgment would carry interest, and interest rates will bear some relationship to local currency values.

date of judgment.[24] A claimant cannot simply ask a court to give judgment in a foreign currency of his preference, but if the loss is sustained in
that currency, there is no longer any reason for reluctance to acknowledge
it. It is a good illustration of how a procedural issue lost its characterization as such when it began to have an adverse effect on the rights it was
meant to help vindicate.

Until the Foreign Limitation Periods Act 1984, the approach to time
bars and their impact on litigation was complicated. A provision which
acted by putting an end to a claim, by prescribing it, was regarded as
substantive, and such a provision of the *lex causae* was applied by an
English court. By contrast, a provision which acted by preventing the
bringing of proceedings, by limiting it, was regarded as procedural, with
the result that such a provision of the *lex fori* was applied by an English
court, but such a provision contained in the *lex causae* would not be.
English time-bar provisions are enacted in the form of limitation statutes.
As a result, English limitation periods, and foreign rules of prescription,
were applied cumulatively, with the shorter of the two having decisive
effect. The justification for this, otherwise than as an arid exercise in
theory, was impossible to see. The Foreign Limitation Periods Act 1984[25]
pre-empted reform by the courts, by providing that time-bar provisions
are governed by the *lex causae* and not by English law unless it is the *lex
causae*. English law on limitation will still apply to identify the point from
which time begins to run;[26] and may still apply to measure and define the
period in cases where the application of the new statutory rule would be
contrary to public policy.[27] Public policy is defined by the Act to include
cases where the operation of the new rule would do undue hardship to a
party, actual or potential. So a period which is too short, and especially
one which does not allow for postponement if the claimant is too ill to
make the decision to litigate, may offend public policy; conversely, a
period which is excessively long, given that an English trial relies on oral
testimony, may also be offensive to public policy. Though the wording of
the Act is hardly pellucid, it has been held that the effect of the public
policy provision, when applicable, is that the English time period applies
without further regard to whether this is substantive or procedural.[28] The
lamentable provision that there is no recourse to *renvoi* on questions of

---

[24] *Miliangos* v. *George Frank (Textiles) Ltd.* [1976] AC 443; *Services Europe Atlantique Sud
(SEAS)* v. *Stockholms Rederaktiebolag Svea of Stockholm (The Despina R)* [1979] AC 685.
[25] S. 1.   [26] S. 4.   [27] S. 2.
[28] *Arab Monetary Fund* v. *Hashim* [1996] 1 Lloyd's Rep. 589, 599–600 (CA).

limitation[29] is just absurd. One can imagine that the intention was to ensure that once the rules for choice of law, including any *renvoi* which they may make and the evidence of foreign law allows, have identified a domestic law to apply, the time-bar provisions of that law will also apply. But if that is what was meant, it is regrettable that the Act does not say so. For it can be read as providing that the law to govern limitation is identified and fixed before any question arises of *renvoi* to another law on the issues of substance. Such dissociation of limitation from rules which actually resolve the substantive question is presumably an interpretation whose adoption would be an unfortunate accident.[30]

PENAL LAWS AND REVENUE CLAIMS

The second broad area in which English private international law applies the *lex fori* and overrides any provision of the *lex causae* is in the area of penal, revenue, and other public laws: the rule is usually stated as providing that an English court will not enforce a foreign penal law or a foreign revenue law; the status of the third category of other public laws is less secure but, subject to careful definition, is wholly sound in principle.[31] The identification of a penal or revenue law is generally straightforward (though it is to be observed that it is an area in which the law arguably requires the process of classification to focus on a rule of law and not on an issue); but more difficulty is encountered in understanding the limits of enforcement.

A penal law is one which imposes a fine or forfeit or other obligation upon a lawbreaker, and which is ordered to be made to the state. Its identification as penal is a matter for English law as *lex fori*.[32] It is probable that a law which requires a payment to be made to a private individual is not a penal law, even though the avowed purpose of the law is to punish wrongdoing by ordering a payment which is a multiple of any loss suffered, or which is unrelated to any loss: on this basis the Roman law action which the owner had against a thief for twice or fourfold the value of the thing stolen, or the award of damages trebling the loss inflicted on the victim by violation of US anti-trust laws, will not be considered as penal laws whose enforcement is prohibited by the common law.[33] It appears to follow that where a regulatory body brings a civil action on

---

[29] S. 1(5).   [30] Just as its legislation was.   [31] Dicey & Morris, above n. 4, Rule 3.
[32] *Huntington* v. *Attrill* [1893] AC 150.
[33] But in the case of multiple damages, statute now precludes enforcement: Protection of Trading Interests Act 1980, s. 5.

behalf of a class of persons who have sustained losses, this will not involve
the enforcement of a penal law. It is irrelevant that the defendant agrees
to make the payment, so the forfeit of a voluntary bail bond involves
enforcement of a penal law;[34] and the payment of an agreed sum to
prevent prosecution will be treated likewise.

It is not very illuminating to define a revenue law as a tax law, but it is
hard to improve on this general definition; and in this context the rule is
sometimes described as the 'revenue rule'. Income and capital taxes, sales
and service taxes will be revenue laws, and their enforcement cannot take
place by action in the English courts. More marginal cases may arise from
the collection of state medical insurance payments from employees, for it
may be thought that if the state is providing a service in return for the
payment, the demand is not a tax but a charge for services; the same
analysis may be applied to payments made to a state monopoly utility. But
such an argument would be misconceived, not least because it is capable,
if with a little strain, of being applied to all income taxes: every taxpayer
is said to get something in return for his payment. The more incisive
question is whether the payment is voluntary in the sense that the law
which imposes the charge also permits the person to renounce the benefit
and thereby avoid liability to pay. Whatever the practicalities may otherwise be, if a person is not entitled to disclaim the right to take advantage
of the hospitals, national defence etc. which are paid for and provided to
him from his income taxes and national health insurance and, having
done so, be released from liability to pay for them, the laws will be
revenue laws. Likewise, if he is not entitled to renounce whatever it is
which is provided to the public from value added tax takings and thereby
escape liability to pay VAT, this identifies a revenue law. In the case of a
state supplier, however, matters may be different: if a homeowner is
legally entitled to tell the water utility that he does not want its services,
and as a result avoid the liability to pay a charge, the payment will not be a
revenue law, no matter how unlikely it is that the person could take
advantage of his technical freedom of contract. But if the owner of a
television remains liable in law to pay the licence fee even though he
forswears any reception of the state broadcasting service, the payment is a
revenue law. It is nothing to the point that a householder can avoid liability for payment by having no television, or that an employee can avoid
income tax by giving up his job, or that a customer can avoid VAT by not
buying shoes, for on that basis only death duties would be true revenue

---

[34] *United States of America v. Inkley* [1989] QB 255 (CA).

laws. Rather the question is whether the person may satisfy the condition which renders him liable to tax, but then renounce the benefit which is offered in return for the payment. If he cannot, it is a tax law and not a contractual liability.

English private international law prevents only the enforcement of such laws; it does not deny them recognition[35] unless they are so offensive that even to notice that they have been enacted would be repellent to public policy.[36] It is easy to see the action as an enforcement one when a foreign attorney general sues for sums due on a dishonoured bail bond, or when a foreign collector of taxes brings an action on an unpaid tax demand.[37] As the exclusionary rule also applies to indirect enforcement, the analysis is the same if the state first obtains a judgment in regular civil form from its courts, and then seeks recognition of the judgment and enforcement of the judgment debt: a coat of whitewash will not deceive the court.[38] The same is probably true if the collection action is brought by an agent of the state, such as the Director-General of Fair Trading. By contrast, recognition of a penal or revenue law is unobjectionable, so that if performance of a contract is made illegal under the criminal law of the place where performance is due, that will render the contract unenforceable in the English courts: a result which would be impossible if the penal law were denied even recognition.[39] The problematic cases arise on the line which separates indirect enforcement from recognition, not least because some loosely-reasoned authorities have stated that if judgment in the action would increase the likelihood that a tax would be paid, the action is prohibited by this rule.[40] For example, a claim brought by a seller or provider of services upon an invoice which contained an element of value added or service tax might be thought to involve the indirect (because brought at the instance of a person obliged by law to levy the charge and collect the dues on behalf of the state, to which an account

---

[35] *Re Emery's Investment Trusts* [1959] Ch. 410. And the reasoning in *Ralli Bros.* v. *Compania Naviera Sota y Aznar* [1920] 2 KB 287 and *Regazzoni* v. *K. C. Sethia (1944) Ltd.* [1958] AC 301 could not have been used if no account at all had been taken of the penal laws of Spain and India, respectively.

[36] Cf *Kuwait Airways Corp.* v. *Iraqi Airways Co.* [2001] 1 Lloyd's Rep. 161 (CA), where the court refused to recognize Iraqi legislation purporting to seize the assets of the Kuwaiti state airline, in flagrant breach of international law.

[37] *Government of India* v. *Taylor* [1955] AC 491.

[38] *United States of America* v. *Harden* (1963) 41 DLR (2d) 721 (Can. SC).

[39] *Ralli Bros.* v. *Compania Naviera Sota y Aznar* [1920] 2 KB 287; *Regazzoni* v. *K. C. Sethia (1944) Ltd.* [1958] AC 301.

[40] *Rossano* v. *Manufacturers' Life Insurance Co. Ltd.* [1963] 2 QB 352; *QRS 1 ApS* v. *Fransden* [1999] 1 WLR 2169 (CA).

must be made) enforcement (because it seeks an order to pay money which in law belongs to the defendant) of a revenue law. Plausible as this may be, it cannot possibly be correct. If it were, and the court were to deduct the tax element from the judgment sum, the claimant would presumably still have to account to the state for the stipulated percentage of this reduced sum, which would then have to be further reduced, and so on, *ad absurdam*; a similar analysis would make impossible an action to be brought by an employee for any sum due as unpaid but taxable wages. A preferable analysis would ask whether, when the proceedings were commenced, there was an accrued and outstanding liability to the revenue.[41] If on a true analysis there was not, albeit that a liability will arise when the defendant has satisfied the judgment of the court, the action will not be for the enforcement of a revenue law, but for its recognition as having contributed to the invoiced sum or level of salary. The answer will be the same if the liability has accrued but has already been discharged. A similar need for careful differentiation will be encountered in relation to governmental seizure of property, where close attention needs to be paid to whether law providing for the seizure is being pleaded for enforcement[42] or for mere historical recognition of an accomplished fact.[43]

It is striking that in no case in which the revenue rule defeated a claimant's action was the claimant asking the court to apply its own domestic law as *lex causae*: the exclusionary rule appears to strike only when the choice of law principles of the court would require it to apply a foreign law as *lex causae*, the result of doing which would be to enforce a revenue law. If by contrast the court is asked to apply its own domestic law to the action, it is hard to see how this can engage the revenue rule. So if a foreign state brings an action in England founded on English tort law alleging a conspiracy to damage the revenue of the claimant state, this should not be seen as the enforcement of a foreign revenue law: the foreign law may have to be recognized to explain the losses inflicted by the conspirators, but if the action is sustainable under the tort law of the forum, there should be no recourse to the revenue rule. This may be the true reason why an application made pursuant to an English Act for the taking of evidence at the behest of a foreign tax authority will not be refused: the *lex causae* for such a procedural application is English law, and no question of enforcement of a foreign revenue law is involved.[44]

[41] *Williams & Humbert Ltd.* v. *W. & H. Trade Marks (Jersey) Ltd.* [1986] AC 368.
[42] *Banco de Vizcaya* v. *Don Alfonso de Borbon y Austria* [1935] 1 KB 140.
[43] *Williams & Humbert Ltd.* v. *W. & H. Trade Marks (Jersey) Ltd.* [1986] AC 368.
[44] *Re State of Norway's Application (Nos 1 and 2)* [1990] 1 AC 723.

True, the foreign law has to be recognized in order to establish the basis for the application against the respondent in the first place, but recognition of such laws has never been prohibited.

To describe this as a rule where the *lex fori* supervenes to defeat a claim which was otherwise well-founded under a foreign *lex causae* may, however, not be particularly helpful. In the light of the observation that the rule appears limited to cases where a foreign law is the *lex causae*, it may be more instructive to reformulate the rule as providing that penal and revenue claims are governed by the *lex fori*: if the claim is a penal or revenue one, it must be founded on the domestic law of the court in which it is brought. So liability for a crime may be enforceable by the domestic English law of extradition, or under those rare English laws which criminalize conduct taking place overseas, or under those even rarer English laws which give effect in England to the penal laws of another state. A revenue claim may be enforceable by recourse to the provisions of a treaty with the foreign state given effect in England by domestic legislation. Seen in these terms the application of the *lex fori* in this context is part of, and does not contradict, the rules for choice of law in the conflict of laws; and the critical question would be whether the *claim* should be characterized as a penal or a revenue one, and not whether the *law* relied on is a penal or a revenue one. Acceptance of this reformulation would have the beneficial effect of integrating this collection of cases into the mainstream of the conflict of laws, and would end their having to be regarded as some sort of overriding exception to the general scheme for choice of law.

As indicated above, some authority maintains that there is a third category, of 'other public laws'.[45] It seems rational that claims based on and calling for the enforcement of foreign laws which are analogous to penal and revenue laws, such as confiscation and nationalization, exchange control, laws regulating the duties of those employed in the security services, and so forth should be dealt with similarly, though whether it is beneficial to call these 'other public laws' must be open to doubt. On the other hand, if a householder is obliged by law to pay water or other utility charges, whether he wishes to take the service or not, to a private or privatized company, it would be unfortunate if the private character of the payee meant the payment was not under a revenue law. If

---

[45] *Att.-Gen. (UK)* v. *Heinemann Publishers Australia Pty. Ltd.* (1988) 165 CLR 30; *Att.-Gen. of New Zealand* v. *Ortiz* [1984] AC 1 (CA); Private International Law (Miscellaneous Provisions) Act 1995, s. 14(3).

it may be treated as quasi-revenue, or as an other public law, the difficulty goes away.

PUBLIC POLICY AND RELATED DOCTRINES

At various points in our examination of private international law we will encounter the proposition that a particular result otherwise provided by choice of law will be departed from by reason of public policy. It is helpful to set out some lines of distinction to demarcate what properly is regarded as public policy and what is not. The public policy engaged is only ever that of English law, but where it is engaged it overrides the application of a foreign *lex causae*. As an illustration which relates to the previous material, if an English court is called upon to recognize a foreign law which is so repellent to English standards that even to take notice of it is intolerable, it will be ignored.[46] So if it is alleged that a contract is unenforceable because illegal in the place of performance, the illegality being one which prevents the performance of acts on racial or other unacceptable discriminatory grounds, the law may be denied recognition and the contract enforced according to its terms. Similarly if a supplier sues on an invoice on which tax is imposed at a rate which discriminates against a particular ethnic group, so offensive a law will be treated as if it had never been made, on the ground that even to recognize it as datum will conflict with the public policy of English law. With that illustrative introduction, we may examine three separate, though linked, issues: where English public policy overrides a foreign rule; where an English statute precludes the application of a foreign rule; and the public policy of a foreign law.

ENGLISH PUBLIC POLICY

As indicated above, where *foreign rules* are picked out for application by choice of law rules, a rule of the *lex causae* will not be applied if its content is repugnant to English public policy, or if the result of its application in the given context is contrary to English public policy. 'Public policy' in this sense refers to the fundamental values of English law. Though it is often said that it generally has a restrictive meaning, the Human Rights Act 1998 seems certain to broaden the scope of, but also to provide a clearer and more fertile definitional basis for, English public policy. The history of prejudice has given a few ghastly illustrations. A

---

[46] *Oppenheimer* v. *Cattermole* [1976] AC 249.

law depriving a racial group of its property,[47] or one invalidating marriage between members of a dominant ethnic group and a subjugated ethnic group will, or should, be regarded as so offensive to English public policy that it will be treated as if it did not exist and had never been enacted, no matter the context in which it arises. Iraqi laws purporting to seize Kuwaiti assets in time of war and in defiance of United Nations sanctions which demanded to have mandatory effect have also been denied recognition.[48] To take a less obvious example, it has been held that though a contract containing a covenant restricting the freedom of a party to take employment may be valid and enforceable according to the *lex causae*, it may still conflict with the English doctrine that such agreements are illegal restraints of trade;[49] and the English rule may prevail. It has not yet been held that a rule of foreign law which allows a husband to divorce his wife, but not *vice versa*, should not be recognized, but discrimination between the sexes is hardly more acceptable than that between the races.

By contrast with unconditionally immoral or evil laws, others may need to be evaluated in their context and the facts shown to have a sufficient connection to England before any similar conclusion can be drawn about them. For instance, to recognize a law giving a husband a unilateral right to divorce his wife on a whim, while giving her no right to prevent this (and still less a reciprocal right to divorce him) may already be considered to be contrary to public policy when said to apply to a wife who is habitually resident in England[50] but may be regarded differently, and not disqualified from application, when applied as between parties who have no connection with England. Likewise, a law which allows marriage between husband and niece will not be regarded as so objectionable that it will be overridden by English public policy when the marriage has nothing to do with England.[51] Much confusion is reduced when the two senses of public policy—the first absolute, the second contextual—are distinguished; and it may be that the restraint of trade example considered above would be better seen as falling into the contextual category.

Another way to express this idea might be that the first category of public policy applies whatever the *lex causae* or connection to England, whereas the second applies only if England is a country with which the issue has a real and substantial connection. This could be seen either as a

---

[47] Ibid.
[48] *Kuwait Airways Corp.* v. *Iraqi Airways Co.* [2001] 1 Lloyd's Rep. 161 (CA).
[49] *Rousillon* v. *Rousillon* (1880) 14 Ch. D 351.
[50] Cf *Chaudhary* v. *Chaudhary* [1985] Fam. 19 (CA).
[51] *Cheni* v. *Cheni* [1965] P 85.

disguised choice of law rule, or as analogous to the 'sufficient connection' principle which must be satisfied before an English court will grant some forms of equitable relief. And if this were to be accepted, attention could be focused on the question which ought to lie at the heart of the analysis, namely what degree of connection with England ought to be required before this contextual form of public policy would be invoked.

In the interest of balance, it is necessary also to observe that English public policy may also override the *lex causae* in the interest of a fundamental but illiberal value enshrined in English law. For example, English law once took the view that a polygamous marriage was not to be regarded as, or as equivalent to, marriage, even though the personal laws of the parties, and the law of the place of celebration, considered it a valid marriage.[52] Only gradually was this whittled away to the point where almost all trace of it had gone. No court has yet been called upon to decide the point, but there is reason to fear that English public policy may be invoked to deny recognition to marriages between people of the same sex validly celebrated under the law of a foreign country[53] which has elevated the humane values of equality and parity of esteem above bigotry and discriminatory spite; but it may well be that if such cases are defensible at all (which is much to be doubted) there must be a sufficient connection with England to justify the alleged interest of English public policy.

ENGLISH STATUTES WITH OVERRIDING EFFECT

The operation of public policy as thus described may amount to the superimposition of a rule of common law on the choice of law process. The second category to examine is the statutory equivalent, where English legislation is framed in such a way that it instructs the judge to apply it to any case which falls within its terms, without regard to choice of law. Where a rule of English law is cast in statutory form, and the statute is framed as a direction to the judge that it is to be applied to all cases coming before his court, the true explanation does not lie in the common law or public policy, but in parliamentary sovereignty: the legislator has in this specific instance overridden the general rules of the conflict of laws.[54] Now what Parliament can do expressly it can also do by implication, albeit that deducing the intention where Parliament has been delphic is difficult. As a general guide to the construction of the parliamentary intention, a rule which may be interpreted as one of absolutely fundamental importance and insistence may be held to override in every case;

---

[52] *Hyde* v. *Hyde* (1866) LR 1 P & D 130.　　　[53] e.g. Denmark, the Netherlands.
[54] e.g. Carriage of Goods by Sea Act 1971.

one which may be thought of as less imperative applies only if the facts disclose enough of a connection to England for it to be supposed that this is what the legislator had in mind. The extent to which the Human Rights Act 1998 will be interpreted as applicable regardless of the connection to England, or as applicable only if the facts have a sufficient connection to England, or as inapplicable unless English law is the *lex causae* remains to be tested. But it is very unlikely indeed that the last proposition could ever be correct; and as between the first two it may depend on the relative importance of the guarantee in question: in principle, the guarantee of respect for private life may not be interpreted as being as peremptory as that which demands a fair trial.[55]

THE PUBLIC POLICY OF THIRD COUNTRIES

No mechanism exists at common law for applying the rules of public policy of a country whose law is not the *lex causae*, or one of the *leges causae*. It is true that statute may provide what the common law cannot reach: in the contractual context, Article 7(1) of the Rome Convention[56] offered the opportunity to do this very thing. Problems of uncertainty laid aside, there is a good case to be made for such a statutory provision. The *lex causae* may be such by reason of the parties' choice; and they may have made the choice for the very purpose of sidelining the law which would otherwise have applied, and a particular provision of that law which is regarded as of mandatory effect, such as one protecting consumers from unfair or unequal contractual terms, or protecting investors from unauthorized providers of financial services. One way of dealing with such evasive choices of law is to annul the right to choose, or to limit the right to choose,[57] the law. But another would have been to maintain the choice of law (which may have been for a variety of reasons, not all of them improper), while allowing the public policy of a third law to be applied. But perhaps because it would have been an unprecedented novelty for English judges, and a disconcerting novelty for litigants, Article 7(1) was not enacted into English law.[58] Of course, where a provision of the *lex causae* is described under that law as, or as enshrining, a rule of public policy, there is no reason whatever for an English court to decline to give it effect, for it is still part of the *lex causae*, whatever else it may be.

---

[55] Cf *Williams & Humbert Ltd. v. W. & H. Trade Marks (Jersey) Ltd.* [1986] AC 368, 428.

[56] Contracts (Applicable Law) Act 1990, Sch. 1.

[57] By providing, as in some circumstances the Rome Convention does for the additional application of certain laws from third countries, often called 'mandatory rules'.

[58] Contracts (Applicable Law) Act 1990, s. 2(2).

3

Jurisdiction of English Courts

TYPES OF JURISDICTION

To say that a court has jurisdiction means that the law has conferred on it the power to hear and determine a case against a defendant.[1] It is implicit that the court must have jurisdiction over the subject matter of the claim and personal jurisdiction over the defendant to it. But in English law, it does not follow that, just because a court has jurisdiction, it will invariably exercise it at the behest of the claimant. A pervasive characteristic of common law private international law is that a court may decline to exercise the jurisdiction which it admittedly has, with the result that the claimant, if he wishes to sue, may have to have recourse to a foreign court. By contrast with this common law flexibility, where jurisdiction is conferred on the courts by Convention or by Council Regulation (EC) 44/2001,[2] this discretion is largely excluded. Such discretionary matters, however, impinge only on the complex rules which govern the personal jurisdiction of the court. By contrast with this, the topic of subject matter jurisdiction, which is is not well developed in English private international law, contains no element of discretion. It needs to be examined at the outset of any account of jurisdiction.

SUBJECT MATTER JURISDICTION

There are few instances in which an English court lacks jurisdiction over the subject matter of a claim, but where this is so it is irrelevant that the parties are willing to submit to the personal jurisdiction of the court: the absence of subject matter jurisdiction lies beyond their power or control. A potentially difficult question, however, will arise where the common law denies subject matter jurisdiction, but a Convention or the Regulation nevertheless ascribes personal jurisdiction over the defendant.

---

[1] See generally Dicey & Morris, chaps. 11 and 12; A. Briggs and P. J. Rees, *Civil Jurisdiction and Judgments* (2nd edn., Lloyd's of London Press, London, 1997).

[2] [2001] OJ L12/1. See the next section below for details of these jurisdictional instruments.

At common law, there was no jurisdiction to adjudicate questions of title to foreign land, and therefore no jurisdiction to hear claims which involved determining a question of title.[3] Most systems consider such jurisdiction the exclusive prerogative of the courts at the *situs* of the land. Statute has amended this so that a court may now hear a claim in tort unless it is one principally concerned with title to foreign land.[4] It has been held that this requires the question of title to be quantitatively the dominant issue for decision,[5] but this may be to restrict the rule more than its underlying justification properly allows. But the result is that if the defence to an allegation of trespass is that the defendant had a licence to enter, or the defence to a claim for nuisance is that the claimant had no sufficient title to the land, the court will lack jurisdiction to adjudicate the claim. It is unnecessary to ask whether the exclusionary rule would apply where no question arises of legal title but equitable title is disputed, such as a claim about shares in the beneficial ownership of land subject to a trust. As a matter of ancient authority, where there was a contract or an equity between the parties, the court always had jurisdiction to adjudicate on and enforce the personal obligations arising from it, even if the subject of this personal right was foreign land.[6] So a court may determine the shares in a tenancy in common in foreign land arising from the trust of that land, and may decree the specific enforcement of a contract to mortgage or to convey foreign land.

Sparse but persuasive authority[7] also held that a court lacked jurisdiction at common law to adjudicate on foreign patents or copyright, especially where issues of validity were raised, no doubt for the reason that, unless affected by international treaty, the grant or extent of such rights was a matter for the foreign sovereign alone. But the better view may be that this is not a matter touching the jurisdiction of the court, making any adjudication a nullity. Instead, a court should decline to exercise its jurisdiction, or should apply English domestic law as the *lex causae* to produce a like result.

Where the courts have personal jurisdiction over the defendant because of an international treaty or instrument, the prevailing judicial

---

[3] *British South Africa Co.* v. *Companhia de Moçambique* [1893] AC 602; *Hesperides Hotels Ltd.* v. *Aegean Turkish Holidays Ltd.* [1979] AC 508; cf Civil Jurisdiction and Judgments Act 1982, s. 30.

[4] Civil Jurisdiction and Judgments Act 1982, s. 30.

[5] *Re Polly Peck International plc (in administration)(No 2)* [1998] 3 All ER 812, 828 (CA).

[6] *Penn* v. *Baltimore* (1750) 1 Ves. Sen. 444.

[7] *Potter* v. *Broken Hill Pty. Ltd.* (1906) 3 CLR 479; *Norbert Steinhardt & Son* v. *Meth* (1961) 105 CLR 440; *Tyburn Productions Ltd.* v. *Conan Doyle* [1991] Ch. 75.

view is that the common law limitations on subject matter jurisdiction are no longer applicable. So a court is obliged to hear a claim against an English defendant which seeks determination of title to land in New York, or of the validity of patent rights under the law of Brazil.[8] This is problematic. As we shall see, if the land had been French, the court would have no jurisdiction:[9] what principle justifies an opposite result when the land lies further afield is a complete mystery; and in the context of intellectual property rights, the courts have even doubted whether the exclusionary rule has ever been well-founded.[10] But the common law is to be preferred to this revisionism. The economic analysis required to assess intellectual property rights, especially where their validity is concerned, is rarely appropriate for a foreign court. Nevertheless, if it has to be accepted that a court cannot deny that it has jurisdiction, it is hoped that it will conclude that it is still entitled to decline to exercise it,[11] and achieve by discretion that which it cannot achieve by plain rules of law.

PERSONAL JURISDICTION

The principles of state and diplomatic immunity serve to limit the exercise of jurisdiction over non-commercial claims brought against states and diplomats.[12] Indeed, in these cases it may be subject matter jurisdiction, rather than personal jurisdiction, which is lacking, on the footing that appraisal of the act of a foreign sovereign lies beyond the competence of the English court.[13] In relation to international organizations, the instrument establishing the organization as a juridical person for the purposes of English law will usually also define the extent of any immunity from the processes of the court.[14] If the organization is not accorded personality by English legislation, its personality may still be recognized if this has been conferred under the law of another state, rather as if it were a corporation created under the law of that state.[15]

Subject to that exception, a court will have jurisdiction over a defendant when process has been or is deemed to have been served on him, and

---

[8] *Pearce v. Ove Arup Partnership Ltd.* [2000] Ch. 403 (CA); *QRS 1 ApS v. Fransden* [1999] 1 WLR 2169 (CA).

[9] Below, p. 62.   [10] *Pearce v. Ove Arup Partnership Ltd.* [2000] Ch. 403 (CA).

[11] See below, p. 86.

[12] State Immunity Act 1978; *Holland v. Lampen-Wolfe* [2000] 1 WLR 1573 (HL).

[13] *Kuwait Airways Corp. v. Iraqi Airways Co.* [2001] 1 Lloyd's Rep. 161 (CA), at para. 319.

[14] International Organisations Act 1968.

[15] *Arab Monetary Fund v. Hashim (No 3)* [1991] 2 AC 114. What happens if it is given legal personality under the laws of more than one state is not very clear.

rules as to jurisdiction *in personam* are therefore rules which define whether and when it is lawful to serve the defendant.[16] As a matter of common law, any defendant present within the territorial jurisdiction of the court was liable to be served with process by or on behalf of the claimant, who might do so as of right; but no defendant was liable to be served if he was outside England. To overcome this latter difficulty, successive Rules of Court permitted a claimant to apply for permission to serve process on a defendant out of the jurisdiction: the cases in which this may be done are currently set out in Part 6 of the Civil Procedure Rules ('CPR').[17] For convenience, these provisions are referred to as 'traditional' rules of jurisdiction, even though some are very recent indeed.

Since 1987, a series of European instruments,[18] enacted into English law and required to operate alongside the traditional rules, has radically altered the jurisdiction of English courts in civil and commercial matters. In such cases, a claimant must now consider whether these instruments confer jurisdiction on, or withhold it from, an English court. Only if these instruments are wholly inapplicable, or if they themselves direct recourse to the traditional jurisdictional rules, will the latter apply. For civil or commercial disputes, these European rules are at the heart of the subject, the traditional rules applying only in the gaps which they leave. It will be shown that coexistence between these jurisdictional systems, both of them complex to begin with, leaves a number of difficult issues unresolved.

In this chapter we examine jurisdiction over defendants in civil or commercial matters, this being the principal concern of the modern conflict of laws. Jurisdiction in family matters, the administration of estates, bankruptcy and insolvency, and so on is treated in the chapters which deal with those substantive topics. In summary, where the dispute arises as a civil or commercial matter, the rules set out in Council Regulation (EC) 44/2001, though at one point incorporating by reference the traditional rules of jurisdiction, will determine the jurisdiction of an English court, or its lack.

---

[16] For the procedure for effecting service see Civil Procedure Rules 1998 ('CPR') Pt. 6. Personal service and service by first class post will be the most common methods.

[17] In force from 2 May 2000, replacing Rules of the Supreme Court, Order 11. Care must be taken to notice alterations to the wording of these provisions from one incarnation to the next.

[18] Examined in detail in the following para.

COUNCIL REGULATION (EC) 44/2001 AND THE BRUSSELS AND LUGANO CONVENTIONS

THE REGULATION AND THE EARLIER CONVENTIONS

The interest of the European Community in civil jurisdiction grew from Article 293[19] of the EC Treaty, which committed the six original Member States[20] to develop a system for the mutual recognition and enforcement of judgments in civil and commercial matters. It was decided that the best way to ensure swift and automatic enforcement of sister-state judgments—creating a free market in judgments, as some are pleased to call it—was to limit the power of the judge to review the judgment of which enforcement was sought; and that the best way to achieve that result was to adopt a uniform set of rules for the taking of jurisdiction in the first place. The Brussels Convention of 27 September 1968[21] was adopted to perform this dual function.

As new states joined the European Community, they acceded to the Brussels Convention, which was successively amended on the accession of the United Kingdom,[22] Denmark, and Ireland; Greece; Portugal and Spain; and Austria, Finland, and Sweden. By the end of 2000, the re-re-re-amended text[23] of the Brussels Convention served as the common jurisdictional text of the fifteen Member States. In addition, a parallel Convention, signed at Lugano on 16 April 1988,[24] bound the states of the European Union and of the European Free Trade Area (Austria, Finland, and Sweden), which later acceded to the Brussels Convention, and thereby ceased to be 'Lugano states'; and Iceland, Norway, and Switzerland, which remain outside the European Union, as 'Lugano states'.[25]

With effect from 1 March 2002, however, the position is rather more complex. As between fourteen of the Member States of the European Union, that is, all except Denmark, the Brussels Convention is replaced by Council Regulation (EC) 44/2001, adopted under Article 65 EC. It makes considerable changes to the rules contained in the Convention, and

[19] Formerly Art. 220 EC.
[20] Belgium, France, Germany, Italy, Luxembourg, the Netherlands.
[21] In force in the six states from 1 Jan. 1973.
[22] This version being enacted as Sch. 1 to the Civil Jurisdiction and Judgments Act 1982 (the '1982 Act'), which has been amended on each subsequent accession.
[23] SI 2000/1824, in force from 1 Jan. 2001.
[24] Civil Jurisdiction and Judgments Act 1982, Sch. 3C, as inserted by Civil Jurisdiction and Judgments Act 1991, Sch. 1.
[25] For the position of Poland see the following para.

enacts the amended arrangements as a Council Regulation which is directly effective in the Member States. This may have been done to tighten the grip of the institutions of the EU, by removing effective authority from the states acting as parties to a convention, and vesting it in the institutions of the EU as a bureaucracy, though it will also make for swifter amendment when the provisions reveal shortcomings: a regulation will be easier to amend[26] than a new convention is to make. On the other hand, issues arising for decision between the Member States and Denmark will continue to be governed by the Brussels Convention, and between the Member States and Iceland, Norway, Switzerland, and Poland[27] by the Lugano Convention. The result—whether interim or final is uncertain—is a fragmentation of jurisdictional schemes, all slightly and treacherously different one from another. One may wonder whose interest is served by making the picture so much more complex than it was. It is certainly not that of a litigant or adviser, not that of a writer trying in his own way to meet the statutory goals of transparency and high predictability.[28]

Until a customary terminology emerges, we will use the terms 'Regulation jurisdiction' and 'Member State' to refer to the rules established by, and parties to, the Regulation.[29] References to the Brussels Convention, unless the context makes it plain that something else is intended, are to the rules of the Brussels Convention as in force until 1 March 2002, and still effective in relation to Denmark.[30] 'The Court' is the Court of Justice of the European Communities, or European Court. Though all the relevant authorities were decided under the provisions of the Brussels and Lugano Conventions, the account which follows has its focus on the Regulation, and terminology has been adjusted accordingly.

THE REGULATION: GENERAL SCHEME

The Regulation deals with jurisdiction in civil or commercial matters. It serves as the basic jurisdictional statute for the Member States, and national courts may make references to the European Court for a

---

[26] Especially as amendment will be permitted by majority voting.

[27] Which acceded to the Lugano Convention on 1 Aug. 2000: SI 2000/1824.

[28] Recital 11 to the Reg.

[29] That is, all the Member States of the EU except Denmark: Art. 1(3) of the Reg. For the purposes of the Reg., Gibraltar is treated as a part of the UK.

[30] The Lugano Convention has not been amended since its adoption, save for the accession of Poland. References to the Arts. of these Conventions, to distinguish them from the Reg., are given in the form 'Art. 17 BC'.

preliminary ruling on its interpretation.[31] It is drafted in many languages, though these versions are not, perhaps, in every nuance and respect, identical, and occasionally parties may exploit the differences. The Brussels Convention has the same scope but different wording. Where the Regulation confers jurisdiction on an English court, process may be served on the defendant as of right, whether in England or (with the appropriate certification of the court's jurisdiction under the Regulation) outside it.[32]

Where the Regulation confers international jurisdiction upon the courts of a Member State, it confers it on the courts of the United Kingdom, not England, for England is not a state. To deal with this, internal rules of national jurisdiction, resembling but sometimes deliberately diverging from the Regulation, allocate jurisdiction between the courts of England, Scotland, and Northern Ireland.[33] These rules of internal United Kingdom law are not the concern of the European Court.[34]

Most definitional terms used in the Regulation bear 'autonomous' meanings, distinct from those accorded to the same terms in national law, developed in the jurisprudence of the Court for the Brussels Convention, and which remain authoritative.[35] The meanings of 'contract' and 'tort', used for the jurisdictional purpose of the Regulation,[36] do not mirror these terms when used in English private international law to characterize issues and choose laws. The former is a jurisdictional matter of European law; the latter a substantive matter of national law. It follows that a court which has Regulation jurisdiction on the basis of the 'contract' rule may proceed to determine the merits by using its private international law of tort.[37] In addition, certain general canons of interpretation have

---

[31] Art. 234 (ex Art. 177) EC. The 1971 Protocol which empowered the Court to interpret the Brussels Convention (1982 Act, Sch. 2) will be almost entirely redundant; the Lugano Convention is not subject to the interpretation of the Court.

[32] CPR r. 6.19. For the form of the certification, see CPR 6PD para. 3.5.

[33] 1982 Act, Sch. 4, as amended by Civil Jurisdiction and Judgments Order 2001, Sch. 2.

[34] Case C–364/93 *Kleinwort Benson Ltd.* v. *City of Glasgow DC* [1995] ECR I–415. The extent to which preliminary rulings on the Reg. (and, prior to that, the Convention) are conclusive on the interpretation of the internal UK rules is uncertain, but they must be strongly influential: *Kleinwort Benson Ltd.* v. *Glasgow City Council* [1999] 1 AC 153; *Agnew* v. *Länsförsäkringsbolagens AB* [2001] 1 AC 223, 245.

[35] So, except where the provisions have been materially altered, will the expert reports on the various conventions: Jenard Report [1979] OJ C59/1; Schlosser Report [1979] OJ C59/71; Evrigenis Report [1986] OJ C298/1; Cruz Report [1989] OJ C189/35; Jenard and Möller Report [1990] OJ C189/61.

[36] Art. 5.

[37] Case C–26/91 *Soc. Jakob Handte GmbH* v. *Soc. Traîtements Mécano-chimiques des Surfaces* [1992] ECR I–3967, 3984.

emerged over the years. First, as the basic principle is that a defendant is entitled to defend in the courts of the state where he is domiciled any provision of the Regulation derogating from this right will tend to receive a restrictive construction.[38] This was established by the Court in its jurisprudence on the Brussels Convention, and will continue to underpin much of the interpretation of the Regulation.[39] Secondly, as the Regulation seeks to make judgments obtained in one Member State freely enforceable in other Member States, rules which mandate non-recognition of judgments will be given a restrictive construction, whereas those which prevent parallel litigation will be construed amply.[40] Thirdly, the courts of the Member States are mutually trusted to be of equal competence, and it is generally inadmissible to invite the courts of one state to conclude that the courts of another state erred in considering that they have or had jurisdiction.[41]

Where a claim falls within the domain of the Regulation, this instrument determines the jurisdiction of an English court. Its application is not dependent on whether the claimant is domiciled in a Member State: it is not a statute which is available to be taken advantage of by only a chosen few,[42] and if the defendant is out of the jurisdiction, service of process does not need the permission of the court.[43] The hierarchy of its provisions is reflected in the order in which they are examined below.

The domain of the Regulation: Articles 1, 66–68, and 71

The point of departure is to define the domain of the Regulation in its three elements, that is to say, its material, or subject-matter scope; its temporal scope; and its relationship with other legal instruments.

Subject matter

Article 1 of the Regulation states that it applies, like its forerunners, to 'civil and commercial matters'. It will often be obvious whether the claim falls within this expression, but where it is not obvious it will be measured

---

[38] e.g., Case C–220/88 *Dumez France SA* v. *Hessische Landesbank* [1990] ECR I–49; Case C–364/93 *Marinari* v. *Lloyd's Bank plc* [1995] ECR I–2719.

[39] Now see Recitals 10 and 11 to the Reg.

[40] Recital 15. See also Case 144/86 *Gubisch Maschinenfabrik KG* v. *Palumbo* [1987] ECR 4861.

[41] Case C–351/89 *Overseas Union Insurance Ltd.* v. *New Hampshire Insurance Co.* [1991] ECR I–3317. But, as will be seen, the English courts (*Turner* v. *Grovit* [2000] QB 345 (CA)) have not shown complete fidelity to this proposition.

[42] Case C–412/98 *Universal General Insurance Co.* v. *Groupe Josi Reinsurance Co. SA* [2000] ECR I–5925.

[43] CPR r. 6.19(1).

against an autonomous interpretation of the terms. It may include claims made by public authorities, or by other public-law bodies, where the rights relied on are part of the general law, rather than being peculiar to public law. So a town council which fails to pay a contractor who has repainted its offices will be sued in a civil and commercial matter; but a claim by a local authority against a houseowner whose overhanging and dangerous tree has been removed by the council acting under special statutory powers is not civil or commercial.

But the fact that the court hearing the case does not regard the claim as a matter of public law is not enough to disqualify it as civil or commercial. Rather, the question is whether such claims are in general, and across the Member States, regarded as civil or commercial: a process of examination which, if taken seriously, seems designed to complicate the jurisdictional inquiry. In one case, a Dutch local council brought a claim founded on Dutch law of tort or unjust enrichment against a shipowner whose sunken vessel was removed by the council from an international water-way. It had acted under powers conferred by an international treaty, but the claim was framed as a civil or commercial one. Even though it was a private law claim as a matter of Dutch law, this did not make it civil or commercial for the purpose of Article 1, because across the Member States as a whole this would not be seen as a private-law matter.[44] By contrast, a negligence claim against a German schoolteacher, who was in some respects a public servant with a clear status in public law, was civil or commercial, because the duty of care of a schoolteacher was neither more nor less than that of citizens under ordinary private law, whatever other powers and duties a German teacher might have.[45] But were the teacher to rely on a right or immunity which was special and peculiar to teachers as state servants, the raising of such a defence might serve to remove the claim from the domain of the Regulation, for if the claim and defence are indivisible, and the one is excluded from the Regulation, the other cannot bring it back within Article 1.[46]

The requirement to look across the Member States to ascertain whether the matter in question is generally a civil or commercial one may be particularly difficult if a claim is brought against a body which has emerged from the denationalization of infrastructural industries, such as the railways in the United Kingdom. Would a claim against the body

---

[44] Case 814/79 *Netherlands State* v. *Rüffer* [1980] ECR 3807.
[45] Case C–172/91 *Sonntag* v. *Waidmann* [1993] ECR I–1963.
[46] Cf Case 145/86 *Hoffmann* v. *Krieg* [1988] ECR 645.

which now owns the railway tracks alleging damage caused by its negligent failure to maintain the rails, or against a privatized water company
in respect of injury caused by its failure to prevent contamination, be civil
or commercial? The fact that the claim lies against a company owned by
its shareholders may suggest one answer; the fact that the company is
charged by legislation and kept under statutory regulation to perform its
duties suggests another; but if it is necessary to look across the Member
States to see how legal responsibility for the running of the railway and
the provision of water is dealt with there, the task becomes all but impossible. As a result, the temptation to limit the inquiry to English law will
be hard to resist.

A claim is outside the domain of the Regulation if it concerns customs,
revenue, or administrative matters;[47] likewise status or legal capacity of
natural persons, matrimonial property, or succession; bankruptcy and the
winding up of insolvent companies or other legal persons; or social security.[48] It is uncertain whether, if such an issue arises only incidentally, the
claim as a whole may be outside the Regulation. There is English authority[49] for the proposition that the Regulation will apply unless the principal component in the dispute is an excluded matter, and that this follows
from the need to construe exceptions to the Regulation restrictively. But
there is no convincing warrant for this, for though the outer edges of the
Regulation must be well defined, it is not necessary that they be far flung;
and there is an apparent distinction between the Regulation 'not applying
to X' and 'not applying to a matter principally concerned with X'. The
point may be illustrated by examination of 'arbitration' which, as a single
and unelucidated word, is excluded from the Regulation.[50] All agree that
arbitration as a means of dispute resolution, and judicial measures which
regulate and control it, and the enforcement of arbitral awards, fall outside
the Regulation;[51] but what of the enforcement of judgments obtained in
breach of an agreement to arbitrate? On the one hand, if the subject
matter of the dispute, and hence the judgment, is civil or commercial, it
may fall within the domain of the Regulation. But on the other, for a
court to be obliged to recognize the judgment would mean it having to
contradict its own laws on arbitration, a matter untouched by the

---

[47] Art. 1(1).   [48] Art. 1(2)(a)–(c).
[49] *Ashurst* v. *Pollard* [2001] Ch. 595 (CA) (bankruptcy); *The Ivan Zagubanski*, 16 Nov.
2000, not yet reported (arbitration).
[50] Art. 1(2)(d).
[51] Case C–190/89 *Marc Rich & Co. AG* v. *Società Italiana Impianti PA* [1991] ECR
I–3855.

Regulation. The cases conflict. In one, it was held that a Dutch court was not bound to recognize a German order for maintenance (a matter within the scope of the Regulation) where this would mean it had to contradict its own law on the marital status of the parties (a matter excluded from the Regulation).[52] But if a court in another Member State has heard and given judgment in a case, having refused to give effect to an arbitration clause, it is sometimes argued that an English court may be obliged to recognize the judgment and to that extent contradict its own law on arbitration.[53]

Proceedings for enforcement of a judgment from a non-member state are not within the Regulation,[54] nor are ancillary or incidental procedures which arise in the course of such proceedings, such as the trial of an issue whether the judgment creditor obtained his judgment by fraud.[55] The same reasoning serves to exclude judgments which make an order in terms of an arbitral award.[56] In all these cases, the exclusion reflects the fact that the effective adjudication was not by a judge of a Member State. In all cases falling outside the domain of the Regulation, the jurisdiction of the English courts over the defendant is a matter for the traditional jurisdictional rules of English law, and the Regulation can thereafter be ignored.

Temporal scope

Article 66 provides that the Regulation applies to the taking of jurisdiction by courts in legal proceedings instituted after 1 March 2002.[57] In England, at least, the institution of proceedings will mean the issue of process, rather than its service on a defendant.[58] For proceedings instituted before that date, the Brussels and Lugano Conventions remain in force, as they also do in relation to the contracting states to the Brussels or Lugano Convention but not bound by the Regulation.

---

[52] Case 145/86 *Hoffmann* v. *Krieg* [1988] ECR 645.

[53] The question is examined in Chap. 4 below. But the effect of Case C–391/95 *Van Uden Maritime BV* v. *Deco Line* [1998] ECR I–7091 is that the existence of an agreement to arbitrate means that a state has no jurisdiction to adjudicate even though the dispute is within the scope of the Reg., and jurisdictional error is no basis for denying recognition to a judgment.

[54] Judgments from Denmark will be within the scope of the Brussels Convention; those from Lugano states will be within the scope of that Convention. The proposition in the text refers to judgments from countries outside any of these territories.

[55] Case C–129/92 *Owens Bank plc* v. *Bracco* [1994] ECR I–117.

[56] Schlosser Report [1979] OJ C59/71.

[57] See Art. 76 for the commencement date.

[58] *Canada Trust Co.* v. *Stolzenberg (No 2)* [2000] 3 WLR 1376 (HL).

Other conventions

As regards the relationship with other conventions, one might have expected that existing international agreements, especially those which implicate non-member states, would remain unaffected by the Regulation. The reality is not quite so rational. Though Article 71 provides that the Regulation 'shall not affect any conventions . . . which in relation to particular matters, govern jurisdiction' it goes on, rather ineptly, to explain that this means that if a convention allows for the taking of jurisdiction, that provision shall continue to be effective, even though the defendant is domiciled in a Member State which is not party to that convention. Accordingly, if another convention, such as those in maritime law which deal with the arrest of sea-going ships, and with cargo claims, authorize the taking of jurisdiction, the Regulation appears not to impede it. But unless the particular convention contains its own provisions for the prevention of parallel litigation, the provisions of the Regulation[59] will apply 'to fill the gap'. It is as if the particular convention is absorbed into the Regulation, with the result that it may then be modified in its operation.[60] The result is hard to reconcile with the proposition that the Regulation does not affect the assumption of jurisdiction under the particular convention; and Article 71(2) of the Regulation is deceptive. Even so, what Article 71 completely fails to say is that, where a convention expressly forbids the taking of jurisdiction, that provision shall continue to be effective, whatever the Regulation would otherwise have decreed. The relevant international obligations of the United Kingdom in relation to arbitration include obligations to *refuse* to accept jurisdiction, rather than to exercise it, and for this to be ignored by the Regulation is inexplicable.

In relation to community instruments which make provision for jurisdiction in relation to specific matters, Article 67 provides that these are not prejudiced in their application by the Regulation. So Directive 96/71/EC[61] on workers temporarily posted abroad and Directive 93/13/EC on unfair terms in consumer contracts[62] may to this extent prevail over the Regulation.

[59] Arts. 27–30; p. 81 below.

[60] Case C–406/92 *The Tatry* [1994] ECR I-5439.

[61] [1997] OJ L18/1, Art. 6 of which deals with jurisdiction.

[62] Unfair Terms in Consumer Contracts Regulations 1999, SI 1999/2083, applicable to arbitration and jurisdiction agreements: Case C–240/98 *Océano Grupo Editorial SA* v. *Quintero* [2000] ECR I-4941; *Standard Bank London Ltd.* v. *Apostolakis*, 9 Feb. 2001, not yet reported. The Directive can be found at [1993] OJ L95/29.

Domicile: a preliminary examination

Many of the provisions contained in the Regulation turn upon whether
the defendant is domiciled in the United Kingdom or another Member
State. It is necessary to distinguish natural persons from companies or
other legal persons or associations of persons, and from trusts, for the
definition of domicile is not uniform. To determine whether an individual is domiciled in the United Kingdom, Article 59(1) of the Regulation tells a court to apply the law of the United Kingdom. In this context,
domicile in the United Kingdom is determined by Civil Jurisdiction and
Judgments Order 2001, Sch. 1, para. 9, which re-enacts section 41 of the
Civil Jurisdiction and Judgments Act 1982, not by the common law.
According to this, an individual is domiciled in the United Kingdom if he
is resident in the United Kingdom, and this residence indicates that he
has a substantial connection with the United Kingdom (a fact which may
be presumed from three months' residence). Similar rules, *mutatis
mutandis*, determine whether an individual is domiciled in a part of the
United Kingdom. But to determine whether an individual is domiciled in
another Member State, Article 59(2) provides that a court must apply the
law of the Member State of the proposed domicile. So whether he is
domiciled in France is a matter of French law; in Italy, a matter of Italian
law, and so on. It follows that an individual may have a domicile in more
than one Member State. This is unproblematic, for though it would be
very inconvenient for concurrent domiciliary laws to determine capacity
to marry, for example, it is much less surprising if a person's connections
with two Member States are sufficient for these each to be proper places
in which to sue him in matters of general[63] jurisdiction.

There has been pressure to provide a single autonomous definition of
domicile, or to abandon it *holus bolus* and move instead to the concept of
habitual residence, not least because of variation in the separate national
law definitions of domicile. But in the absence of a public register of
status, however defined, it is difficult to see that such a change would
accomplish very much of value. There will be occasional difficult cases,
typically where a person maintains a residence or some other establishment, but manages to cast a veil of secrecy over his movements.[64] In such
a case his domicile would probably be no more difficult to ascertain than
his habitual residence, and it is unlikely that the change would have
brought much about.

---

[63] Chap. II, Sect. 1 of the Reg. is entitled 'General provisions'.
[64] Cf *Canada Trust Co.* v. *Stolzenberg (No 2)* [2000] 3 WLR 1376 (HL).

For a *company*, *other legal person*, or *association of natural persons*, Article 60(1) provides that it has a domicile in any one or more of three places: where it has its statutory seat, or its central administration, or its principal place of business. For the purposes of the United Kingdom, 'statutory seat' is defined as the registered office or, where there is none anywhere, the place of incorporation or, where there is none anywhere, the place under the law of which the formation took place. The purpose[65] of Article 60 is to move the law towards a more uniform definition of the domicile of a corporation or other legal person. Previously each national law had supplied its own definition of the domicile of a company,[66] etc., and the result was a complexity which served no useful purpose; the contrast with the domicile of individuals is that for companies and other legal persons distinctive national law definitions of domicile are redundant.

By contrast, to ascertain whether a *trust* is domiciled in the United Kingdom, Article 60(3) provides that the court will apply the law of the United Kingdom. Accordingly, a trust is domiciled in England if English law is that with which the trust has its closest and most real connection.[67] It is never necessary to determine whether a trust is domiciled in another Member State, for no jurisdictional rule is formulated on this basis.

Jurisdictional rules of the Regulation

Suppose that proceedings in a civil or commercial matter are instituted after the coming into effect of the Regulation on 1 March 2002. If this happens, the Regulation alone serves to determine whether the court has, or does not have, jurisdiction; and to obtain a reliable answer, it is necessary to examine the provisions of the Regulation in the order in which they are set out below.

Exclusive jurisdiction, regardless of domicile: Article 22

Article 22 of the Regulation[68] gives exclusive jurisdiction, regardless[69] of domicile, to the courts of a Member State, in five areas. In the rare case where it confers exclusive jurisdiction on the courts of two Member States, Article 29[70] provides that the first court seised alone has exclusive jurisdiction. Where Article 22 confers exclusive jurisdiction on a court, no other court has jurisdiction, even if both parties purport to submit to

---

[65] Recital 11. [66] Cf Art. 53 BC.

[67] 2001 Order, Sch. 1, para. 12, re-enacting 1982 Act, s. 45.

[68] Sect. 6 of Chap. II; cf Art. 16 BC, which contain minor divergences.

[69] That is to say, whether the defendant is domiciled in any Member State or none.

[70] Cf Art. 23 BC.

it;[71] and a judgment which conflicts with Article 22 must be denied recognition.[72] For Article 22 to be engaged, the connection must lie with a Member State. If the land, public register, etc., is in a non-member state, Article 22 has no application, and the relevant question is whether the Regulation gives a court with jurisdiction under some other Article a discretion to decline it by pointing to a non-member state; the issue is not straightforward and is considered below.

Article 22(1) covers proceedings which have as their (principal[73]) object rights *in rem* in, or tenancies of, immoveable property in a Member State: exclusive jurisdiction is vested in the state where the land is situated. To this two ancillary rules are added. First, where the proceedings have as their object a tenancy of immoveable property concluded for temporary private use for no more than six consecutive months, Article 22(1) provides that the courts of the Member State in which the defendant is domiciled shall also[74] have exclusive jurisdiction, provided that the tenant is a natural person, and landlord and tenant are domiciled in the same Member State, which is useful if the dispute is a small one concerned with a holiday letting in another Member State. Secondly, Article 6(4) allows a contractual action to be combined with the action *in rem* against the same defendant, which is useful in a mortgage action.

It is not enough that the proceedings concern or are even fought over land or a tenancy of immoveable property; the policies which underpin Article 22(1) require a more careful analysis than that. But these policies are capable of pointing in conflicting directions. Three can be proposed: most Member State laws regard jurisdiction over land as a matter for only the courts of the *situs*; land law, and especially tenancy law, is complicated and is better applied by a local court; and as the Article derogates from a person's right to defend at home it is to be read restrictively. This last point has been taken to mean that proceedings in which a tenancy is only part of the background to the dispute, or is only a minor part of a more complex contract (such as an all-inclusive holiday[75]) and not the principal aspect of the claim, fall outside Article 22(1). Likewise, claims to enforce obligations contained in or associated with leases but which are not themselves peculiar to tenancies, such as a covenant to pay for the business

---

[71] Art. 23(5).   [72] Art. 35(1).
[73] This word does not appear in the text of the Art., but was read in: Case C–280/90 *Hacker* v. *Euro-Relais* [1992] ECR I–1111; cf *Ashurst* v. *Pollard* [2001] Ch. 595 (CA).
[74] Joint exclusive jurisdiction may occasion the use of Art. 29.
[75] Case C–280/90 *Hacker* v. *Euro-Relais* [1992] ECR I–1111.

goodwill in a lease of commercial premises[76] or the statutory obligations of the provider of consumer credit after the landlord has defaulted on his obligation,[77] fall outside it as well. By contrast, a claim in respect of unpaid rent or utility charges,[78] or for the cost of cleaning up behind departing tenants who made a ruin of the premises,[79] are founded on obligations inherent in any tenancy, and no matter how narrow the interpretation of Article 22(1), these fall within it.

Rather more difficulty surrounds the question whether proceedings 'have as their object rights *in rem*' where the claimant cannot assert that he is already legal owner of the land and suing as such but claims, for example as contractual purchaser, to be entitled to be made legal owner[80] or claims, for example, as beneficiary under a resulting trust of the land already to be equitable owner of the land. The conclusion of the Court in such a case[81] that a beneficiary under a resulting trust has only an interest *in personam* and not one *in rem* was wrong, at least as a matter of English law, by several centuries;[82] and its further holding that a suit does not have a right *in rem* as its object when brought to acquire legal title from a resulting trustee is almost inexplicable: if an action brought to acquire legal title does not have legal title as its object, what does it have?[83] And in the context of Article 27, 'the object of proceedings' means 'the end in view':[84] the end in the beneficiary's view is the acquisition of title to the land. On the other hand, the outcome, if not the reasoning, can be defended from two very different points of view: first, that where the substantive law which the court will apply is not specifically land law or tenancy law, there is no need to engage Article 22(1), any more than if the same principles of resulting trust or of insolvency[85] were to be deployed against the owner of a yacht or of shares, and, secondly, that the common

---

[76] Case 73/77 *Sanders* v. *Van der Putte* [1977] ECR 2383.

[77] *Jarrett* v. *Barclays Bank plc* [1999] QB 1 (CA).

[78] Case 241/83 *Rösler* v. *Rottwinkel* [1985] ECR 99.

[79] Case C–8/98 *Dansommer A/S* v. *Götz* [2000] ECR I–393.

[80] Or as contractual vendor, seeking rescission of unperformed contract of sale: Case C–518/98 *Gaillard* v. *Chekili* [2001] ECR I–2771.

[81] Case C–294/92 *Webb* v. *Webb* [1994] ECR I–1717.

[82] The interest of the beneficiary can be enforced against all the world except the *bona fide* purchaser for value without notice; it is unreal to see this as a mere right *in personam*.

[83] Not least because it is brought on the basis that the claimant beneficiary does have pre-existing (and exclusive) equitable title.

[84] Case C–406/92 *The Tatry* [1994] ECR I–5439.

[85] *Ashurst* v. *Pollard* [2001] Ch. 595 (CA) (which was not excluded from the material scope of the Reg. because the claim of the trustee did not arise in the course of, but after, the insolvency).

law drew a similar jurisdictional distinction between determining legal title to foreign land (which it had no power to do) and enforcing a contract or other equity between the parties, albeit in the context of a land dispute (which it had).[86] But this just goes to illustrate the manner in which the various policies behind Article 22(1), all sensible in themselves, can collide, and that their reconciliation is not always possible.

Article 22(2) covers proceedings which have as their object the validity of the constitution, the dissolution or winding up, of companies, or the decisions of their organs. Exclusive jurisdiction is given to the Member State of the seat of the company, but this means the seat as defined by national law, not that in Article 60(2).[87] Where the winding up is a hoped-for remedy, such as on proof of minority shareholder oppression,[88] as opposed to an ongoing process, Article 22(2) is probably inapplicable.[89] Authority suggests that claims that an organ of the company has acted without authority will fall under the Article, at least where this is the principal component of the claim; but that allegations of abuse of authority will not:[90] a distinction in which is hard to believe.

Article 22(3) gives exclusive jurisdiction to the Member State in which a public register is kept if the proceedings have as their object the validity of an entry in that register. An action to rectify an entry on a land register will be covered;[91] and there is no rational[92] reason to exclude any action which seeks the amendment of an entry in such a register. The Article may also apply to a register maintained by a public limited company if it is open for inspection by the public, but the point is debatable.[93]

Article 22(4) gives exclusive jurisdiction to the Member State in which a patent or trade mark is registered or deposited if the proceedings have as their object the registration or validity of that right. An action for infringement will not fall within the Article,[94] but if the validity of the patent is raised as a defence it has been held that Articles 22 and 25 combine to give exclusive jurisdiction to the courts of the state of

---

[86] *Penn v. Baltimore* (1750) Ves. Sen. 444.

[87] Final sentence of Art. 22(2); see Civil Jurisdiction and Judgments Order 2001, Sch. 1, para. 10.

[88] Companies Act 1985, s. 459.

[89] Cf Case C–294/92 *Webb v. Webb* [1994] ECR I–1717.

[90] *Grupo Torras SA v. Sheikh Fahad Mohammed al Sabah* [1996] 1 Lloyd's Rep. 7 (CA).

[91] *Re Hayward* [1997] Ch. 45.

[92] The decision in *Ashurst v. Pollard* [2001] Ch. 595 (CA) that an application to procure amendment to the register of land ownership in Portugal was not within the predecessor of Art. 22(3) is beyond comprehension.

[93] *Re Fagin's Bookshop plc* [1992] BCLC 118.

[94] Case 288/82 *Duijnstee v. Goderbauer* [1983] ECR 3663.

registration and to disseise the other court.[95] The practice in some other Member States, however, would be to stay the infringement proceedings, to allow the issue of validity to be determined in the court with exclusive jurisdiction over it, the infringement action then being resumed. It is arguable that this divergence in national practice distorts the effect of the Regulation.

Article 22(5) gives exclusive jurisdiction to the Member State in which a judgment from a Member State is being enforced if the proceedings are concerned with that enforcement. There must have been a judgment: proceedings which seek to pave the way for enforcing a prospective judgment, such as by obtaining a freezing injunction, are outside the Article.[96] It is possible that applications against a non-party for an order that there be a contribution to payment of the winning party's costs fall within this provision, for these are concerned with the enforcement of the court's original judgment.[97]

Jurisdiction by appearance: Article 24

Unless Article 22 applies, if the defendant enters an appearance before a court, Article 24[98] provides that the court thereupon has jurisdiction; any prior agreement on jurisdiction will be considered to have been waived or varied by consent.[99] But if the appearance was entered[100] to contest the jurisdiction of the court, which in England will mean following the procedure in CPR Part 11, the appearance will not confer jurisdiction. One of the bedrock principles of the Regulation is that a defendant must be allowed to appear, without prejudice, to argue for its proper application to his case, and that he must do this *in limine*, and not by opposing recognition of the judgment *ex post*. So long as he does what is necessary to contest the jurisdiction at the first opportunity which the procedural law of the court allows him, he will not lose this protection if he is required in practice to plead his defence to the merits of the claim at the same time.[101] But if he takes a step towards defending the claim on the merits, which

---

[95] *Coin Controls Ltd.* v. *Suzo International (UK) Ltd.* [1999] Ch. 33.

[96] Case C–261/90 *Reichert* v. *Dresdner Bank (No 2)* [1992] ECR I–2149.

[97] Cf *The Ikarian Reefer* [2000] 1 WLR 603 (CA) where the point was not taken. But the Art. does not require it to be a judgmenr from *another* Member State.

[98] Sect. 7 of Chap. II; cf Art. 18 BC.

[99] Case C–150/80 *Elefanten Schuh GmbH* v. *Jacqmain* [1981] ECR 1671.

[100] The predecessor to Art. 24 (Art. 18 of the Conventions) required, in the English language at least, that the appearance be *solely* to contest the jurisdiction. If the law was ever that restrictive, it is not now.

[101] Case 27/81 *Rohr SA* v. *Ossberger* [1981] ECR 2431.

was not in this sense required, he will have thrown away the shield which Article 24 gave him.[102]

Insurance, consumer and employment contracts

Where disputes arise out of insurance contracts,[103] certain consumer contracts,[104] or individual contracts of employment,[105] and where the insurer, supplier, or employer is domiciled in a Member State (or is not, but made the contract by a local branch or agency which is so domiciled[106]), there may well have been such inequality between the parties that the insured or policyholder, consumer, or employee will need special jurisdictional privileges if his rights are to be effectively safeguarded. These three Sections of Chapter II establish a pattern of rules in which the policy-holder,[107] consumer, or employee has the right to sue and be sued in the courts of his domicile. In certain cases the policyholder or insured, consumer, or employee may elect to sue in a Member State other than that of his domicile; but the insurer, supplier, or employer is generally restricted to suing where the defendant is domiciled. Jurisdiction agreements are generally binding only if entered into after the dispute arose, or if they widen the choice given to the policyholder,[108] consumer,[109] or employee.[110] By way of reinforcement, a judgment which violates any of the juris-dictional provisions governing insurance and consumer contracts will be denied recognition, though for an inexplicable reason this safeguard is not extended to employment contracts.[111] Where the insurer, supplier, or employer neither has, nor is deemed by reason of his having a branch or

---

[102] Cf (in a case not governed by the Reg.) *Marc Rich & Co. AG* v. *Società Italiana Impianti PA* [1992] 2 Lloyd's Rep. 624 (CA).

[103] Arts. 8–14; Sect. 3 of Chap. II; cf Arts. 7–12A BC, from which some divergence has been made.

[104] Arts. 15–17; Sect. 4 of Chap. II; cf Arts. 13–15 BC, from which some divergence has been made.

[105] Arts. 18–21; Sect. 5 of Chap. II. This has no immediate precursor in the Conventions, though Arts. 5(1) and 17 BC did make piecemeal provision for these contracts.

[106] For the definition of domicile in the UK in this context see Civil Jurisdiction and Judgments Order 2001, Sch. 1, para. 11.

[107] In addition to those general rules described in the text there is specific provision for co-insurance (Art. 9(1)(c)), liability insurance or insurance of immoveables (Art. 10), direct actions by an injured party against an insurer (Art. 11), joinder of parties (Art. 11), counterclaims (Art. 12). Jurisdiction agreements are regulated by Arts. 13 and 14.

[108] Art. 13.

[109] Art. 17; and see Unfair Terms in Consumer Contracts Regulations 1999, SI 1999/2083, enacting Dir. 93/13/EC on unfair terms in consumer contracts [1993] OJ L95/29; Case C–240/98 *Océano Grupo Editorial SA* v. *Quintero* [2000] ECR I–4941.

[110] Art. 21.

[111] Art. 35(1), which omits reference to Sect. 5 of Chap. II.

agency to have, a domicile in a Member State, Article 4 will apply to claims against him.[112]

More particularly, the *insurance* provisions do not apply to reinsurance, which is not a relationship of inherent inequality,[113] but they do apply to direct actions by the injured party against the insurer.[114] The restrictions on jurisdiction agreements are relaxed in the cases of marine insurance and in the case of large risks.[115] A *consumer* contract is one in which an individual concludes the contract for a purpose outside his trade or profession and is one which in general secures the needs of an individual in terms of private consumption.[116] There is no exclusion of investment or other middle-class contracts so long as they fall within the definition,[117] for any rule which sought to differentiate between weak consumers and strong consumers would be terribly subjective. Within that general definition, the types of consumer contracts actually covered by Section 4 of Chapter II are more restrictive than might be expected: Article 15(1) applies it only to (a) a contract for the sale of goods on instalment credit terms, or (b) a contract for a loan repayable by instalments, or other credit, made to finance the sale of goods, or (c) a contract concluded with a person who pursues commercial or professional activities in the Member State of the consumer's domicile or, by any means, directs such activities to that Member State or to several states including that Member State, and contracts falling within the scope of such activities. And in any event Article 15(3) excludes contracts of transport except for package holiday contracts. Point (c) replaces an earlier version which focused on targeted invitations or advertising; and it remains to be seen what this more general wording will cover. Prior to the adoption of the Regulation there had been much discussion of whether contracts made by computer-literate consumers from the comfort of their spare bedrooms would be routinely included or excluded. But it seems plausible that the intention is for a supplier who uses the

---

[112] Case C–412/98 *Universal General Insurance Co.* v. *Groupe Josi Reinsurance Co. SA* [2000] ECR I–5925.

[113] Ibid.

[114] Art. 11(2). In England this will most commonly arise under the Third Parties (Rights Against Insurers) Act 1930.

[115] Arts. 13(5) and 14.

[116] Case C–269/95 *Benincasa* v. *Dentalkit Srl* [1997] ECR I–3767; and see also Case C–99/96 *Mietz* v. *Intership Yachting Sneek BV* [1999] ECR I–2277.

[117] Case C–318/93 *Brenner* v. *Dean Witter Reynolds Inc.* [1994] ECR I–4275. But if the consumer has assigned his rights to a body which is not itself a consumer, the jurisdictional privilege is lost: Case C–89/91 *Shearson Lehmann Hutton* v. *TVB* [1993] ECR I–139.

Internet as the way to bring his goods and services to the attention of potential customers in a Member State or elsewhere as well as to be someone whose contracts may fall within (c) above. The suggestion, occasionally heard, that this will so intimidate suppliers that it will at a stroke put an end to electronic commerce in the European Union is manifestly absurd.

The *employment* contract provisions of Section 5 are substantively new. They represent the culmination of a series of steps, judicial and legislative, to protect workers from the inevitable inequalities under contracts written by the bosses. The employee may sue where he is domiciled or in the Member State in which he habitually carries out his work, so as to give him the benefits of local[118] employment law.

Agreements on jurisdiction: Article 23

Apart from the cases mentioned above, where their effect is restricted, agreements on jurisdiction for the courts of a Member State are validated by Article 23.[119] A compliant agreement is required to be respected both by the court chosen and by the courts whose jurisdiction is excluded: the agreement serves to prorogate and derogate. Only if no party to the agreement is domiciled in a Member State may it be overridden, and then not before the nominated court has declined jurisdiction. But there is otherwise no discretion to override a valid jurisdiction agreement, say on grounds of overall trial convenience.[120] An agreement to confer jurisdiction on the courts of the United Kingdom is effective so far as the Regulation is concerned, but raises some practical difficulties: it probably gives jurisdiction to the courts in any part of the United Kingdom unless it can be construed as being more particular than first appears.[121] An agreement nominating the courts of two Member States will probably be effective;[122] one which is construed as giving non-exclusive jurisdiction to a court will do exactly what it says.[123] But an agreement for the courts of a non-member state is outside Article 23, not least because the Regulation cannot bind such a court to accept jurisdiction: the relevant question is

---

[118] There is not much likelihood of this attracting much business to the courts of the UK.

[119] Sect. 7 of Chap. II; cf Art. 17 BC, from which some departure has been made.

[120] *Hough* v. *P&O Containers Ltd.* [1999] QB 834.

[121] Cf *Komninos S, The* [1991] 1 Lloyd's Rep. 370 (CA).

[122] Case 23/78 *Meeth* v. *Glacetal Sàrl* [1978] ECR 2133 (but each court had exclusive jurisdiction over particular actions; there was no overlapping of competences).

[123] Art. 23(1), which thereby removes the uncertainty about such clauses under Art. 17 BC: *Kurz* v. *Stella Musical Veranstaltungs GmbH* [1992] Ch. 196 had held them to be effective, but the reconciliation of this with Art. 17 BC was not easy.

whether this gives a court with jurisdiction under some other provision of the Regulation a discretion to decline it in favour of a non-member state. The issue is considered below.

To ensure that the parties have a proper opportunity to be aware of the effect of the agreement they are making, the agreement must be in writing or evidenced in writing (which includes electronic means which provide a durable record in writing[124]), or in a form which accords with the parties' established practice, or in a form which is well known to accord with international trade usage of which the parties were or should have been aware. So a printed term in standard conditions of business will be ineffective unless the parties have signed their agreement to it;[125] but a settled course of dealing or a trade usage will establish a binding form. An inevitable tension exists between the desire to ensure fair dealing by strict application of the rules on form, and awareness that this may be inappropriate where both parties were perfectly well aware that they were dealing on the basis of an agreement on jurisdiction. Though the Court has insisted on strict interpretation of these formalities,[126] it has also approved a more flexible approach where it would be bad faith for a party to plead the formal invalidity.[127] More radically, a shareholder was bound by a jurisdiction agreement contained in the company's constitution on the ground that he knew or should have known of it, and had assented to be bound by his becoming a shareholder.[128] Whether this example of constructive notice will be extended to other contexts remains to be seen. But it is the original contracting parties whose consent needs to satisfy the formal requirements. If a third party succeeds to the contractual rights or liabilities of one of the parties, as under a bill of lading,[129] it is not a requirement that his consent be written or evidenced in writing: a series of French cases had held the contrary, and they are wrong.[130] But

---

[124] Which certainly includes fax, and presumably includes a printed or printable message by e-mail.

[125] Case 24/76 *Estasis Salotti* v. *RÜWA Polstereimaschinen GmbH* [1976] ECR 1831, a proposition reiterated in Case C–159/97 *Trasporti Castelletti Spedizioni Internazionali SpA* v. *Hugo Trumpy SpA* [1999] ECR I–1517 (a case decided on an earlier version of Art. 17 BC; *Lafarge Plasterboard Ltd.* v. *Fritz Peters & Co. KG* [2000] 2 Lloyd's Rep. 689.

[126] Case 24/76 *Estasis Salotti* v. *RÜWA* [1976] ECR 1831, reiterated in Case C–105/95 *MSG* v. *Les Gravières Rhénanes Sàrl* [1997] ECR I–911.

[127] Case 221/84 *Berghofer* v. *ASA SA* [1985] ECR 2699; Case 313/85 *Iveco Fiat* v. *Van Hool* [1986] ECR 3337 (previous course of dealing).

[128] Case C–214/89 *Powell Duffryn plc* v. *Petereit* [1992] ECR I–1745.

[129] Case 71/83 *Partenreederei M/S Tilly Russ* v. *Haven- en Vervoerbedrijf Nova NV (The Tilly Russ)* [1984] ECR 2417.

[130] Case C–387/98 *Coreck Maritime GmbH* v. *Handelsveem BV* [2000] ECR I–9337.

where a third party acquires rights under the contract otherwise than by means of succession, it may be that the formal requirements will be applied in relation to claims involving him.

An agreement which complies with the formalities may not be impeached on the ground that it fails to comply with some provision, whether as to form[131] or substance,[132] of national (as distinct from European[133]) law which would otherwise deprive it of effect; and an argument that the contract containing it is ineffective or void will not immediately defeat the jurisdiction agreement either, for it is to be regarded as severable from and independent of any contract containing it.[134] But if one party claims that his writing was procured by force, fear, or fraud, a court must be allowed to find that there was no 'agreement' to confer jurisdiction. Whether it does this by recourse to its own contract law or to the law which governs the jurisdiction agreement or in accordance with some autonomous definition of agreement is uncertain, but the last of these seems most likely to be held to be correct.[135]

The jurisdiction given by Article 23 is exclusive unless the agreement stipulated otherwise, but it is intended to be of a lower potency than that conferred by Article 22: a judgment which violates Article 23 may not be denied recognition.[136] Yet this has not prevented the English courts from giving Article 23 a high profile: if an English court has been nominated by an agreement on jurisdiction, it will exercise it even if another court has been seised first; and an injunction may go to restrain the respondent from continuing in the other court.[137] We will look at this again in the context of discretion and the Regulation, but it is well to point out that there is nothing in the structure of Article 23 to warrant it, however desirable it may be as a matter of commercial sense.

General jurisdiction over defendants domiciled in the United Kingdom: Article 2

If none of the provisions examined so far serves to confer or deny the

---

[131] Case 150/80 *Elefanten Schuh GmbH* v. *Jacqmain* [1981] ECR 1671 (wrong language).

[132] Case 25/79 *Sanicentral GmbH* v. *Collin* [1979] ECR 3423 (ousting the jurisdiction of the local employment tribunal was illegal).

[133] Art. 67; cf the Unfair Terms in Consumer Contracts Regulations 1999, SI 1999/2083 enacting Dir. 93/13/EC on unfair terms in consumer contracts [1993] OJ L95/29.

[134] Case C–269/95 *Benincasa* v. *Dentalkit Srl* [1997] ECR I–3767.

[135] The point was left wide open in *Benincasa*, above n. 133.

[136] Art. 35(1) does not mention Sect. 7 of Chap. II.

[137] *Continental Bank NA* v. *Aeakos Compania Naviera SA* [1994] 1 WLR 588 (CA); *The Angelic Grace* [1995] 1 Lloyd's Rep. 87. (CA).

jurisdiction of the court, the rule in Article 2,[138] that general jurisdiction exists where the defendant is domiciled, will apply: general jurisdiction means that it is not limited by reference to its subject matter or the form of the action. The definition of United Kingdom, and of English, domicile has been given above.[139] It is striking that though this is said to be the fundamental principle of the Regulation, its place in the hierarchy of rules is relatively low.

Special jurisdiction over defendants domiciled in another Member State: Articles 5–7

If none of the provisions examined so far serves to confer or deny the jurisdiction of the court, the defendant must be domiciled outside the United Kingdom. Articles 5 to 7[140] confer special jurisdiction over defendants who are domiciled in another Member State. Article 5 reflects an indirect awareness of *forum conveniens*, but jurisdiction based on the wording of Article 5 may not be contradicted by showing that the court is, in the particular case, not a *forum conveniens*: the role of *forum conveniens* was exhausted when the Article was drafted. Article 5 may not be used as the anchor to join claims over which the court would not otherwise have had jurisdiction: such general jurisdiction is conferred only by Article 2, and this may impair the utility of Article 5.[141] Article 6 deals with some forms of multipartite litigation; and Article 7 with proceedings to limit liability in maritime claims.

Matters relating to a contract: Article 5(1)

In matters relating to a contract, Article 5(1)(a) gives special jurisdiction to the courts for the place of performance[142] of the obligation in question. A matter does not relate to a contract for the purpose of this jurisdictional rule unless it involves obligations freely entered into with regard to another,[143] but if it does it is not decisive that it would not be regarded as contractual by national law. So a claim to enforce the rules of an

---

[138] Sect. 1 of Chap. II. [139] Pp. 60–1.

[140] Sect. 2 of Chap. II; cf Arts. 5 and 6 BC, from which some departure has been made.

[141] It has been convincingly argued that where parties to a contract sue on it, all associated claims should be 'channelled' into that one action, in the interests of efficiency and because the contract rule is of a higher order: Case 189/87 *Kalfelis* v. *Bankhaus Schröder, Münchmeyer, Hengst und Co.* [1988] ECR 5565, where this was proposed by the AG but rejected by the Court.

[142] The French text renders this as the place where the obligation was or should have been performed, and this is the sense in which it must be understood.

[143] Case C–26/91 *Soc. Jakob Handte GmbH* v. *Soc. Traîtements Mécano-chimiques des Surfaces* [1992] ECR I–3967.

association,[144] or the obligation of a shareholder to a company[145] is contractual even though a national law may disagree; a claim by a sub-buyer against a manufacturer is not contractual, even if it is regarded as contractual under national law;[146] it is uncertain whether liability to someone to whom advice was negligently given, but for which responsibility was voluntarily assumed though regarded as tortious in English law for substantive purposes[147] would satisfy the autonomous definition of contract for the purpose of jurisdiction under the Regulation. If the validity of the contract is disputed, the Article is not precluded from operation,[148] and this is so even if the claimant is asserting, contrary to the submission of the defendant, that an alleged contract is ineffective or that it has been rescinded for misrepresentation, non-disclosure, or duress.[149] But it may be different if both parties accept that a supposed contract is invalid and are parties to a claim only for consequential relief.[150] However, once the issue of jurisdiction under the Regulation has been settled, the national court will apply its own substantive law.[151]

The place of performance of the obligation in question, which locates the court with special jurisdiction, has to be selected from a menu of four items. The first three are given by Article 5(1)(b): in a contract for the sale of goods it is where under the contract the goods were delivered or should have been delivered; in a contract for the provision of services where under the contract the services were provided or should have been

---

[144] Case 34/82 *Peters* v. *ZNAV* [1983] ECR 987.

[145] Case C–214/89 *Powell Duffryn plc* v. *Petereit* [1992] ECR I–1745.

[146] Case C–26/91 *Soc. Jakob Handte GmbH* v. *Soc. Traîtements Mécano-chimiques des Surfaces* [1992] ECR I–3967. But the French cour de cassation has now accepted that the claim of the sub-buyer is not contractual as a matter of French law, after all: *Dragon Rouge*, Cass civ 1ère, 6 July 1999; [2000] Rev. Crit. 67.

[147] Under the principle in *Hedley Byrne & Co.* v. *Heller & Partners* [1964] AC 465. There may be a difference between two- and three-party cases, such as *Hedley Byrne* and *Smith* v. *Eric S. Bush* [1990] 1 AC 831, where reliance is predictable and the identity of the relier known, and cases where this is not so, such as *Caparo Industries plc* v. *Dickman* [1990] 2 AC 605. But actions for damages under the Misrepresentation Act 1967, s. 2(1), and alleging that misrepresentation induced a contract, have been held to be not contractual: *Alfred Dunhill Ltd.* v. *Diffusion Internationale de Maroquinerie de Prestige SARL* [2001] CLC 949.

[148] Case 38/81 *Effer SpA* v. *Kantner* [1982] ECR 825.

[149] *Agnew* v. *Länsförsäkringsbolagens AB* [2001] 1 AC 223; *Boss Group Ltd.* v. *Boss France SA* [1997] 1 WLR 351 (CA). If the case falls within Art. 5(1)(c), the obligation in question will be the one not to misrepresent or to coerce.

[150] *Kleinwort Benson Ltd.* v. *Glasgow City Council* [1999] 1 AC 153 (a case on the intra-UK provisions, and a decision whose scope is curtailed by *Agnew*, above n. 149).

[151] Case C–26/91 *Soc. Jakob Handte GmbH* v. *Soc. Traîtements Mécano-chimiques des Surfaces* [1992] ECR I–3967, 3984.

provided; and in either of these two classes of contract, it will be the place of performance which the parties otherwise agreed if this is what they did.

The fourth choice is given by Article 5(1)(c): in the case of other contracts, it is the place of performance of the primary[152] obligation on the basis of which the claimant brings his claim: the question is which is the obligation whose non-performance forms the basis of his claim.[153] Despite the possibility of disagreement, which will probably be reinforced by the wording of Article 5(1)(b),[154] the obligation referred to by Article 5(1)(c) need not be one created by the contract and required by the terms of the contract to be performed: an obligation not to use misrepresentation or non-disclosure to procure a contract of reinsurance, for example, is not created by the contract but will be covered by the rule.[155] If the contract does not specify the place of performance of the critical obligation, this has to be identified by the court first applying its choice of law rules to ascertain the law which governs the contract, and then using this to locate the place of performance.[156] Though it is sometimes said that this can make the location of special jurisdiction unpredictable, all Member States have the same choice of law rule for contracts,[157] and it is unlikely that this criticism needs to be taken too seriously. And after all, if the parties have not troubled to specify the place of performance of an obligation, the only safe assumption is that they are content to have the default option provided by the governing law.

Though in many cases it will produce an easy answer, Article 5(1)(b) is cast in this complex form as a result of departure from its predecessor in the Conventions, which invariably fastened on the obligation on which the claimant founded his claim.[158] Where the claimant was an unpaid seller, the obligation in question would therefore be the payment of the price, which was not always due somewhere with a close connection to the facts giving rise to the dispute.[159] In the case of a seller under a contract

---

[152] That is to say, a performance obligation, not a secondary obligation to compensate for breach of a primary obligation.

[153] Case 14/76 *De Bloos Sprl* v. *Bouyer SA* [1976] ECR 1497.

[154] Which refers to obligations 'under the contract', as if to exclude reference to those arising outside it.

[155] *Agnew* v. *Länsförsäkringsbolagens AB* [2001] 1 AC 223 (HL).

[156] Case 12/76 *Industrie Tessili Italiana Como* v. *Dunlop AG* [1976] ECR 1473; Case C–440/97 *GIE Groupe Concorde* v. *Master of the Vessel 'Suhediwarno Panjan'* [1999] ECR I–6307.

[157] The Rome Convention, examined in Chap. 5, is common to all Member States.

[158] That is, on the provision which is now Art. 5(1)(c).

[159] Case C–288/92 *Custom Made Commercial Ltd.* v. *Stawa Metallbau GmbH* [1994] ECR I–2913.

governed by English law, this would allow the action to be brought in the seller's home courts, as under English law a debt is payable where the creditor resides,[160] and this flew in the face of the principle that it was defendants, not claimants, who were intended to have home advantage. So for the two major classes of contract, sale of goods and supply of services, the obligation is defined as the performance one, not the payment one, no matter how the claim arises. If the parties have not specified the place of delivery or provision, it will be necessary to fall back on the technique of identifying the law which governs the contract, and then using it to determine the place for performance. So if a contract for the sale of goods is governed by English law, the general rule is that the place of delivery is the manufacturer's place of business.[161] And it is unclear what is intended by the provision in Article 5(1)(b) which allows for contrary agreement, for the place of performance of these obligations is always a matter of agreement between the parties. However, although an agreement on place of performance need not be reduced to writing,[162] a wholly artificial stipulation of a place of performance will be treated as if it were a jurisdiction agreement, and required to comply with Article 23.[163]

The law has therefore embarked on the task of sub-classifying contracts, as opposed to having an omnibus special jurisdictional rule for them all. Presumably Article 5(1)(b) will include contracts for the supply of goods, for example on hire or hire purchase, and the supply of goods and services, as in a contract for work and materials. But there will be many others which do not so easily conform to the assumed pattern of a payment of money[164] in return for a transfer of property: commission agency, a barter contract, contracts of reinsurance, goods paid for by cheque, distributorship, and many arrangements in the realm of financial services will fit uneasily if at all within Article 5(1)(b); and it may be expected that considerable difficulties of definition will arise.

Where the relevant obligation was to be performed in more places than one: delivery to sites in Belgium and the Netherlands, sales representation[165] to be performed in the United Kingdom and Ireland, and so on, one asks where this obligation was principally to be performed, and

---

[160] *The Eider* [1893] P 119.   [161] Sale of Goods Act 1979, s. 29(2).

[162] Case 56/79 *Zelger v. Salinitri* [1980] ECR 89.

[163] Case C–106/95 *MSG* v. *Les Gravières Rhénanes Sàrl* [1997] ECR I–911 (contract for carriage by barge; place of performance specified as a place not on a waterway).

[164] See the definition in Sale of Goods Act 1979, s. 61.

[165] But if this were seen as a contract of employment, it would have fallen under Arts. 18–21.

locates it there;[166] likewise in a case within Article 5(1)(c), if there are two obligations relied on, that which is principal will be the critical one.[167] But if it is not possible to regard one as ancillary to the other as principal, there will be special jurisdiction over only a fraction of the claim.[168] A wise judge will avoid so inconvenient a result.

Matters relating to tort, delict or quasi-delict: Article 5(3)

Article 5(3) gives special jurisdiction to the courts for the place where the harmful event occurred or may occur. The addition of the words 'or may occur' is new and welcome; the place where a harmful event may occur will be subject to the same interpretation as that which identifies where it did occur, differing only in chronology. The place where the harmful event occurred means the place where the damage occurred, or of the event giving rise to it: the claimant may elect between them if they diverge.[169] So when a waterway was polluted and the water used by a gardener downstream with disastrous consequences, the damage occurred where the crop was ruined; the event giving rise to the damage was the original pollution; and the claimant was entitled to elect between them.[170] Locating the place of damage can be an artificial exercise, but the cases offer some guidance. In principle, damage occurs where the damage or loss first materializes, and not, if this is different, where it or its consequence is subsequently felt.[171] So if property is wrongfully taken, the damage occurs where the taking occurred, as distinct from where the claimant's financial records of the loss are kept;[172] or—assuming the case not to fall within Article 5(1)—where the negligent advice is acted on so as to cause loss, as distinct from where it was initially received and read,[173] and as further distinct from where the adverse financial consequences of acting on it are eventually felt;[174] where damaged goods were delivered

---

[166] Case C–125/92 *Mulox IBC* v. *Geels* [1993] ECR I–4075; Case C–383/95 *Rutten* v. *Cross Medical Ltd.* [1997] ECR I–57.

[167] Case 266/85 *Shenavai* v. *Kreischer* [1987] ECR 239.

[168] Case C–420/97 *Leathertex Divisione Sintetici SpA* v. *Bodetex BVBA* [1999] ECR I–6747.

[169] Case 21/76 *Handelskwekerij G. J. Bier BV* v. *Mines de Potasse d'Alsace* [1976] ECR 1875; Case C–364/93 *Marinari* v. *Lloyd's Bank plc* [1995] ECR I–2719; Case C–68/93 *Shevill* v. *Presse Alliance SA* [1995] ECR I–415.

[170] *Handelskwekerij Bier*, above n. 169.

[171] Case C–220/88 *Dumez France SA* v. *Hessische Landesbank* [1990] ECR I–49.

[172] Case C–364/93 *Marinari* v. *Lloyd's Bank plc* [1995] ECR I– 2719. It is probable that this also excludes the jurisdiction of the place where the claimant's shares are traded.

[173] *Ibid.*

[174] *Domicrest Ltd.* v. *Swiss Bank Corporation* [1999] QB 548; *Alfred Dunhill Ltd.* v. *Diffusion Internationale de Maroquinerie de Prestige SARL* [2001] CLC 949.

and not where the damage later came to light;[175] or where people read defamatory material and lower their opinion of the victim, as distinct from where the victim lives.[176] But in identifying and locating the damage, an autonomous interpretation of the cause of action must be used, as distinct from one which is taken from the substantive tort law of the court seised; a similar principle applies to identify the event giving rise to it. So the event giving rise to the damage caused by defamation in the press is the production of the newspaper and not (as it would be seen in domestic English law) the sale of the newspaper to its readership;[177] the compilation of negligent advice and not (as it would be seen in English domestic law) its receipt by the person who acts on it.[178] Any uniformity of jurisdictional result which this may eventually create will be preceded by an era of uncertainty while it is decided whether, for example, it is the failure properly to test, or the marketing without adequate warning, which gives rise to the damage in product liability cases.[179] In effect an entire book of tort will need to be written to fill in the blanks created by the preference for autonomous definitions of causes of action, all to be paid for by hapless litigants.

A 'matter relating to tort' means any action which seeks to establish the liability of a defendant and which is not a matter relating to a contract within Article 5(1);[180] and there should be no difficulty in using it to encompass equitable wrongs like dishonest assistance of a breach of trust,[181] or breach of confidence, or statutory wrongs such as patent infringement.[182] Despite the width of this formulation, and despite the fact that there is no clear line which separates it from restitutionary claims,[183] especially in respect of wrongs, it is probably limited to cases where the claim is based on some semblance of wrongdoing and does not extend to claims for restitution where it is alleged to be simply unjust to retain the gain made at the expense of another: there will not usually be special jurisdiction over such claims which are only casually connected to

---

[175] Case C–51/97 *Réunion Européenne SA* v. *Spliethoff's Bevrachtingskantoor BV* [1998] ECR I–6511.

[176] Case C–68/93 *Shevill* v. *Presse Alliance SA* [1995] ECR I–415.   [177] Ibid.

[178] *Domicrest Ltd.* v. *Swiss Bank Corporation* [1999] QB 548.

[179] Cf *Distillers & Co. Ltd.* v. *Thompson* [1971] AC 458 (PC).

[180] Case 189/87 *Kalfelis* v. *Bankhaus Schröder, Münchmeyer, Hengst und Co.* [1988] ECR 5565.

[181] *Casio Computer Co. Ltd.* v. *Sayo* [2001] CA Civ. 661, 11 Apr. 2001, not yet reported.

[182] *Mecklermedia Corp.* v. *DC Congress GmbH* [1998] Ch. 40.

[183] Indeed, the AG in Case C–89/91 *Shearson Lehmann Hutton Inc.* v. *TVB* [1993] ECR I–139 was clear (at 178) that the effect of *Kalfelis* was to include claims alleging unjust enrichment within Art. 5(3).

a particular place. So a claim for the repayment of money handed over in the mistaken belief that there was a contract will not be within Article 5(3).[184] If this is indeed correct, it proceeds not from a theological view about the nature of restitution in English domestic law, but from the fact that other language versions of what in English is rendered as 'liability' connote rather more clearly the sense of liability for doing wrong or inflicting loss.[185]

Other cases of special jurisdiction under Article 5
In relation to *maintenance claims*, Article 5(2) gives special jurisdiction to the maintenance creditor's place of domicile or habitual residence; the term maintenance creditor includes an original applicant for maintenance.[186] In England, a court dealing with the aftermath of a marriage will usually make an order for a single, undifferentiated, sum by way of financial provision. But for the purposes of the Regulation, maintenance, which falls within its domain, needs to be separated from the adjudication of rights in property arising out of a matrimonial relationship, which does not. It therefore behoves a judge to mark this distinction within the order which he makes, especially if it may require to be enforced in another Member State.[187] For *civil claims in criminal proceedings*, Article 5(4) allows a court hearing a criminal claim to order damages or restitution to a claimant who, in accordance with the procedure of the court, has intervened as a 'civil party'. This has little practical relevance in England where this is not a common form of procedure.

Article 5(5) deals with *liability arising out of the operation of a branch, agency, or other establishment*: such claims may be brought in the place where it is situated. The concept of a branch, agency, or establishment has to occupy a slippery patch of territory between being too dependent and too independent.[188] A useful test is probably to ask whether it has power on its own account to make contracts which will bind its principal. If it does, it will probably be a branch.[189] It is worth noting that the jurisdictional exposure of the defendant is only to the extent that the

---

[184] *Kleinwort Benson Ltd.* v. *Glasgow City Council* [1999] 1 AC 153.
[185] In *Kalfelis*, above n. 180, the language of which was German, the term is '*Schadenshaftung*', where the sense of loss caused by wrong is more palpable.
[186] Case C–295/95 *Farrell* v. *Long* [1997] ECR I–1683.
[187] Case C–220/95 *Van den Boogaard* v. *Laumen* [1997] ECR I–1147.
[188] Case 218/86 *SAR Schotte GmbH* v. *Parfums Rothschild Sàrl* [1987] ECR 4905.
[189] Opinion of the AG in Case C–89/91 *Shearson Lehmann Hutton Inc.* v. *TVB* [1993] ECR I–139, 169.

claim arises out of the operations of the branch, but it is not implicit that the acts of the defendant must have been performed in that place.[190] The equivalent common law rule asks whether the defendant is present within the jurisdiction; and, if he is, allows the bringing of any claim against him, whether or not connected to activities undertaken in that place.[191] There is much to be said for the more limited rule contained in Article 5(5).

In relation to *trusts*, Article 5(6) gives special jurisdiction over a settlor, trustee, or beneficiary who is sued as such to the courts of the Member State where the trust is domiciled. For this provision to apply, the trust must be created by the operation of a statute, or by a written instrument, or created orally but evidenced in writing. In relation to claims for payment in respect of *salvage of cargo or freight*, Article 5(7) gives special jurisdiction to the place of the court under the authority of which the freight was arrested to secure payment or could have been arrested but for the fact that bail or other security was given.

Multipartite litigation and consolidated claims: Articles 6 and 7
The Regulation does not confer special jurisdiction over a claim on the simple basis that the court has jurisdiction over another claim to which the first is connected. If a claimant wishes to join separate claims against a single defendant, this has to be done under the general domiciliary jurisdiction of Article 2. Articles 6 and 7[192] go some way towards allowing the consolidation of separate claims in the interest of co-ordinating the judicial function and avoiding inconsistent judgments, but the limits on their operation are rigid, and at this point the Regulation operates less than perfectly. There are five cases to consider.

Where a claim is brought against *multiple defendants*, Article 6(1) allows them all to be joined in the one action if it is brought where one of them is domiciled and it is necessary to join the claims so as to avoid the risk of irreconcilable judgments resulting from separate trials. It is not necessary that the defendant who is used as the anchor be the principal target of the claim; indeed, it may even be that there is no actual intention to proceed against him at all once he has performed his jurisdictional function; it is unsatisfactory that a defendant who could have challenged the jurisdiction of the court over him[193] can prejudice the position of co-defendants

---

[190] Case C–439/93 *Lloyds Register of Shipping* v. *Soc. Campenon Bernard* [1995] ECR I–961.
[191] P. 91–2, below.   [192] Sect. 2 of Chap. II; cf Arts. 6 and 6A BC.
[193] e.g., on the ground that he is not actually domiciled in that state.

by declining to do so.[194] On the other hand, if it were required that the local defendant be the main defendant, there would be endless scope for argument. As for the degree of connection between the claims, an exercise in judgment is called for; but the predominant need to avoid irreconcilable judgments should incline a court to err on the side of joinder, and not of taking a restrictive view.[195] There is, however, no analogous right to join co-defendants into proceedings in a court having only special jurisdiction under Article 5, or having jurisdiction by agreement or submission under Article 23 or 24. It is very difficult to see the rational[196] policy which excludes these cases from Article 6(1), probably because there is none. It goes without saying that there is no joinder under Article 6(1) where jurisdiction is founded on Article 4.[197]

Article 6(2) allows a claim against a *third party* for a warranty, guarantee, contribution, or indemnity, or brought in some other third party proceeding, to be brought in the court[198] hearing the original action unless the latter was instituted with the sole object of allowing the defendant to ensnare the third party with special jurisdiction. It seems probable that the original action must still be live,[199] but, by contrast with Article 6(1), the jurisdictional basis of the original action is irrelevant to the operation of Article 6(2). The court has a discretion to refuse joinder of the third party so long as this is not done for reasons which, in effect, contradict the general scheme of the Regulation.[200] But if there is an Article 23 jurisdiction agreement between defendant and third party, this will prevent reliance on Article 6(2) by the defendant, no matter how inconvenient the overall result may be, for, by contrast with the common law position, there is no discretion to override Article 23.[201]

Article 6(3) allows a *counterclaim* to be brought in the court in which the original action is pending. The Article is limited to claims which arise

---

[194] Cf *Canada Trust Co.* v. *Stolzenberg (No 2)* [2000] 3 WLR 1376 (HL).

[195] But Case C–51/97 *Réunion Européenne SA* v. *Spliethoff's Bevrachtingskantoor BV* [1998] ECR I–6511 seems to take a very restrictive view, as observed in *Watson* v. *First Choice Holidays*, [2001] CA Civ. 972, 22 June 2001, not yet reported; referred to the Court of Justice.

[196] There is an irrational one of seeking at all costs to bolster the general jurisdiction of the domicile.

[197] Case C–51/97 *Réunion Européenne SA* v. *Spliethoff's Bevrachtingskantoor BV* [1998] ECR I–6511.

[198] But not if it is in Germany or Austria, where the provisions of the local Codes of Civil Procedure have to be used instead: Art. 60e.

[199] *Waterford Wedgwood plc* v. *David Nagli Ltd.* [1999] 3 All ER 185; cf *The Ikarian Reefer* [2000] 1 WLR 603 (CA).

[200] Case C–365/88 *Kongress Agentur Hagen GmbH* v. *Zeehaghe BV* [1990] ECR I–1845.

[201] *Hough* v. *P&O Containers Ltd.* [1999] QB 834.

out of the same relationship or other essential facts as the original claim, but a pleaded set-off which will not overtop the claim is a defence, not a counterclaim, and there is no need to justify it by reference to this rule.[202] It is not clear whether Article 6(3) extends to a counterclaim against a party other than the original claimant, but in the context of insurance, at least, it has been held that it does not where to allow it would deprive an insured or policyholder of his special jurisdictional privileges.[203] Article 6(4), which deals with contract actions joined with actions against the same defendant in *matters relating to rights in rem in immoveable property*, has already been mentioned.[204] It is obviously sensible that an action against a mortgagor should be able to deal with the security right as well as with the personal covenant to repay, and this is, in effect, what Article 6(4) allows. (Article 7 allows a court which has jurisdiction 'by virtue of this Regulation'[205] in an action relating to liability from the use or operation of a ship to entertain a claim for the limitation of such liability.)

It still appears that Article 6 takes only a few steps in the direction of the efficient co-ordination of claims, and that if its provisions are to be given a restrictive interpretation, it will be even less successful than it currently is. But rules in this area need to give the judge substantial discretion, something which is alien to much of the modern legal tradition on the continent of Europe. If it is now expected that courts will trust each other to interpret the Regulation properly, it may be time to reconsider whether judges may not be given a little more flexibility in this area, and the provisions for the co-ordination and consolidation of claims made a little more generous.

Residual jurisdiction over defendants not domiciled in a Member State: Article 4

If none of the rest of the Regulation has applied, the defendant must be someone who lacks a domicile in a Member State. At this point, the Regulation does not prescribe in detail when jurisdiction may be taken over a defendant whose only connection is with a non-member state. Article 4 therefore expressly authorizes the claimant to rely on the traditional jurisdictional rules of the court[206] in which he wishes to sue:

---

[202] Case C–431/93 *Danvaern Productions A/S v. Schuhfabriken Otterbeck GmbH & Co.* [1995] ECR I–2053.
[203] *Jordan Grand Prix Ltd. v. Baltic Insurance Group* [1999] 2 AC 127.
[204] P. 62, above.
[205] Which presumably includes a reference to other conventions by way of Art. 66.
[206] Some of which are set out in Annex 1 to the Reg.

service of process on an Australian defendant present in England, service
out of the jurisdiction on an American defendant with the permission of
the court under the CPR, Part 6, and so on. But the Regulation has not
washed its hands of the dispute. Article 4 is still an integral part of
Chapter II, and it is expressly provided that Articles 22[207] and 23[208] prevail over and limit it. Moreover, as Article 4 still leads to judgments
enforceable under Chapter III of the Regulation, its operation is also
subject to Article 27[209] on *lis alibi pendens*. So a claimant may not rely on
Article 4 if proceedings between the same parties and involving the same
cause of action were instituted in a court which was seised earlier in time,
not even if that court has based its jurisdiction on Article 4 as well.[210] It is
therefore wrong to picture Article 4 as opening a door back into the world
outside the Regulation. It is better understood as incorporating by reference traditional jurisdictional rules; and the effect of their incorporation
into the Regulation means that they have to be adjusted to fit into their
new surroundings. Even so, there is room for unease at the combination
of traditional jurisdictional rules, many of which will appear to defendants as being outrageously wide in their sweep, and the automatic recognition under Chapter III, of judgments based on such provisions. The
point will be examined in the chapter on the recognition of foreign
judgments.

Loss of jurisdiction: *lis alibi pendens* and related actions: Articles 27–30

The aim of the Regulation, that judgments should be enforceable in other
Member States without impediment, would be imperilled by concurrent
litigation of identical or similar, disputes. Articles 27 to 30[211] provide the
means of control. Where the *same action and between the same parties* is
brought before the courts of two Member States, Article 27 requires the
court seised second to dismiss its action. The rule is simple and clear,
entirely dependent on which action was first out of the starting blocks. It
takes no account of considerations of comparative appropriateness: all
courts with jurisdiction[212] under the Regulation are equally appropriate.

---

[207] Exclusive jurisdiction regardless of domicile.
[208] Jurisdiction agreements for the courts of a Member State: this specific provison did
not appear in Art. 4 BC.
[209] And presumably Art. 28 on related actions.
[210] Case C–351/89 *Overseas Union Insurance Ltd.* v. *New Hampshire Insurance Co.* [1991]
ECR I–3317.
[211] Sect. 9 of Chap. II; cf Arts. 21–23 BC; though Art. 30 had no precursor.
[212] Including Art. 4 jurisdiction.

It takes no account of the particular rule relied on by each claimant: despite their hierarchy, all jurisdictional rules[213] applicable under the Regulation are equally proper. Moreover, the court seised second may not investigate whether, still less rule that, the first erred in concluding that it had jurisdiction: all courts are equally competent to apply the Regulation, and where the competences are equal, the first in time prevails.[214] An exception is made where the second court has exclusive jurisdiction under Article 22,[215] but in such a case the second court is in effect ruling on its *own* jurisdiction and deducing the lack of jurisdiction of the first court only consequentially. Only if the defendant in the first court has contested its jurisdiction is the second court permitted to stay its hand; but once the first court has confirmed its jurisdiction the second court must dismiss the action. This brutal solution to the problem may produce an unseemly rush to commence litigation and seise the court of a party's choice; it may be catastrophic to tell the opposite party that proceedings will be commenced after a period of days.[216] 'Speak softly and hurry a big writ', as Theodore Roosevelt nearly said.

For its operation, Article 27 requires three 'identities': identity of parties (but procedural differences between the formulation of the claimants and defendants are not decisive); identity of object (the two actions must have the same end in view): and identity of cause (they must be based on the same facts and rules of law).[217] So in relation to the identity of parties, an action brought *in rem* against a vessel may still be between the same parties as one *in personam* against those with an interest in the vessel; the critical test is whether the interests of the parties are identical and indissociable.[218] As regards object and cause, an action for damages for breach of contract shares identity with one for a declaration that the contract had been lawfully rescinded;[219] an action by a cargo-owner in respect of damage to cargo shares identity with one against the cargo-owner for a declaration of non-liability.[220] But an action for damages for breach of warranty of quality is not identical to an action for the price of goods delivered, and Article 27 will not apply to it.[221]

Prior to the Regulation, the Conventions made only a general attempt

---

[213] Including Art. 4.

[214] Case C–351/89 *Overseas Union Insurance Ltd.* v. *New Hampshire Insurance Co.* [1991] ECR I–3317.

[215] Ibid.   [216] *Messier Dowty Ltd.* v. *Sabena SA* [2000] 1 WLR 2040 (CA).

[217] Case C–406/92 *The Tatry* [1994] ECR I–5439.

[218] Case C–351/96 *Drouot Assurances SA* v. *CMI* [1998] ECR I–3075.

[219] Case 144/86 *Gubisch Maschinenfabrik KG* v. *Palumbo* [1987] ECR 4861.

[220] *The Tatry*, above n. 217.   [221] Art. 28 may, though.

to define the point at which a court was seised for the purpose of these Articles. The Court held that the date on which a court was seised was determined by asking on what date the matter was definitively pending in the particular court, and the question was answered by recourse to the procedural laws of the several courts in which the actions were brought.[222] As a matter of English law, it was decided that a court was not seised, even though the action had been commenced, until process had been served on the particular defendant.[223] Service on a co-defendant would not suffice to seise the court in relation to an unserved defendant,[224] nor did the obtaining of interlocutory relief prior to service of process.[225] In other states the rules were different, and in some a court would be seised prior to service of process. The result was chaotic and confusing, not least because it could be difficult for litigants to obtain reliable advice about the seisin of foreign courts for the purpose of this jurisdictional rule: this is not the daily business of the average practitioner. Proceeding from this concern, Article 30 provides a solution to cases governed by the Regulation: (a) in countries where the claimant lodges a document with the court before serving it, it is the date of lodgment (assuming the claimant has not failed to take the subsequent steps he needs to take for service to be effected); (b) in countries where the document has to be served before being lodged with the court, at the time when it is received by the authority responsible for service (assuming the claimant has not failed to take the subsequent steps he needs to take for lodgment to take place). England is a category (a) country, and the date stamped on the claim form by the court will identify the date of seisin. It appears to be assumed that there is no Member State in which service precedes the lodging of the document with the court, service being made by the claimant himself: if this is an unsound assumption it will reveal itself in time; and there may be cases which do not fit easily into this framework at all, such as where an amendment[226] is made to add a fresh claim, or a new cause of action, or an additional defendant, into proceedings which are already pending *inter alios*. But it would be ungrateful to cavil. The confusion before this

---

[222] Case 129/83 *Zelger v. Salinitri (No 2)* [1984] ECR 2397.

[223] *Dresser UK Ltd.* v. *Falcongate Freight Management Ltd.* [1992] QB 502 (CA).

[224] *Grupo Torras SA* v. *Sheikh Fahad Mohammed al Sabah* [1996] 1 Lloyd's Rep. 7.

[225] *Neste Chemicals SA* v. *DK Line SA (The Sargasso)* [1994] 3 All ER 180 (CA).

[226] It may not be possible to say there has been seisin until the application for amendment has been heard and granted, and seisin will not happen until the amended claim form is reissued (assuming it is later re-served). It is unclear whether the application notice in respect of the proposed amendment could count as an 'equivalent document' to seise the court with the proposed amendment, but it seems improbable.

reform was indefensible, and if problems emerge with Article 30, they can be addressed when within five years[227] the operation of the Regulation is reviewed.

If Article 27 is inapplicable, Article 28 may apply if there are *related actions* in the two courts: that is, actions so closely connected that it is expedient to hear them together to avoid the risk of irreconcilable judgments resulting from separate proceedings. If the actions are related, the second court may dismiss its action if this may be consolidated with the proceedings pending in the first court, or it may stay its proceedings to await the outcome in the first court, or it may do neither. Where relief is granted, the English practice appears to be to prefer dismissal for consolidation in the first court.[228] This may well be appropriate if the two actions involve different parties but have essentially the same cause of action: to bind all concerned into the one hearing and one judgment is sensible, and if the cause of action is substantially the same, the joinder of parties may not lengthen the trial in the first court. But if the same parties are litigating different causes of action in the two Member States, it may be more efficient to stay the second action to await the outcome of the first, and apply Chapter III of the Regulation to curtail the second action. By contrast, if the second action is dismissed for consolidation with the first, the effect will be to lengthen the first trial by the length of the second; had there instead been a stay, the second trial may never need to take place.

Where two courts have exclusive jurisdiction regardless of domicile, Article 29 provides that the court seised second must decline jurisdiction in favour of the first court. Though a court with jurisdiction under a jurisdiction agreement is said by Article 23 to have exclusive jurisdiction, it has never been considered that Article 29, as opposed to Article 27, is applicable to such cases.

Procedural modification of Regulation jurisdiction

A troublesome question concerns the extent to which an English court may supplement or modify the jurisdictional scheme of the Regulation by recourse to its rules on *forum conveniens*, anti-suit injunctions, and so forth. To this question there is no clear and easy answer; much avoidable confusion has arisen from the search for wide and general solutions. The picture must be painted with a fine brush.

---

[227] Art. 68.   [228] *Sarrio SA* v. *Kuwait Investment Authority* [1999] 1 AC 32.

Disputes about jurisdiction

When contesting jurisdiction *in limine*, a defendant may deny that the court has the jurisdiction asserted by the claimant. Factual doubt on any material point is resolved by the claimant[229] demonstrating a good arguable case that the ground on which he relies is satisfied:[230] this is the reason a simple denial by the defendant of the existence of the contract, or whatever, is not conclusive against the existence of jurisdiction. As this has been established by the House of Lords, it may be taken for correct, but it is open to question. A good arguable case means that the court need not be persuaded on a balance of probabilities, but that there is a reasonable, but lower, probability of it.[231] Whilst this may make sense in the context of the common law, where the rules of jurisdiction determine only whether the English court has jurisdiction, those of the Regulation determine the presence and (because one court has it) the denial of every other court's jurisdiction. It seems wrong that an English court may hear a case though it considers that it probably does not have jurisdiction under the Regulation and that a court in another Member State probably does. As it has no power to hear the evidence on the merits, postponing a ruling on jurisdiction[232] until after it has done so, there is no opportunity for correction if it appears that the defendant was right all along and the basis for jurisdiction was absent after all. The result cannot be satisfactory: either the court should be able to adopt the practice in certain Member States, and in a marginal case postpone ruling on jurisdiction until it has heard the evidence, or it should not be able to act on the basis of a good arguable case if it considers that on balance another court does have, and it does not have, jurisdiction. But it appears that it will require legislation, or the Court, to bring it about.

Forum (non) conveniens

When the claimant relies on a jurisdictional rule other than Article 4, a court has no general discretion to stay its proceedings and encourage the claimant to proceed instead in another Member State on the ground that it is the natural forum;[233] and it makes no difference that the claimant is

---

[229] By the procedure under the CPR Pt. 11.

[230] *Canada Trust Co. v. Stolzenberg (No 2)* [2000] 3 WLR 1376 (HL).

[231] *Seaconsar Far East Ltd. v. Bank Markazi Jomhouri Islami Iran* [1994] 1 AC 438.

[232] Going on to give a ruling on the merits if it concludes that there was jurisdiction; dismissing the case on jurisdictional grounds otherwise.

[233] Schlosser Report [1979] OJ C59/71 at para. 78.

not domiciled in a Member State.[234] But where the natural forum is in a non-member state, two classes of case may be considered. First, if the claim concerns title to land, etc., in a non-member state or was covered by a jurisdiction agreement for a non-member state or is brought when there are proceedings already pending in a non-member state, it may be permissible to order a stay on the ground that (as a matter of English law) the foreign court is the natural forum, reinforcing this by analogy with Article 22, 23, or 27 and giving them, as is sometimes said, a 'reflexive effect'.[235] Secondly, if a non-member state is the natural forum, the Court of Appeal has held[236] that the Regulation does not prevent an English court staying its proceedings on the ground of *forum non conveniens*, reasoning that the Regulation[237] did not touch or concern jurisdictional issues which arose between Member States and non-member states. This is undeniable if there is a treaty with the non-member state but, that apart, the compatibility of this with the scheme of the Regulation is acutely controversial, and has been said in the House of Lords to require a reference to the Court for a ruling.[238] After all, in ordering a stay, the English court is not acting by reference to an international obligation owed to the non-member state, but is instead allowing a rule of national procedural law to contradict a claimant's right of access to a court which has jurisdiction under the Regulation: a claimant who has read the Regulation may be taken aback. Not only that, but the claimant will lose the prospect of a judgment capable of enforcement under Chapter III of the Regulation, and this may furnish a separate reason why as a matter of *English* law a stay should not be granted in any event.[239]

Where jurisdiction is founded on Article 4, a court may certainly take into account issues of *forum conveniens* in determining whether to grant or to set aside permission to serve out of the jurisdiction, for, as a matter of English jurisdictional law, service out may only be made, and jurisdiction will only therefore exist, if England is the natural forum.[240] This is uncontroversial. It has also been held that a stay of proceedings

---

[234] For the Reg. applies indifferently: Case C–412/98 *Universal General Insurance Co.* v. *Groupe Josi Reinsurance Co. SA* [2000] ECR I–5925.
[235] *Ace Insurance SA-NV* v. *Zurich Insurance Co.* [2001] 1 Lloyd's Rep. 618 (CA).
[236] *Re Harrods (Buenos Aires) Ltd.* [1992] Ch. 72 (CA).
[237] It was in fact a case on the Brussels Convention.
[238] *Lubbe* v. *Cape plc* [2000] 1 WLR 1545 (HL).
[239] *International Credit and Investment (Overseas) Ltd.* v. *Adham* [1999] ILPr. 302 (CA).
[240] CPR r. 6.21(2A).

commenced as of right under Article 4 may be granted on the basis of *forum non conveniens*. Where the natural forum is a non-member state, this is correct if a stay of proceedings is taken to be an integral part of the jurisdictional rules which Article 4 absorbs into the Regulation: a less uncontroversial proposition, where the effect of a stay is not to deny the existence of jurisdiction.[241] Most controversially, a stay has been ordered where the natural forum lies in another Member State: whether this is right depends upon two main questions. First, if the English court grants a stay of proceedings it still remains seised of them,[242] and may at a later stage lift the stay. Taken together with Article 27, this may mean that the courts of the natural forum are invited to become second seised in a dispute of which the English court was, and still is, first seised, with the result that they are not available for the trial of the action. It has been suggested that this may be overcome by the English court dismissing the action rather than staying it,[243] but this would be a novelty, and one which contradicts the proposition that a stayed action is still pending, and that the stay can be lifted in an appropriate case.[244]

Secondly, there is a larger question, concerning the jurisdictional scheme which the Regulation and the Conventions before it actually set out to create; and two broad views are tenable. If the fundamental distinction is a defendant-centric one, which divides Article 4 jurisdiction from that derived from the rest of the Regulation, it would be defensible to allow a stay in favour of the courts of a Member State, because Article 4 jurisdiction is different in kind from that conferred by the rules contained in the rest of Chapter II of the Regulation. This appears to be the current view of the English courts;[245] and it would be ironic if it were otherwise, for the Regulation would have served to widen the reach of Article 4 jurisdiction, by removing part of the power to stay proceedings founded on it. But if the fundamental distinction is a territory-centric one, which divides the single legal area of the Member States from the outside world, it would not be correct to use a stay of proceedings to send a claimant from a court in one part of that law district to another, whether on the basis of Article 4 or otherwise, because Article 4 jurisdiction is an integral part of its overall scheme. There is no incontestable basis for preferring

---

[241] If *Re Harrods (Buenos Aires) Ltd.* [1992] Ch. 72 (CA), is correct in relation to Art. 2 jurisdiction, this must be an *a fortiori* case.

[242] *Rofa Sport Management AG* v. *DHL International (UK) Ltd.* [1989] 1 WLR 902 (CA).

[243] *Haji-Ioannou* v. *Frangos* [1999] 2 Lloyd's Rep. 337 (CA).

[244] It is also complicated if undertakings have been given by the defendant in support of his application for a stay, and it is later sought to enforce these.

[245] *Haji-Ioannou* v. *Frangos* [1999] 2 Lloyd's Rep. 337 (CA).

the one to the other, but as Article 4 gives the claimant an entitlement to rely on the jurisdictional rules identified in Annex I, he would appear to have a *right* to rely on jurisdiction asserted by service within the jurisdiction. Such a right is diminished if the action may then be stayed on procedural grounds. Moreover, the scheme established by Chapter III for the recognition and enforcement of judgments does not exclude, or treat differently, judgments based on Article 4: it treats the territories of the Member States as a single geographical unit, within which judgments circulate freely and without discrimination. If it is legitimate to draw any analogy from this, the better to understand the basic jurisdictional scheme of Chapter II, it would be that the Member States comprise a single jurisdictional territory, albeit with locally variable rules, but that jurisdiction established before a court somewhere within that territory may not be defeated by the argument that it would be more appropriate that the claimant proceed in another part of that single jurisdictional area. If that were accepted as correct, a stay for the courts of another Member State would contradict the economy of the Regulation. An authoritative answer remains to be given.

Anti-suit injunctions

Given that a court seised second has no right to assess the jurisdiction of a court seised first,[246] it may appear that it has no right to order a respondent who is suing as claimant in another Member State to discontinue his action, for this would involve not only ruling on the foreign court's jurisdiction, but granting relief on the back of a finding that it was lacking. But an English court will cheerfully grant such an order if it finds that a jurisdiction agreement valid under Article 23 gave it, and should have been interpreted by the foreign court as denying its, jurisdiction; and it is irrelevant whether the foreign court was seised first or second or not at all.[247] Despite the fact that there is much to be said for summary enforcement of such commercial agreements,[248] the problems are formidable. In the first place, if the foreign court is seised first, Article 27 may remove the court's jurisdiction over the respondent. Perhaps this does not follow if the application for an anti-suit injunction (which seeks to prevent the merits being investigated in the foreign court) does not have the same

---

[246] Case C–351/89 *Overseas Union Insurance Ltd.* v. *New Hampshire Insurance Co.* [1991] ECR I–3317.
[247] *Continental Bank NA* v. *Aeakos Compania Naviera SA* [1994] 1 WLR 588 (CA); *The Angelic Grace* [1995] 1 Lloyd's Rep. 87 (CA).
[248] *OT Africa Line Ltd.* v. *Hijazy* [2001] 1 Lloyd's Rep. 76.

cause of action[249] as the foreign action on the merits of the dispute. But this is problematic, for an application for an order that a trial be aborted, whatever the underlying merits may be, does appear to have the same (but opposite) end in view as proceedings for a trial of the underlying merits. Moreover, if the English court is precluded from reasoning that the foreign court has no jurisdiction, on what other basis can it move to restrain the respondent? It is possible that an argument which proceeds by conceding that the foreign court has jurisdiction, but that proceedings brought in it are nevertheless vexatious or oppressive, might just navigate the shoals, but the foreign court will have its own remedies to prevent abusive recourse which are presumptively sufficient.[250] Nor is that all. Article 22(5) gives the court where a judgment is to be enforced exclusive jurisdiction over proceedings concerned with it. It may well be that no-one thought to legislate that the court where a trial is to take place has exclusive jurisdiction over proceedings concerned with that trial, because it was too obvious to need saying. In the end, it is most unlikely that this dramatic and interventionist remedy, no matter how commercially useful it is, will withstand the scrutiny of the European Court. For even if it does not actually violate Article 27, such injunctions show scant respect for the principle of mutual trust in the administration of justice in the Community, and are designed to prevent the free circulation of judgments.[251] For a judgment obtained in defiance of an English injunction will be precluded on grounds of public policy[252] from recognition in England; and as the injunction is in principle entitled to recognition in other Member States, the eventual result may be a complete mess.

Applications for provisional or protective measures: Article 31

Provisional or protective measures obtained before the trial may critically affect the way the dispute is resolved: measures freezing assets and ordering disclosure of their whereabouts, orders for an interim payment, and so on, will affect the balance of power prior to the trial. Yet the jurisdictional regulation of these measures is touched only lightly by Article 31[253] of the Regulation, which contents itself with the principle that so long as they are guaranteed to be provisional and reversible, there is no need to impose any jurisdictional restriction on where, nor on in how

---

[249] Case 406/92 *The Tatry* [1994] ECR I–5439.

[250] This could have been (but was not) the reasoning used by the Court of Appeal in *Turner* v. *Grovit* [2000] 1 QB 345 (CA) in ordering an injunction to restrain proceedings before the Spanish courts.

[251] Recital 15.   [252] Art. 34(1).   [253] Sect. 10 of Chap. II; cf Art. 24 BC.

many states at the same time, they may be obtained. Where the substantive claim to which they are ancillary falls within the domain of the Regulation, that is, within Article 1, it is necessary to distinguish two types of case in which provisional, including protective, measures may be applied for. If the court applied to has jurisdiction over the merits, there is no restriction upon the relief it may order, provisional or otherwise.[254] But if it does not, an application may still be made under Article 31 of the Regulation. The only jurisdictional requirement to be satisfied is any which national law places upon the applicant, and there is no objection to the use, in this context, of traditional or exorbitant grounds of personal jurisdiction. In England, therefore, all that is needed is to serve the respondent with the claim form by which the relief is sought: within the jurisdiction as of right, or out of it with the prior permission of the court[255] (though in deciding whether to grant permission to serve the court may take account of the fact that the trial will not be taking place in England and may ask whether this makes it inexpedient to grant the relief applied for[256]). But Article 31 has been held[257] to impose two further limitations, though not strictly jurisdictional in nature. First, the measure must be one which is truly provisional, in that it is guaranteed to be reversible if it turns out not to have been warranted once the merits have been tried. An English freezing order, which will require an undertaking in damages often fortified by a bank guarantee, is a good example of what is meant. Secondly, its scope may not extend to assets within the territorial jurisdiction of another Member State. This is more problematic, for though this limitation makes sense if the order is expressed to take effect directly against assets,[258] an English freezing order does not do so, but merely orders an individual who is or has been brought within the personal jurisdiction of the court not to dissipate his assets. It remains unclear whether the presence or residence of the respondent within England immunizes such an order from this limitation,[259] or whether the

---

[254] Case C-391/95 *Van Uden Maritime BV* v. *Deco Line* [1998] ECR I-7091 (where the court did not have merits jurisdiction, an agreement to arbitrate having denied every court merits jurisdiction).

[255] CPR r. 6.20(4).

[256] Civil Jurisdiction and Judgments Act 1982, s. 25(2). For analysis of this, see *Crédit Suisse Fides Trust SA* v. *Cuoghi* [1998] QB 818 (CA).

[257] Case C-391/95 *Van Uden Maritime BV* v. *Deco Line* [1998] ECR I-7091.

[258] Which is understood to be the way in which a French order of *saisie conservatoire* operates.

[259] This appears to have been the view in *Crédit Suisse Fides Trust SA* v. *Cuoghi*, above n. 256.

order must instead be taken as one which, in substance and notwithstanding its form,[260] does affect assets in another Member State so that, to that extent, it may not be sought under cover of Article 31.

COMMON LAW AND RULES OF COURT

We turn to examine the traditional rules of jurisdiction.

DOMAIN OF THE TRADITIONAL RULES

If the dispute is not a civil or commercial matter, the traditional rules of English law, as established by common law and legislation, alone determine the jurisdiction of the court. In such a case the Regulation has no bearing on the existence or the exercise of jurisdiction, even in the event of a *lis alibi pendens*; and the judgment will not qualify for recognition in other Member States under Chapter III of the Regulation.

If the dispute is in a civil or commercial matter, where Article 4 of the Regulation specifies that the traditional rules of English law are to be applied, it is, as was explained above, misleading to contend that the Regulation is inapplicable. The control of parallel litigation in the courts of Member States and the recognition of judgments will still be governed by the Regulation, as will an application for provisional or protective measures. This context may require the traditional rules to 'receive shape from the subject matter and wording of the Convention itself'.[261] But with that proviso we can proceed to examine the traditional approach to the jurisdiction of an English court.

JURISDICTION BASED ON SERVICE OF PROCESS WITHIN ENGLAND

Jurisdiction is established by service of process.

Establishing jurisdiction by service

A person who is present in England can be served with process as of right; and this simple fact serves to establish the jurisdiction of the court over him. The manner of service is prescribed by the Civil Procedure

---

[260] For an analogous refusal by the Court to accept that the precise form of an English admiralty action *in rem* renders it different from an action *in personam* in the context of Art. 27 see Case C–406/92 *The Tatry* [1994] ECR I–5439.

[261] Mance LJ in *Raiffeisen Zentralbank Österreich AG* v. *Five Star Trading LLC* [2001] CA Civ. 68, [2001] 2 WLR 1344, at para. [33]. The case concerned the impact of the Rome Convention on common law rules on assignment of intangibles, but the point is important and general.

Rules ('CPR'). It now includes personal service, service by post, and service by certain electronic means,[262] but the need for a measure of formality is justified by the significant consequences of an action having been commenced. Service on a partnership is also regulated by the CPR. Legislation provides that an English company may be served at its registered office[263] (though if in liquidation on its liquidator, and then only with permission of the court[264]). An oversea company with a registered branch in England may be served by serving the person notified to the Registrar of Companies as authorized to accept service in relation to the business of the branch;[265] service on other oversea companies may be made on the person notified to the Registrar of Companies as authorized to accept service, in default of which process may be served at a place of business within the jurisdiction.[266] In this context, a place of business denotes a fixed and definite place from which the business of the company is carried out.[267] If at this place contracts are made which bind the company, the company will probably have a place of business within the jurisdiction.[268] But the procedures for service on corporations set out in CPR Part 6 are alternatives to statutory service, and these widen and relax the methods of service on a company.[269]

Contesting jurisdiction

A defendant who considers that as a matter of law the court has no jurisdiction over him or over the subject matter of the claim, or who contends that service was irregular, or on some other ground seeks to have service set aside, must first acknowledge service. This is a purely formal step, for he may then apply under CPR Part 11,[270] within the time limited for the service of his defence, for a declaration that the court has no jurisdiction, and for relief consequential on that ruling: as the submission is that he should not have been served, the usual relief will be the

---

[262] CPR r. 6.2. [263] Companies Act 1985, s. 725.
[264] Insolvency Act 1986, s. 130(2).
[265] Companies Act 1985, s. 694A; *Saab v. Saudi American Bank* [1999] 1 WLR 1861 (CA).
[266] Companies Act 1985, ss. 694A(3), 695.
[267] *South India Shipping Corp. Ltd. v. Export-Import Bank of Korea* [1985] 1 WLR 585 (CA); *Re Oriel Ltd.* [1986] 1 WLR 180 (CA).
[268] Cf *Adams v. Cape Industries plc* [1990] Ch. 433 (CA) a case on the recognition of foreign judgments.
[269] CPR rr 6.2(2), 6.5(6); CPR 6 PD, para. 6.2; *Saab v. Saudi American Bank* [1999] 4 All ER 321 (CA).
[270] This procedure for contesting the jurisdiction is applicable whether the case is one to which the Reg. applies, one based on service within the jurisdiction, or one based on service out of the jurisdiction.

setting aside of service. Where he has been served within the jurisdiction, the most common ground for objection is that the Regulation provides that he is not liable to be sued in the English courts; he may also plead a personal immunity from the jurisdiction of the courts or that the subject matter of the claim is something over which the court has no jurisdiction: in any such case service should be set aside. But if he acknowledges service but makes no application under Part 11, or if he takes a step in the action otherwise than to contest the jurisdiction, he will be taken to have submitted to the jurisdiction, and this submission will itself become the basis for the jurisdiction of the court, no matter that a challenge could have been made successfully.[271]

Applying to stay the proceedings

A defendant who has no basis for arguing that the court lacks jurisdiction and that he should not have been served may still apply to stay the proceedings on the ground that, though the court does have jurisdiction over him, the claimant should nevertheless sue in the courts of another country. Confusingly, perhaps, the application is also made under CPR Part 11 and within its time frame even though the defendant is not contesting the jurisdiction of the court.[272] If his argument succeeds, the English action will not be dismissed[273] but will remain pending but held in abeyance;[274] though he cannot be compelled to do so, the claimant will have no practical alternative to suing in a foreign court. In principle a stay may be lifted if some problem arises, or if an undertaking given to the court by the defendant is not performed: as the action remained pending throughout, there is no problem of limitation. Where service was made within the jurisdiction, two main grounds exist for seeking a stay of proceedings: that the *forum conveniens* is elsewhere, and that bringing the English action is a breach of contract. The relief is common to both, but the principles which lead to it are sharply distinct.

---

[271] The exception to this proposition is that where there was no subject matter jurisdiction (see above, p. 48), personal submission cannot remedy the deficiency, and jurisdiction remains non-existent.

[272] This represents a clear departure from the practice prior to 1999, when a challenge to the jurisdiction and an application for a stay were made by distinct mechanisms, reflecting their distinct intellectual bases. But it is undeniably convenient to have a single procedure for all objections to being sued in England.

[273] Though for the proposition that it may be dismissed if a stay would leave the claimant unable to sue in the foreign court see *Haji-Ioannou* v. *Frangos* [1999] 2 Lloyd's Rep. 337 (CA), discussed above at p. 87.

[274] *Rofa Sport Management AG* v. *DHL International (UK) Ltd.* [1989] 1 WLR 902 (CA).

Forum (non) conveniens

If the defendant can show that there is another court which is available to the claimant, and which is clearly more appropriate than England for the trial of the action, a stay will generally be ordered unless the claimant can establish that it would be unjust to require him to sue there. The two limbs of the test are distinct, with separate burdens of proof, but the test overall asks what the interests of justice require.

The English[275] development of this doctrine, principally by the House of Lords, has made a distinctive contribution to common law juris-dictional thinking.[276] What underpins it is the proposition that if the parties are content to have a trial in England, no-one will stop them;[277] but if they are not in agreement, there is no compelling reason why the claimant, rather than the defendant, should get his way and have the trial in England. Once that is accepted, all that remains is to elaborate the test which will give effect to the principle. In England this is done by looking to a court which is shown to be clearly more appropriate than England for the trial of the action, and asking whether there would be any injustice in having the trial take place there. In Australia, the same broad principle is accepted but is applied rather differently: the immediate focus is not on the comparative appropriateness of the foreign court as against the local one, but on whether the Australian court is clearly *in*appropriate for the trial:[278] this may be considered a more seemly question for an Australian judge to answer. This approach also reflects a view that, if a court is given jurisdiction, it should require clear and convincing grounds before it declines to exercise that jurisdiction; and this is therefore halfway to the civilian view that if the legislator has vested the judge with jurisdic-tion, he has a duty to exercise it, and has no power to set aside the law, whether on grounds of *forum conveniens* or otherwise. But if this is indeed the general civilian view, it misunderstands the common law doctrine, not least because it is a necessary counterpart to rules of

---

[275] Though it was developed much earlier in Scotland, and was incorporated into the American constitutional guarantee of due process, long before it was accepted in England.

[276] The leading authorities are *Spiliada Maritime Corp.* v. *Cansulex Ltd.* [1987] AC 460, *Connelly* v. *RTZ Corp. plc* [1998] AC 854, and *Lubbe* v. *Cape plc* [2000] 1 WLR 1545 (HL). For the steps which led to *Spiliada*, see *The Atlantic Star* [1974] AC 436, *MacShannon* v. *Rockware Glass Ltd.* [1978] AC 705, and *The Abidin Daver* [1984] AC 398.

[277] Unless there is an absence of subject matter jurisdiction, or if Art. 22 of the Reg. denies the jurisdiction of the English court.

[278] *Oceanic Sun Line Special Shipping Co.* v. *Fay* (1988) 165 CLR 197 (Aust. HC); *Voth* v. *Manildra Flour Mills Pty. Ltd.* (1990) 171 CLR 538 (Aust. HC). It may be clearly inappropriate if the dispute was already pending in the courts of another country: *Henry* v. *Henry* (1996) 185 CLR 571 (Aust. HC).

jurisdiction based on service which are otherwise too broad and insensi-
tive to be acceptable by themselves; is confirmed by statute;[279] has been
warmly embraced by the profession; and has been taken up throughout
the common law world. The distrust of judicial discretion which such
criticism betrays gives no ground for objection to the common law. Lord
Goff of Chieveley, the principal architect of the developed law, described
the doctrine as the 'most civilised of legal principles',[280] and he is right:
it allows a judge in one country to yield to the submission that the
courts of another country are better placed than he is to adjudicate, and
to give effect to that judicial comity which acknowledges that where
sovereignties collide, a sensitive solution is vastly preferable to an abrupt
one.

More criticism is sometimes offered by arguing that the doctrine
allows parties to litigate about where to litigate, and that this is
unwelcome when what they ought to be doing is to devote their resources
to trying the merits of the claim. But this is far from convincing. A brisk
preliminary skirmish on jurisdiction may well allow each side to gauge
the strength of the other's case and the stomach each has for the fight.
After the issue has been decided, the case may well settle and, if it does,
settle on better informed terms than would otherwise have been the case.
If this is so, the doctrine of *forum conveniens* also justifies itself as a
species of alternative dispute resolution. But as it has been embraced
with such enthusiasm by the broad profession, further justification is
probably unnecessary.

Descending to the detail of the test, the first limb requires that the
foreign court be clearly or distinctly more appropriate than England.
Attention will focus on the location of the events and the witnesses to
them, the law which will be used to determine the case, general issues of
trial convenience, the relative strength of connection with England and
with the alternative forum, and so on. The assessment of these factors is a
matter for the trial judge.[281] In order to show that the foreign court is
available as well as appropriate, all that is required is that the court have
jurisdiction over the defendant, which may be founded on the defendant's undertaking to submit given as late as the hearing of the application

---

[279] Civil Jurisdiction and Judgments Act 1982, s. 49.
[280] *Airbus Industrie GIE* v. *Patel* [1999] 1 AC 119.
[281] A point made by Lord Templeman in *Spiliada Maritime Corp.* v. *Cansulex Ltd.* [1987]
AC 460 (HL), and reiterated periodically since. For a matchless appreciation of the issues as
they are seen from the courthouse in Galveston, Texas, see *Smith* v. *Colonial Penn Insurance
Co.* 943 F Supp. 782 (1997) (US Dist. Ct.).

for a stay.[282] The fact that the claimant lacks the resources to sue in the foreign court does not make that court unavailable (though it may well be relevant under the second limb[283]).

Once the defendant has shown the natural forum to be overseas, the claimant may oppose a stay by seeking to show that it is unjust to leave him to his remedies in the foreign court. Arguments that damages will be lower or civil procedure less favourable to him will be generally[284] inadmissible, for as long as the foreign court has a developed system of law, it is inappropriate for the English courts to pass judgment on it, and still less on individual rules extracted from it. But if there is cogent[285] evidence that the claimant will not receive a fair trial, especially on racial or religious grounds, it will probably be unjust to stay the proceedings. And if it is impossible for the claimant to fund an action in the foreign court, whereas legal aid or a conditional fee arrangement would be available to him in England, it will be unjust to stay, at least in a case which requires a substantial sum of money to prepare the evidence and conduct the trial: this may make a significant, but limited, inroad on the principle that adverse comparison with the foreign court's procedure will not be invited.[286]

If the claimant will lose in the foreign court, because the claim he makes in England will not be open to him in the foreign court or because the defendant will have a good defence to the action, it ought to follow that this is an irrelevance: after all, this is just an application of the rule that differences in relief play no part in the decision whether to grant a stay, where impartiality should be the watchword. But there is some authority[287] for the view that in this case it would be unjust to order a stay,

---

[282] Though this may bear on the issue of costs. An earlier suggestion, that a court is not available unless a claimant was able to proceed there as of right, made in *Mohammed* v. *Bank of Kuwait and the Middle East KSC* [1996] 1 WLR 1483 (CA), was rejected by *Lubbe* v. *Cape plc* [2000] 1 WLR 1545 (HL).

[283] Ibid.

[284] *Spiliada*, above n. 281, at 482. Though from time to time a court fails to respect this principle, and finds an injustice in, e.g., the effect of the costs rules of the foreign court (for example, *Roneleigh Ltd.* v. *MII Exports Inc.* [1989] 1 WLR 619 (CA)), such cases must be wrong in principle. For a ringing statement of orthodoxy see *The Herceg Novi* [1998] 4 All ER 238 (CA).

[285] *The Abidin Daver* [1984] AC 398: attack by innuendo is absolutely inadmissible.

[286] *Lubbe* v. *Cape plc* [2000] 1 WLR 1545 (HL), explaining *Connelly* v. *RTZ Corp. Ltd.* [1998] AC 854. Were the common law otherwise, there would have been an argument about its consistency with Art. 6 of the European Convention on Human Rights.

[287] *Britannia SS Insurance Association Ltd.* v. *Ausonia Assicurazioni SpA* [1984] 2 Lloyd's Rep. 98 (CA); *Banco Atlantico SA* v. *British Bank of the Middle East* [1990] 2 Lloyd's Rep. 504 (CA). Moreover, the distinction makes a shadowy appearance in the cases on anti-suit injunctions, such as *Airbus Industrie GIE* v. *Patel* [1999] 1 AC 119.

and that a stay will be refused. Such favouring of claimant over defendant is unprincipled and wrong: the idea that the rules are different in a case where the claimant has only one court in which he can expect to win is as wrong as it would be if a defendant were to say that the foreign forum is the only court in which his defence can be successfully advanced. No account whatever ought to be taken of this fact, save perhaps where, in a contract dispute, the foreign court will disregard an express choice of law, so that to try to relocate the case to a foreign court would be for the defendant to engineer a constructive breach of the parties' contract.[288]

If relief is granted, the case is stayed, and remains pending. The stay may well be on terms which reflect undertakings given to the court by the defendant, so that if these turn out to be ineffective the stay can be lifted and the action allowed to proceed. If, by contrast, the action were to be dismissed, it is difficult to see how these undertakings could be enforced, or the action revived.

Breach of contract in suing in England
The second basis on which the defendant may seek a stay of proceedings is the existence of a contract by which the claimant bound himself to sue in a foreign court and not in England.[289] Here, rather than the burden lying on the defendant to persuade the court, a stay will be ordered unless the claimant can establish strong reasons for the court not to do so. Though it might have been possible to adapt the ordinary *forum non conveniens* test to cover this kind of case,[290] the courts have been reluctant to do this, for fear that it would tend to weaken the effect of agreements on choice of court.[291] There are two parts to the analysis. First, the agreement must be examined. It will have to be shown that the alleged agreement on choice of court is valid[292] and effective; that it applies to the particular action brought by the claimant; and that it provides for the exclusive jurisdiction of the chosen court. If so, the bringing of the action in England is a breach of contract for which a stay, rather than damages, is the most appropriate remedy. These three questions of construction and

---

[288] This may be the explanation for the cases mentioned in the previous note.

[289] If the argument is that there is a valid and binding arbitration agreement, the Arbitration Act 1996, s. 9 makes a stay mandatory, and no element of discretion arises.

[290] By using the test as it applies in service out of the jurisdiction, which is examined below, and where the claimant bears the burden of proof on all points.

[291] If it were clear that it was the service out version of *Spiliada* (above n. 281) which applied here, there would be small chance of this dilution. But maybe even that is enough to demand a separate test.

[292] Invalidity may be brought about by the Unfair Terms in Consumer Contracts Regulations 1999, SI 1999/2083.

validity are undertaken by reference to the law which governs the jurisdiction agreement, which will commonly be the law governing the contract of which it forms a part, and any overriding provision of the *lex
fori*.[293] But as a contractual promise, the jurisdiction agreement is construed like any other term of the contract and the law which governs it
will determine its effectiveness. So far as concerns its scope, it will be
necessary for the defendant to show that the words were wide enough to
encompass the action brought by the claimant: a term which says it
applies to 'all actions under this contract', for example, may not extend to
a claim alleging pre-contractual misrepresentation or claims in respect of
equitable obligations. But where the law governing the contract is English, there will be a strong judicial instinct to construe the clause and the
intentions of the parties widely and inclusively, so that the untidiness, or
worse, of there being two courts with competence over parts of the matter
will not usually arise.[294] As regards the exclusivity of jurisdiction, there is
no breach of contract unless the parties obliged themselves and each
other to sue in the foreign court.[295] They do not need to have used the
word 'exclusive', but it certainly helps if they do: more inept wording, as
when 'the parties submit to the jurisdiction of the courts of X' or 'the
courts of Y are to have jurisdiction over all disputes', is harder to construe
with any sense of confidence, and defeats the whole object of making
jurisdiction a matter of certainty rather than lottery. But again, where
English is the governing law, there will be a preference for finding that the
agreement was exclusive.[296]

If the clause is held to be exclusive and to cover the particular claim
advanced in England, the grant of a stay is probable but not automatic.[297]
If England is the natural forum, and if there are additional powerful

---

[293] *Hoerter* v. *Hanover Telegraph Works* (1893) 10 TLR 103 (CA). Though Art. 1(2)(d) of
the Rome Convention means that the Convention makes no claim to govern this question,
the common law rule is that the agreement is governed by the law of the contract in which it
is contained.

[294] *Harbour Assurance Co. (UK) Ltd.* v. *Kansa General Insurance Co. Ltd.* [1993] QB 710
(CA); *Pacific Resources Corp.* v. *Crédit Lyonnais Rouse*, 1 Oct. 1994, not yet reported (CA);
The Pioneer Container [1994] 2 AC 324 (PC); *Donohue* v. *Armco Inc.* [2000] 1 Lloyd's Rep.
579 (CA).

[295] If they did not, the principles governing a stay will be the ordinary ones examined
under *forum non conveniens*, subject to the point that the claimant may not be permitted to
point to the court he agreed to nominate with a view to establishing the injustice of a stay.

[296] *Sohio Supply Co.* v. *Gatoil (USA) Inc.* [1989] 1 Lloyd's Rep. 588 (CA). But cf
J. Fawcett, 'Non-exclusive Jurisdiction Agreements in Private International Law' [2001]
LMCLQ 234.

[297] *The El Amria* [1981] 2 Lloyd's Rep. 119 (CA); *The Pioneer Container* [1994]
2 AC 324 (PC).

reasons why the claimant should nevertheless be permitted to break his contractual promise, the action will be allowed to continue. Perhaps the most compelling reason for not staying the proceedings may be if there are non-parties also implicated by the facts of the dispute but who are not privy to the particular agreement: it may be very inconvenient for the litigation to take place in international fragments.[298] After all, a court has a duty to secure the proper administration of justice, and this may mean that a private agreement on jurisdiction has to be subordinated to the wider public interest. But otherwise, the claimant should not be heard to complain about particular aspects of the legal system which he chose, and for which consideration may have been asked and given. If the action is nevertheless allowed to proceed in England despite the agreement on exclusive jurisdiction, it is unclear what, if anything, prevents the defendant counterclaiming for damages for any proven loss flowing from the breach of contract. To allow the action to continue despite a valid and binding choice of court agreement is only to refuse relief by way of specific enforcement; a remedy for damages for breach of contract is a common law right which, in principle, the defendant may assert, by counterclaim if necessary. It may be difficult to obtain proof of loss, and it is also apparent that there may be some judicial embarrassment in allowing such a claim to proceed. But damages for breach of contract remain a common law right; and if the agreement on jurisdiction was bought and paid for, it would denature it to withhold the usual remedy for its breach.

JURISDICTION ESTABLISHED BY SERVICE OUT WITH THE PERMISSION OF THE COURT

If the defendant is not in England, so that he cannot be served as of right, process must be served on him overseas in order to found the jurisdiction of the court. Prior to 1 May 2000 the procedure was set out in Order 11 of the Rules of the Supreme Court. But from that date these provisions were replaced by the CPR Part 6; the authorities on the interpretation of the earlier rules are still pertinent.[299] The procedure is for the claimant to apply without notice to his opponent for permission to serve in accordance with the CPR Part 6. He must state the grounds on which the

---

[298] *Bouygues Offshore SA* v. *Caspian Shipping Co. (Nos 1, 3, 4, 5)* [1998] 2 Lloyd's Rep. 461 (CA). But where the non-parties are allies ('friends and relations') of one party, egged on to bring actions designed to create a picture of fragmentation, this will be disregarded: *Donohue* v. *Armco Inc.* [2000] 1 Lloyd's Rep. 579 (CA).

[299] *Petroleo Brasiliero SA* v. *Mellitus Shipping Inc.* [2001] CA Civ. 418, [2001] 1 All ER (Comm.) 993.

application is made, and must identify the paragraphs of Rule 6.20 relied on.[300] In principle he will not be allowed to add new claims to supplement or to amend those which were advanced when permission was sought;[301] a fresh application for permission will be required. And he must be full and frank in drawing to the attention of the court arguments which would be made by the defendant in opposition to application.[302] Once permission has been granted and service has been made, the defendant is required to acknowledge it, but may then apply under the CPR Part 11 to have the order granting permission, and the service of process, set aside. On the hearing of this application, the claimant bears the burden of proof on all those issues which determine whether permission should have been given in the first place: the fact that the application is by the defendant does not mean that the burden has now shifted to him.[303] The jurisdiction to serve out which is being invoked is arguably an exorbitant one,[304] and the onus of persuasion lies on the party seeking the grant of permission.

The claimant is required to show three things: that each pleaded claim falls within the letter and spirit[305] (for otherwise the paragraphs of an exorbitant jurisdiction would be widened still further) of one or more of the paragraphs of rule 6.20; that England is the proper place in which to bring the claim;[306] and that he believes that his claim has a reasonable prospect of success on its merits.[307] These three elements are distinct and must be individually satisfied: a clear success in one cannot condone marginal failure in another.

The paragraphs of rule 6.20

The paragraphs of rule 6.20 identify the claims in respect of which the court has power to grant permission to serve out. At first sight it makes sense for the law to have categories of case into which the claims must fit

---

[300] CPR r. 6.21(1)(a).　　　　　　[301] *Parker* v. *Schuller* (1901) 17 TLR 299 (CA).

[302] *Electric Furnace Co.* v. *Selas Corporation of America* [1987] RPC 23 (CA); *The Hida Maru* [1981] 2 Lloyd's Rep. 510 (CA). Several cases have considered whether breach of this obligation should lead automatically to the setting aside of permission, but the answers are not completely consistent. Evidently it will be a matter of degree.

[303] *Artlev AG* v. *Joint Stock Co. Almazy Rossii-Sakha*, 8 Mar. 1995, not yet reported (CA). This point appears to have been overlooked by the High Court of Australia in *Oceanic Sun Line Special Shipping Co. Inc.* v. *Fay* (1988) 165 CLR 197.

[304] So said Lord Diplock in *Amin Rasheed Shipping Corp.* v. *Kuwait Insurance Co.* [1984] AC 50, 65. But the High Court of Australia did not agree: *Agar* v. *Hyde* (2000) 173 ALR 665, [2000] HCA 41, and it is probably right, now that service out is limited by considerations of *forum conveniens*.

[305] *The Hagen* [1908] P 189 (CA); *Johnson* v. *Taylor Bros.* [1920] AC 144, 153; *Mercedes-Benz AG* v. *Leiduck* [1996] 1 AC 284, 289 (PC).

[306] CPR r. 6.21(2A).　　　　　　[307] CPR r. 6.21(1)(b).

before permission can be given, but at second sight this proves to be an illusion. Permission will not in any event be granted unless England is the proper place, or natural forum, to bring the claim. If this condition, which emerged as a specific and discrete requirement only recently,[308] is satisfied, it is difficult to see exactly what value is added to the law by these more primitive, pigeonhole, criteria, or why there should not be an additional, open-ended, rule for any other case in which permission should be given, such as that under the law of New South Wales, which allows service out 'where the proceedings are founded on a cause of action arising in the State'.[309] The law needs to be re-thought. The critical question is whether, had the central role of *forum conveniens* been appreciated from the outset, the law would have devised these pigeon-holes as well, and insisted on compliance with their letter and their spirit before permission to sue in the natural forum was granted. A rational answer would be negative. Nevertheless, the paragraphs of rule 6.20 are the law. If there is any uncertainty about any fact which is required to bring the claim within the paragraph relied on, the claimant is required to make out a good arguable case, which is less than satisfying a balance of probability, upon it.[310] So if he applies for permission to serve on the basis that the claim arises from a contract made within the jurisdiction but the defendant, whilst admitting that there is a contract, denies that it was made in England, the claimant must show a good arguable case that England is where it was made. These locational elements are matters of English domestic law; the broad legal concepts are defined by English law, including its private international law. So in the case just mentioned, if the defendant were to concede that there was a contract as a matter of English domestic law, but deny that it was a valid contract according to its governing law, the plea is tested by reference to the law which governs the contract. But if he puts in issue the proposition that it was made in England, this will be tested by reference to English domestic law.

Each separate claim must fall within a paragraph of rule 6.20; any which do not will be deleted.[311] In the account which follows we will deal with only those which are of practical importance. Those dealing with commercial cases are given first; then those less frequent in commercial litigation; and then the remainder.

---

[308] In *Spiliada Maritime Corp.* v. *Cansulex Ltd.* [1987] AC 460, though there had been occasional trailers for it in earlier cases.

[309] Pt. 10 r. 1A(1).

[310] *Seaconsar Far East Ltd.* v. *Bank Markazi Jomhouri Islami Iran* [1994] 1 AC 438.

[311] For otherwise the scope of the para. would be extended: *Metall und Rohstoff AG* v. *Donaldson Lufkin & Jenrette Inc.* [1990] 1 QB 391 (CA).

Contract claims

Three paragraphs deal with contractual claims. Under paragraph 5, service out may be ordered where a claim is made in respect of a contract where that contract was made within the jurisdiction, or was made through an agent trading or residing within the jurisdiction, or is governed by English law, or contains a term to the effect that the court shall have jurisdiction to determine any claim in respect of the contract. Under paragraph 6, service may be ordered when a claim is made in respect of a breach of contract committed within the jurisdiction. Paragraph 7 provides for service where a claim is made for a declaration that no contract exists where, if the contract were found to exist, it would have fallen within paragraph 5.

As said above, if it is not admitted, there must be a good arguable case that there is a contract, valid according to rules of English private international law,[312] but whose place of making is determined by reference to English domestic law.[313] Though the paragraphs are drawn widely, the contract must be one by which the claimant and defendant are alleged to be bound: it is not enough that a contract *inter alios* forms the background to the claim.[314] For the purposes of paragraph 6, breach by a repudiatory act occurs where the act was done; breach by non-performance where the required act was to have been performed. Paragraph 7 is a new addition to the rules, which is designed to make it easier to bring a claim for a declaration of non-liability under an alleged contract, a claim which fell only uncertainly under the predecessor of paragraph 5. It probably applies generally to claims which deny that a contractual duty is owed to the defendant, but which the defendant alleges is owed, rather than being limited to cases in which it is claimed that no contract ever existed.[315] It is also to be expected that a claim for relief which is consequential upon holding that there is no contract is also within paragraph 7. Convenience suggests that it should be. Even so, the fact that these submissions have to be made goes to reinforce the question why the jurisdiction of the court

---

[312] *Amin Rasheed Shipping Corp.* v. *Kuwait Insurance Co.* [1984] AC 50; *Bank of Baroda* v. *Vysya Bank Ltd.* [1994] 2 Lloyd's Rep. 87.

[313] *Chevron International Oil Co.* v. *A/S Sea Team (The TS Havprins)* [1983] 2 Lloyd's Rep. 356.

[314] *Finnish Marine Insurance Co.* v. *Protective National Insurance Co.* [1990] 1 QB 1078.

[315] A court will not grant leave to serve a claim for a negative declaration unless it is an appropriate case for the seeking of such relief: *Messier Dowty Ltd.* v. *Sabena SA* [2000] 1 WLR 2040 (CA).

over a claim which has England as its natural forum should be limited by category.

Tort claims

Under paragraph 8, service out may be authorized where a claim is made in tort where the damage was sustained within the jurisdiction, or where the damage sustained resulted from an act committed within the jurisdiction. Under the previous rule, which required that the claim be 'founded on *a* tort', it had been held that this required there to be an actual tort, ascertained by reference to rules of English private international law.[316] The omission of the indefinite article makes it less certain that this is still the way to interpret paragraph 8, and that there must be *a* tort, demonstrated (where it is not admitted) to the level of a good arguable case. If it remains correct, there must be a good arguable case that the defendant is liable to the claimant, for without liability it cannot be said that there is *a* tort. If, by contrast, the paragraph requires only that the pleaded claim be properly formulated in the terminology of tort, or be characterized as tortious, there will be no need to show a good arguable case upon actual liability before service out may be authorized.[317] It is hard to say which view is to be preferred. It does appear odd that because the term 'contract' does not describe a cause of action, but 'tort' does, there is a jurisdictional requirement of liability under paragraph 8 which is absent from paragraphs 5 to 7. No obvious policy requires this and, as a result, it may be preferable to read paragraph 8 as referring to the characterization of the claim and not to the existence of liability. Damage is sustained in England if some significant damage is sustained in England: it need not be all, nor even most, of it.[318] It is unclear whether 'sustained' is intended to reflect or reproduce the interpretation of where damage 'occurred' within Article 5(3) of the Regulation,[319] but if it does, the focus will be on the place of the direct damage done to the immediate victim of it. Moreover, in the case of purely economic losses or damage to reputation, the location of the damage is undeniably artificial. An act is committed within the jurisdiction if the damage resulted from substantial and efficacious acts committed within the jurisdiction, even if other substantial acts

[316] RSC O. 11 r. 1(1)(f), as interpreted in *Metall und Rohstoff AG* v. *Donaldson Lufkin & Jenrette Inc.* [1990] QB 391 (CA). The private international law of torts is examined in Chap. 5.
[317] Though the requirement of CPR r. 6.21(1)(b) will still need to be satisfied.
[318] *Metall und Rohstoff AG* v. *Donaldson Lufkin & Jenrette Inc.* [1990] 1 QB 391 (CA).
[319] It was held in *Batstone & Firminger Ltd.* v. *Nasima Enterprises (Nigeria) Ltd.* [1996] CLC 1902 that it was.

were committed elsewhere.[320] Though it must be the act of the actual defendant, the act of one joint tortfeasor is the act of all.[321]

Constructive trusteeship and restitution

Paragraph 14 allows service to be authorized where a claim is made against the defendant as constructive trustee and his alleged liability arises out of acts committed within the jurisdiction. The former rule made it explicit that the acts committed within the jurisdiction were not required to be those of the defendant; it is unlikely that their omission from paragraph 14 reflects a desire to narrow the scope of the provision. Presumably the acts must still have something to do with the defendant.[322] Only some of the acts, not necessarily the receipt of the assets, need take place within the jurisdiction.[323] So as long as a participant in fraud takes part in a scheme where one of the wrongdoers did acts in the jurisdiction, service out may probably be made on all.[324] Paragraph 15 allows service to be authorized where a claim is made for restitution where the defendant's alleged liability arises out of acts committed within the jurisdiction. This is a new provision, and it is uncertain whether the local acts relied on must be those of the defendant. On the footing that restitutionary claims are not necessarily based on wrongdoing by the defendant, but upon his relationship to acts done by the claimant, it is less likely that the acts of the defendant are those which must take place within the jurisdiction.

Other commercial claims

Paragraph 1 applies if the defendant is domiciled within the jurisdiction,[325] though this will often mean that the jurisdictional rules of the Regulation will apply, and permission to serve will not be needed. Paragraph 2 applies if the claim is made for an injunction ordering the defendant to do or to not do an act within the jurisdiction. The injunction must comprise a substantial element of the relief sought,[326] and it must be an injunction in respect of substantive rights: an application for a freezing order, or other relief not predicated on the existence of substantive rights,

[320] *Metall und Rohstoff*, above n. 318.
[321] *Unilever plc v. Gillette (UK) Ltd.* [1989] RPC 583 (CA).
[322] Cf *Dexter Ltd. v. Harley, The Times,* 2 Apr. 2001 (a case on Art. 5(3) BC).
[323] *ISC Technologies Ltd. v. Guerin* [1992] 2 Lloyd's Rep. 430; *Polly Peck International plc v. Nadir,* 17 Mar. 1993, not yet reported (CA), interpreting RSC O. 11 r. 1(1)(t).
[324] If one can be served as of right, it will also be possible to apply for permission under para. 3 to serve a co-defendant as a necessary or proper party.
[325] Within the meaning of the 1982 Act: CPR r. 6.18(g).
[326] *Rosler v. Hilbery* [1925] 1 Ch. 250 (CA).

is not within the paragraph[327] but is specifically provided for by paragraph 4 instead. Paragraph 3 applies if the defendant is a necessary or proper party to a claim against someone who has been or will be served; the paragraph is a broad one which serves the efficient disposal of claims.[328] Paragraph 9 applies if the proceedings seek the enforcement of any judgment or arbitral award.[329] And paragraph 17 applies when a party seeks an order that costs be awarded to or against a non-party to the proceedings.[330]

Property, trusts, and other cases
Claims concerning property in England fall under paragraph 10; claims to execute English trusts under paragraph 11; claims in the administration of the estate of an English domiciliary under paragraph 12; and probate actions under paragraph 13. And paragraphs 15–19 make up a list of other causes of action, almost all statutory and where the statutory duty is reinforced by the right to apply for permission to serve out.

England is the proper place in which to bring the claim

The second requirement cast on the claimant is in rule 6.21(2A), which echoes, in modified language, the proposition[331] that England must be shown, clearly or distinctly, to be the most appropriate forum.[332] Those factors which are relevant when a stay is sought of English proceedings apply, *mutatis mutandis*, here as well. It is unclear why the draftsman elected not to use the 'natural forum' formula which had been hallowed by judicial and professional usage, but the enumeration and telling reference to natural forum considerations in rule 6.21(3) shows that it was a late insertion to fill a gap which had been inadvertently left. However, it is possible that in an extreme case, England may be the proper place to bring a claim even though England is not the natural forum: if the alternative[333] forum is some war-torn corner of the globe, a trial in

---

[327] *Mercedes-Benz AG* v. *Leiduck* [1996] 1 AC 284 (PC).
[328] *Petroleo Brasiliero SA* v. *Mellitus Shipping Inc.* [2001] CA Civ. 418, [2001] 1 All ER (Comm.) 993.
[329] The judgment or award must have been given by the time permission is sought: *Mercedes-Benz AG* v. *Leiduck* [1996] 1 AC 284 (PC).
[330] Supreme Court Act 1981, s. 51.
[331] But which was never so expressed in statutory form: it was the immediate ratio of *Spiliada Maritime Corp.* v. *Cansulex Ltd.* [1987] AC 460, which held this to be a discrete component of RSC O. 11 r. 4(2) which required that the case be shown to be a proper one for service out.
[332] *Spiliada Maritime Corp.* v. *Cansulex Ltd.* [1987] AC 460, interpreting RSC O. 11 r. 4(2).
[333] In this context this will probably be where the defendant is resident and can, in principle at least, otherwise be sued.

England may be in the proper place. It is less certain whether this condition would be satisfied if financial support for the claim were available only in England and not in the alternative forum. The logic of recent cases on *forum conveniens* would suggest that this is so; and if the defendant is before the court, even though his acknowledgment of service is not counted as his submission, it would be remarkable, and arguably a breach of the European Convention on Human Rights, for a court to set aside service and leave the claimant without effective remedy.[334] On the other hand, there are manifest points of distinction if the courts do not wish to be pushed this far.

The claim has a reasonable prospect of success

Service out will not be authorized unless the claimant gives evidence of his belief that the claim has a reasonable prospect of success. If the defendant considers that the claim falls below this standard, he should probably challenge the obtaining of permission on the ground that the claimant could not properly have held and stated this belief; and if he succeeds on this point the court will set aside the permission and the service of process.[335] It used to be required of a claimant that he show a good arguable case on the merits of his claim, which, though rather nebulous, required a higher standard of probability of winning; this was deliberately relaxed in 1994.[336] It appears to be entirely justified: if England is the natural forum, why should a claimant who wishes to serve out be required to have a higher apparent chance of success than one who has served within the jurisdiction? On the other hand, a defendant served out of the jurisdiction used to know that he could appear and defend the case on its merits, in which case any judgment against him would be likely to be internationally effective, or ignore the summons, and know that though the judgment against him was certain to be enforceable in England it was most unlikely to be enforceable in any other country: there was a choice. But after the United Kingdom acceded to the Brussels Convention, it ceased to be true that a judgment based on service out under CPR Part 6, and given in default of appearance, would be recognized and

---

[334] Cf *Lubbe* v. *Cape plc* [2000] 1 WLR 1545 (HL).

[335] Cf *Seaconsar Far East Ltd.* v. *Bank Markazi Jomhouri Islami Iran* [1994] 1 AC 438. It may be dangerous to make the argument by means of an application under CPR r. 3.4(a) or CPR r. 24.2(a)(i), as these are not challenges to the jurisdiction of the court and may therefore be seen as submission.

[336] *Seaconsar Far East Ltd.* v. *Bank Markazi Jomhouri Islami Iran* [1994] 1 AC 438; followed on this point by the High Court of Australia in *Agar* v. *Hyde* (2000) 173 ALR 665, [2000] HCA 41.

enforceable only in England. Instead, it will be effective in all the Member States and contracting states, and it has therefore raised the stakes, making it much more risky for a defendant to elect not to appear and to allow judgment to be entered against him in default. Yet to do that at the very same time as lowering the bar on the question how convincing need be the case on the merits is to wham the overseas defendant doubly. It is unclear whether these two points were considered alongside each other, but if they were not, the law could benefit from further reflection before confirming that the result is what was intended.

OFFENSIVE FORUM-SHOPPING

The traditional rules of jurisdiction now limit the extent to which a claimant may forum-shop in the English courts. But there are two respects in which the common law responds to the forum-shopping to a foreign court: by granting injunctions to impede the foreign proceedings, and by allowing actions for declaratory relief.

Anti-suit injunctions

As Lord Goff of Chieveley pointed out,[337] the jurisdictional scheme put in place by the Regulation is common to the Member States, and has, in a sense, the Court of Justice sitting above it to promote the proper interpretation of its rules. The common law world is different, and jurisdictional balance and order between states is achieved by the doctrine of *forum non conveniens*, by which a court directly limits its own jurisdiction, and the anti-suit injunction, by which a court indirectly places limits on the jurisdiction of other courts. It is the second of these with which we are now concerned. A court with personal jurisdiction over a respondent may order him not to bring or not to continue proceedings in a foreign court, by the granting of an injunction against suit. The order is not addressed to the foreign judge, who is manifestly not subject to the personal jurisdiction of the English court, but to the respondent, who is. Even so, the foreign judge may not appreciate the subtlety of the distinction,[338] and for this reason, a concern for comity limits the manner in which the court will exercise its discretion.[339] This potent remedy gives the English court an international reach by which to control what it finds to be wrongful recourse to a foreign court. Though the remedy is also

---

[337] *Airbus Industrie GIE* v. *Patel* [1999] 1 AC 119.
[338] For a telling German failure to see the point see *Re the Enforcement of an English anti-suit injunction* (Case 3 VA 11/95) [1997] ILPr. 320 (Regional Court of Appeal, Düsseldorf).
[339] *Airbus Industrie GIE* v. *Patel* [1999] 1 AC 119.

found in other common law systems, albeit with some difference of detail, it is largely unknown in civilian systems. Its compatibility with the jurisdictional scheme of the Regulation is contentious. It is necessary to deal separately with two points: personal jurisdiction over the respondent and the exercise of the court's discretion.

Personal jurisdiction over the respondent

The respondent must be served with process in order to be made subject to the jurisdiction of the court in respect of the claim for an injunction. An anti-suit injunction is an application for final[340] relief in respect of legal or equitable rights, and process must be lawfully served in accordance with the Regulation or the traditional rules, as the case may be. Where personal jurisdiction is founded on the traditional rules, it may therefore be necessary to seek permission to serve out of the jurisdiction. Though there is no paragraph of rule 6.20 which is specifically dedicated to applications for an anti-suit injunction, there is nothing to prevent the cause of action which founds the claim to relief being brought within any particular paragraph which will accommodate it. So if the claim for an injunction is based on the fact that there is a contract falling within rule 6.20(5), which gives a legal right not to be sued, this paragraph may be relied on in the application for permission. In cases where jurisdiction and the right to serve process are governed by the Regulation, the fact that an action between the same parties is already pending in the courts of another Member State may mean that Article 27 negates jurisdiction otherwise derived from Chapter II of the Regulation. The two causes of action may be said to be different: for an injunction to prevent the trial, for substantive relief after the trial on the merits, but may, just as convincingly, be said to be the same: an injunction to prevent the claim being heard in state X, a claim for substantive relief at the trial in state X.[341] However that may be, the fact that there is another Member State seised may well bear on the exercise of the court's discretion whether to grant the relief, whether the other court was seised before or after the English court.

Discretion to grant the injunction

An anti-suit injunction will generally not be ordered unless England is or would be the natural forum for the litigation of the substantive

---

[340] Though it is possible to apply for an interim anti-suit injunction to preserve the status quo until the application for a final injunction can be heard.

[341] The reasoning in Case C-406/92 *The Tatry* [1994] ECR I-5439 does not make it plain which is correct.

dispute.[342] This condition is satisfied if the respondent could and should bring any claim he has before the English courts, but it is also satisfied, in principle at least, even though the respondent would lose if he had to sue in England: the critical question is where the trial of the dispute has its natural home, not where the respondent is able to find a court which will allow his claim to succeed and the defence to be overcome.[343] Though it may be thought that an English court should be able to restrain wrongful behaviour committed by anyone subject to its personal jurisdiction, it has been recognized that some limitation needs to be placed on this power. It could have been done through the development of a choice of law rule,[344] to determine whether the respondent's conduct should be evaluated by reference to English or a foreign law, but it was instead achieved by insisting on a natural forum connection which, when satisfied, makes it appropriate for the English court to exercise its discretion and to apply English law and equity in granting relief. In other words, if England is the natural forum, judicial comity is not infringed by the intervention of the English court applying English law. Subject to his satisfaction of this condition, the applicant must show that the respondent is vexatious or oppressive in his bringing the foreign action.[345] The meaning of these terms retains an element of flexibility, but if the foreign action is brought in bad faith or to harass, in that it is bound to fail if defended but its defence is certain to cause trouble and expense, or its consequences may be unjustifiably involved,[346] it may be restrained. The absence of a real link between the acts complained of and the foreign court may help to indicate that there is oppression;[347] if it is otherwise unconscionable to bring the action it may be restrained. According to Australian equity,[348] the foreign action is unobjectionable if it seeks relief which would not be available from a local court, but this seems problematic:[349] it follows that

---

[342] *Société Nationale Industrielle Aérospatiale* v. *Lee Kui Jak* [1987] AC 871 (PC); *Airbus Industrie GIE* v. *Patel* [1999] 1 AC 119.

[343] This is the effect of *Midland Bank plc* v. *Laker Airways Ltd.* [1986] QB 689 (CA). This decision was conspicuously not approved in *Airbus Industrie GIE* v. *Patel*, but in principle it is right, for the law has no business in preferring the successful claim of the respondent to the successful defence of the applicant. The proposition that there are special rules for 'single forum' cases is unsound.

[344] Cf A. Briggs, 'Anti-suit Injunctions: a Pause for Thought' [1997] *LMCLQ* 90.

[345] *Société Nationale Industrielle Aérospatiale* v. *Lee Kui Jak* [1987] AC 871 (PC).

[346] *Société Nationale Industrielle Aérospatiale* v. *Lee Kui Jak* [1987] AC 871 (PC) (consequential contribution proceedings would be intolerably complex).

[347] *Midland Bank plc* v. *Laker Airways Ltd.* [1986] QB 689 (CA).

[348] *CSR Ltd.* v. *Cigna Insurance Australia Ltd.* (1997) 189 CLR 345.

[349] It is also contrary to *Midland Bank plc* v. *Laker Airways Ltd.* [1986] QB 689 (CA).

the further from the standards of English law the relief is, the less it
would be possible to restrain the action. According to Canadian equity,[350]
before applying for the injunction, the applicant must make any jurisdictional application to the foreign court: an injunction will not be
granted unless the foreign court refuses to apply principles of *forum
conveniens* but then, having refused to observe comity, it can expect no
comity in return. Though this has sometimes been said to be the general
rule in England,[351] clarification of the requirement that England be shown
to be the natural forum makes it an unnecessary, and possibly undesirable,
requirement in England: if England is the natural forum, that is a sufficient recognition of what comity demands.[352] And there is something
unattractive in encouraging an English court to sit as if it were hearing an
appeal from a foreign court;[353] and if the application is delayed until the
issue has been fought in the foreign court, it may mean that the time for
an injunction has passed.

Where the claim to an injunction is founded on a contractual right not
to be sued in the foreign court, it is uncertain whether England must be
the natural forum for the action.[354] If England is the chosen court, there
will be no difficulty,[355] but if the nominated court is in a non-member
state the answer is less clear. On one view the existence of a legal right not
to be sued is enough by itself, but it may also be said that if neither the
nominated court nor the action to be restrained is in England, it is none
of the English court's business to say where the trial should take place,
however much the respondent may appear to be at fault. But where it is
appropriate for the court to exercise its discretion, it is unlikely that there
is a distinct need to demonstrate vexation or oppression: an injunction in
support of a legal right not to be sued in the foreign court will be granted
unless there is good reason not to do so.[356] To say that there is oppression
or vexation whenever there is a legal right not to be sued seems
unnecessary and illiterate: an injunction in equity's auxiliary jurisdiction

[350] *Amchem Products Inc.* v. *British Columbia (Workers' Compensation Board)* [1993] 1 SCR
897, (1993) 102 DLR (4th) 96.
[351] *Barclays Bank plc* v. *Homan* [1993] BCLC 680, 686–7 (Hoffmann J), 703 (CA).
[352] See on this point, and more generally, A. Briggs, 'Anti-suit Injunctions in a Complex
World' in F. D. Rose (ed.), *Lex Mercatoria: Essays on International Commercial Law* (Lloyd's
of London Press, London, 2000), chap. 12.
[353] Cf *The Angelic Grace* [1995] 1 Lloyd's Rep. 87, 95 (CA).
[354] The point was left open in *Airbus Industrie GIE* v. *Patel* [1999] 1 AC 119.
[355] *Continental Bank NA* v. *Aeakos Compania Naviera SA* [1994] 1 WLR 588 (CA).
[356] *Donohue* v. *Armco Inc.* [2000] 1 Lloyd's Rep. 579 (CA); *National Westminster Bank plc* v.
Utrecht-America Finance Co. [2001] CA Civ. 658, [2001] 2 All ER (Comm.) 7.

and in support of legal rights does not need to be founded on an equitable right.

Impact of the Regulation

Where the foreign court is in a Member State in which the Regulation applies, or a contracting state to the Brussels or Lugano Convention, the specific requirements of comity should direct attention to the obligations of mutual trust.[357] It should be accepted that each court will apply the jurisdictional rules, and prevent any abusive exercise of rights, in any proceedings brought before it. If this is taken at its full width, it may lead to the conclusion that there is no room for the anti-suit injunction—part of the jurisdictional scheme of the common law—within the domain of the Regulation at all.[358] But a narrower view can be defended: that an English court is absolutely prohibited from reviewing the jurisdiction of a court in another Member State,[359] and that this line of argument, and any conclusion derived from it, is inadmissible.[360] If, however, it is accepted without question that the other court has jurisdiction, but there are other reasons why the action may be regarded as oppressive or vexatious, by focusing on the wrongful behaviour of the respondent, an injunction might just about be defensible. On the other hand, the effect of its grant will be to risk creating a clash of judgments, for a judgment obtained in defiance of an anti-suit injunction will not be recognized in England,[361] and recognition of the injunction in the Member State where proceedings are taking place may well be contrary to public policy. It is hard to avoid the conclusion that there are just too many objections to the granting of such an injunction, and its compatibility with the scheme of the Regulation appears very doubtful.[362]

Negative declarations

The development of the doctrine of *forum conveniens* was the first substantial means by which a defendant could challenge the jurisdictional

---

[357] Recitals 16 and 17 to the Reg.

[358] This would be consistent with the description of schemes given by Lord Goff of Chieveley in *Airbus Industrie GIE* v. *Patel* [1999] 1 AC 119; it is also the apparent view of the German courts: *Re the Enforcement of an English anti-suit injunction* [1997] ILPr. 320 (Regional Court of Appeal, Düsseldorf).

[359] Case C–351/89 *Overseas Union Insurance Ltd.* v. *New Hampshire Insurance Co.* [1991] ECR I–3317.

[360] It should have led to the refusal to grant the injunction in *Turner* v. *Grovit* [2000] 1 QB 345 (CA).

[361] Art. 34(1) of the Reg.

[362] See further Rose (ed.), above n. 352, *Commercial Law*, chap. 12.

dominance of the claimant; and an anti-suit injunction may be seen as the second: the party sued is not obliged to sit back and take his punishment, but may try to forestall his being sued in a court whose jurisdiction is unwelcome to him. For the sake of completeness, we should mention the third means which may be resorted to: bringing proceedings on the merits of the claim for a declaration that he, the 'natural defendant', owes no liability to the opponent. This, if successful, will either prevent the opponent bringing proceedings of his own or mean that, if he does, the principles of *res judicata* may forestall the enforcement of a foreign judgment.

The early history of such actions was that the courts were hostile to them.[363] They would be very slow to exercise any jurisdictional discretion in support of them;[364] they would be struck out as premature, or abusive, or otherwise impeded. The suspicion that they were open to abuse by forum-shoppers was widely held; and their potential to harass an opponent, who may not have decided whether to sue and who may not be ready for the fight, was considerable. But the sea has changed, and there is now no reason to disparage such actions. Three principal reasons may be given. First, it became the practice of the Commercial Court to entertain such actions, and to find them justifiable: insurers, suppliers, and others will often need to know whether they have legal obligations of an insured (so they can step in and conduct the defence if they do) or a distributor (so they can terminate supplies and retain another if they do not). The practice of the courts seems to have undermined the formal state of the law. Secondly, in the context of the Regulation, it is settled that an action for a declaration of non-liability brought in a court which has jurisdiction cannot be objected to on jurisdictional grounds: there is no wrong in suing in a court with jurisdiction under the Regulation.[365] Thirdly, the Court of Appeal has given its seal of approval to this new approach,[366] favouring such claims, rather than criticizing or obstructing them, as a good and useful means of resolving disputes. It is hard to disagree: the legal certainty which can be brought about by a prompt application for a declaration may be far preferable to the limbo of waiting to see whether proceedings are commenced by the other party. Abusive use of the procedure can still be prevented, but there will now be no presumption of

---

[363] *Guaranty Trust Co. of New York* v. *Hannay* [1915] 2 KB 536 (CA); *The Volvox Hollandia* [1988] 2 Lloyd's Rep. 361 (CA).

[364] By refusing permission to serve out of the jurisdiction.

[365] Case C–406/92 *The Tatry* [1994] ECR I–5439.

[366] *Messier Dowty Ltd.* v. *Sabena SA* [2000] 1 WLR 2040 (CA).

abuse; and as this new wisdom beds down in the law, the need for separate mention of proceedings for negative declaratory relief will become a thing of the past.

JURISDICTION TO OBTAIN INTERIM RELIEF

Interim relief, which includes provisional and protective measures, may be ordered in support of actions in the English courts, or of civil or commercial claims in the courts in another Member State or contracting state (Article 31 cases), or in support of other actions in those courts or elsewhere.[367] If the respondent is present within the jurisdiction of the court he may be served with the claim form as of right: it is irrelevant that he may be domiciled in another Member State and so not be subject to the jurisdiction of the English courts over the merits of the claim. If he is outside the territorial jurisdiction, an application for permission to serve the claim form out of the jurisdiction must be made under CPR rule 6.20(4): this is so even in relation to applications falling within Article 31 of the Regulation. But in all cases, the fact that the court may lack jurisdiction to try the case on the merits is a material factor in determining whether it is expedient to grant the relief;[368] and it will also be relevant in deciding whether the court should grant permission to serve out, as rule 6.21(2A) also applies to applications under rule 6.20(4). As regards whether it may be inexpedient to grant the relief, it has been suggested that where the court seised of the merits could have granted but decided not to grant relief, an English court should be slow to act to contradict it; but where it had no power to grant relief, an English court should be inclined to make an order to assist the foreign court. It must be doubtful, though, whether it is realistic to 'assist' a court whose legislator has, presumably deliberately, withheld certain powers from it.[369]

---

[367] Civil Jurisdiction and Judgments Act 1982, s. 25.
[368] Ibid., s. 25(2).
[369] *Crédit Suisse Fides Trust SA* v. *Cuoghi* [1998] QB 818 (CA).

4

Recognition and Enforcement of Foreign Judgments

RECOGNITION, ENFORCEMENT, AND RELATED MATTERS

The judgments of foreign courts have no direct effect in England. If adjudication is thought of as an incident of state sovereignty, this will come as small surprise. But it has long been recognized that there is a countervailing general public interest. This requires that those who have had a hearing and received judgment should abide by its terms, and that the law should prevent or discourage the re-opening of disputes which have already had a hearing and an adjudication; a variant would force or encourage litigants to put forward all their issues for adjudication at once, rather than holding some back for a subsequent dispute. This broad principle is not limited to cases where the first judgment was obtained in England, but in a shrinking world and subject to conditions applies also to foreign judgments. Accordingly, foreign judgments may be given effect in England according to the rules of the common law and statute, under various schemes examined in this chapter. As will be seen, there are degrees of foreignness, and the schemes accordingly comprise three broad categories. The judgments which are most readily given effect to in England are from other parts of the United Kingdom and from sister states of the European Union or states party to the Brussels or Lugano Convention, where legislation has provided rules which are easily satisfied and procedures for enforcement which are notably swift. In the furthest category are judgments from the whole of the rest of the world, for which the common law alone provides the rules governing recognition and enforcement, and also the procedure for enforcement. Between the two are those from a small number of states which are party to a bilateral treaty with the United Kingdom, and from other territories of Commonwealth and Empire, for which the statutory conditions for recognition and enforcement reflect the common law, but which benefit from a simplified procedure for enforcement.

An important distinction must be drawn at the outset between the recognition of a judgment and its enforcement; and between these and the other effects which can be derived from a foreign judgment. *Recognition* of a judgment means treating the claim which was adjudicated as having been determined once and for all. It does not matter whether it was determined in favour of the claimant or the defendant, though judgments *in personam* are only ever recognized as effective against particular parties: by way of contrast to judgments *in rem*,[1] there is no sense of their being recognized generally or universally. The matter is then *res judicata*, and the losing party will be estopped from contradicting it in subsequent proceedings in an English court.[2] For the foreign judgment to achieve recognition, qualifying conditions have to be met, which regulate the connection between the foreign court and the parties, accommodate and limit the scope of objections to the judgment, and define the nature of the judgment to which this status of *res judicata* will be accorded. The principles of *res judicata* can operate in relation to entire causes of action ('cause of action estoppel') as well as on discrete issues which arose and were determined in the course of the trial of a cause of action ('issue estoppel').[3] Given a *res judicata*, a party bringing proceedings in England to try and obtain a ruling which contradicts this foreign judgment may be met with the plea of estoppel by *res judicata*, and stopped in his tracks.

Recognition serves two purposes. Where judgment has been given in favour of the defendant, dismissing the claim, it operates defensively by allowing the defendant who has won in a foreign court to rely on this to defeat a subsequent action brought by the unsuccessful claimant. But where the foreign judgment was in favour of the claimant, the position is more complex, because the claimant may not have been successful on every part of his claim. To take the easiest case first, if there was judgment for a claimant[4] in respect of the whole of the claim, he may wish to go further, and bring proceedings for the *enforcement* of the judgment, for example, by collecting money which the foreign court ordered to be paid and which remains unpaid. Not every judgment entitled to recognition

---

[1] e.g., on the status of a person, or the ownership of a thing.

[2] See generally G. Spencer Bower, A. K. Turner, and K. R. Handley, *The Doctrine of Res Judicata* (3rd edn., Butterworths, London, 1996).

[3] *Carl Zeiss Stiftung* v. *Rayner & Keeler Ltd. (No 2)* [1967] 1 AC 853.

[4] Which expression includes counterclaimant or party, not excluding a defendant, in whose favour other order has been made.

may be enforced in England,[5] but to be enforced, a foreign judgment must first be recognized. If it is to be enforced at the behest of the successful claimant, the judgment must meet further conditions; but once enforcement is ordered, the judgment may be executed as if it had been given by an English court, either because it is ordered that the judgment be registered pursuant to statute which provides that registration has this effect or (if enforced under the common law) because an English court gives its own judgment which itself becomes the order which will be enforced.

A third possibility is that the claimant was partially successful. If, for example, he succeeds on his claim but recovers a rather smaller sum in damages than he expected, he may seek to improve on the first result by suing on the underlying cause of action in the English courts. In this case neither recognition[6] nor enforcement will stand in his way, but the manifest unfairness of his having a second bite at the cherry led to statutory intervention removing the right to sue again.[7]

The tradition of English textbooks is to concentrate on the enforcement of judgments, and to treat recognition as an afterthought of limited practical importance. But the logic of the law is that recognition is the necessary primary concern, for without it the judgment can have no effect whatever in the English legal order. In relation to the three regimes for recognition and enforcement, therefore, we will start with the criteria for recognition, and will then examine what else is required for enforcement.

We will first examine judgments in civil or commercial matters from the courts of Member States bound by Council Regulation (EC) 44/2001,[8] the instrument which has in very large part replaced the Brussels Convention, and will then look at judgments whose effect in England is governed by the Brussels and Lugano Conventions, the significance of which in England is now sharply reducing. Secondly, we consider recognition and enforcement of judgments at common law, where the rules are restricted neither by geography, nor by subject matter, nor by type of court. Finally we consider the statutory registration schemes developed

---

[5] If the particular judgment cannot be enforced, e.g. because the remedy ordered by the foreign court falls outside those which can be enforced in an English court, there is nothing to prevent the claimant seeking recognition where enforcement is not available, and using the principles of *res judicata* to short-cut his way to victory in the English action.

[6] For there will be no discrete issue on which the defendant won (but if there is, such as a refusal to award a particular head of damages, issue estoppel in the defendant's favour on this issue will be available).

[7] Civil Jurisdiction and Judgments Act 1982, s. 34.   [8] [2001] OJ L12/1.

to simplify procedure in relation to enforcement at common law, but which apply only to specific courts in specified countries. In this chapter the focus of attention will be on judgments *in personam*. The recognition of judgments in family law, the administration of estates, and insolvency are dealt with within the chapters which examine this subject matter.

RECOGNITION AND ENFORCEMENT UNDER COUNCIL REGULATION (EC) 44/2001

The Regulation mostly supplants the Brussels Convention as the instrument by which judgments from the courts of Member States of the European Union will take effect in the English legal order. The Brussels Convention, by contrast, will remain the instrument of enforcement for judgments from and in Denmark and, to some extent, for judgments given before the Regulation came into effect on 1 March 2002. The Lugano Convention will continue to apply to judgments from and in Iceland, Norway, Switzerland, and Poland. But in deference to its dominant position, we will focus on the Regulation, and note the different effect of these other regimes in its light.

RECOGNITION OF THE JUDGMENT: ARTICLES 32–37, AND 72

For a judgment to be recognized under Chapter III of the Regulation, it (i) must be from a court in a Member State,[9] (ii) must be given in a civil or commercial matter, (iii) need not be in proceedings which were instituted after the Regulation came into effect, (iv) must not be impeachable for jurisdictional error, (v) must not be impeachable for procedural or substantive reasons, and (vi) must not be excluded from recognition by another treaty. It is often said that if it fails to meet these criteria, there is no objection to an attempt to obtain recognition and enforcement of a judgment under the rules of the common law, on the footing that Chapter III of the Regulation is a permissive, not an exclusive, regime. This may be correct. But on the other hand, in those cases which fall within the domain of the Regulation but of which Article 34 says they 'shall not be recognized', it is arguable that the Regulation imposes an obligation to withhold recognition, and precludes allowing it by other means. Be that as it may, according to Article 33 it is not necessary to bring any form of action or procedure to obtain recognition of a judgment under the

---

[9] For the purpose of the Reg., Gibraltar is treated as part of the UK.

Regulation beyond pleading it, so if a successful defendant wishes to rely on a judgment to which the Regulation applies, all he need do is plead it as satisfying the criteria for recognition. But there is no objection to his bringing proceedings for a declaration that the judgment be recognized if this would serve a useful purpose.[10] We will first examine the six points listed above.

Judgments: Article 32

For the purposes of the Regulation, a judgment is an adjudication by a court of a Member State, including an order as to costs.[11] This excludes judgments from a non-member state, even after a judge in a Member State has held them to be enforceable:[12] the Regulation applies to original determinations by a judge in a Member State, but not to instances where a judge validates a decision taken by a judge outside the Member States. Many Member States have treaties or other provisions dealing with judgments from non-member states, frequently in relation to former colonies; but such bilateral relationships are not enough to admit such a judgment, via the doorway of the Member State's own private international law, into Chapter III of the Regulation. Similar considerations underpin the fact that a judgment declaring the enforceability of an arbitration award is not a judgment within Chapter III of the Regulation either. Article 32 does include a provisional or interlocutory judgment, and will include the dismissal of a case on jurisdictional grounds, such as by reference to a choice of court agreement for another Member State: there is no requirement that the judgment or order be *res judicata* in the court which pronounced it. It includes a judgment by consent, for this is still an adjudication.[13] A judgment which orders a periodical payment imposed as a penalty for disobedience to a court order is included,[14] though it may be enforced only if the sum due has been finally quantified by the court which ordered it.[15] Settlements which have been approved by courts in the course of proceedings[16] and authentic instruments[17] (unknown to English law, but which are documents authenticated by a public authority or a notary, and which are enforceable under some laws

---

[10] RSC O. 71 Pt. IV.   [11] Art. 32.
[12] Case C–129/92 *Owens Bank Ltd. v. Bracco* [1994] ECR I–117.
[13] *Landhurst Leasing plc v. Marcq* [1998] ILPr. 822 (CA). But it does not include a settlement; and if it is desired to make binding the terms on which a claim is compromised, a judgment is much to be preferred to a contractual disposal: Case C–414/92 *Solo Kleinmotoren GmbH v. Boch* [1994] ECR I–2237.
[14] Art. 49.   [15] Art. 49.   [16] Art. 58.   [17] Art. 57.

without the need for legal action[18]) are enforceable under similar conditions.[19]

It is easy to see the final order of a court as a judgment. It is less clear how this applies to a finding made by a court which is not embodied in its final order: does 'judgment' include a decision upon an issue as well as the disposal of a cause of action? The answer is unclear, but in principle if a judgment qualifies for recognition under the Regulation, it is then integrated into the English legal order. Once that is done, there is nothing to prevent an English court applying principles of issue estoppel to the judgment and to its parts, though as a matter of English private international law, rather than as a requirement of the Regulation, which is *functus officio* once it has brought about the recognition of the judgment.

Civil or commercial matters: Article 1

The judgment must be in a civil or commercial matter, the meaning of which was examined in Chapter 2. Although it has not been stated in clear and explicit terms, it seems that the recognizing court is entitled to decide for itself whether the judgment was given in a civil or commercial matter, and is not bound on this point simply to accept the view of the adjudicating court. After all, the adjudicating court may not have needed to decide the issue for itself: it may have deduced that if the matter was a civil or commercial one, the Regulation gave it jurisdiction, and if it was not, its own domestic law did instead.[20] Even so, it is to be expected that where the adjudicating court has given such a ruling, its conclusion will be persuasive. It follows that a judgment in respect of subject-matter excluded by Article 1 from the domain of the Regulation will not be recognized under Chapter III. Where a single judgment deals with included and excluded matter it may be possible to sever it: this may happen when a judgment has provided for maintenance and has determined rights in property which arise out of a matrimonial relationship, or when a criminal court imposes a criminal penalty and orders compensation to a civil party. Where severance is not possible, the substantial presence of excluded matter in an indivisible judgment may wholly preclude recognition under the Regulation.[21] Where the judgment was

---

[18] Case C–260/97 *Unibank A/S* v. *Chistensen* [1999] ECR I–3715.

[19] But for the points of difference see Case C–414/92 *Solo Kleinmotoren GmbH* v. *Boch* [1994] ECR I–2237.

[20] Case 29/76 *LTU GmbH & Co.* v. *Eurocontrol* [1976] ECR 1541; Case 145/86 *Hoffmann* v. *Krieg* [1988] ECR 645.

[21] Case C–220/95 *Van den Boogaard* v. *Laumen* [1997] ECR I–1147; and see Art. 48.

obtained in defiance of an agreement to arbitrate it is arguable that recognition should be withheld. To do otherwise would oblige a court to contradict its law on arbitration, which lies outside the domain of the Regulation.[22] But if Article 1(2)(d) merely means that no court has adjudicatory jurisdiction over the merits of what is still a civil or commercial claim,[23] and as jurisdictional error furnishes no general basis for denying recognition,[24] recognition of the offending judgment may in principle be required, but may in turn be withheld as conflicting with the public policy of enforcing agreements to arbitrate.[25]

Date of the proceedings and the date of judgment: Article 66

The Regulation applies to the recognition of judgments given in proceedings instituted after 1 March 2002. For judgments in proceedings instituted before that date, the transitional provisions of Article 66 require recognition if the proceedings were commenced after the Brussels or Lugano Convention had come into effect in the two states concerned. In effect, only the most ancient of judgments from courts of Member States will have been obtained in proceedings antedating the Brussels or Lugano Convention, and Article 66 will therefore recognize and enforce judgments which were jurisdictionally founded on the Brussels or Lugano Convention. Even if this is not so, as long as the adjudicating court founded itself on rules of jurisdiction which conform to those of the Regulation, its judgment may be enforced under Chapter III. There is therefore little reason to suppose that the date of the original proceedings will have any significant effect on the application of Chapter III.

Jurisdictional errors: Article 35

The adjudicating court may have erred in its application of the Regulation by accepting jurisdiction when it did not have it. Save in the exceptional cases mentioned below, this is irrelevant to the recognition of the judgment under Chapter III.[26] At a superficial level the reason is clear: it was the responsibility of the defendant to make this very argument to the adjudicating court, and had the chance to make it once, there is no reason to allow him to make it, for what might be a second time, to

---

[22] Cf Case 145/86 *Hoffmann v. Krieg* [1988] ECR 645.

[23] Case C–391/95 *Van Uden Maritime BV v. Deco-Line* [1998] ECR I–7091.

[24] See Art. 35, below the next heading.

[25] *Phillip Alexander Securities and Futures Ltd.* v. *Bamberger* [1997] ILPr. 73, 104; Art. 34(1).

[26] Art. 35.

another court at the point of recognition. Indeed, there is every reason not to, for it could well impede the free circulation of judgments if it were otherwise.

Now this is reasonable for those domiciled in Member States, whose jurisdictional exposure is defined and limited by the Regulation. It is quite disgracefully unfair to those who are sued on the basis of Article 4. They have no chance to complain about the width of the jurisdictional rules asserted against them, either at trial (because Article 4(2) says that they are expressly subject to the traditional and exorbitant jurisdictional rules set out in Annex I to the Regulation) or at recognition (because jurisdictional points may not generally be taken at the point of recognition[27]). No European defendant is laid open to this unprincipled combination of unreconstructed jurisdictional rules, on the one hand, and the absence of right to be heard on the propriety of those rules or their application on the other. That this was the calculated act of those who drafted the Convention[28] and the Regulation which adopts it[29] takes the breath away. By humiliating contrast, the Supreme Court of the United States has long held that the constitutional guarantees[30] of due process and equal treatment apply to foreigners as well as to American nationals.[31] It would be very welcome indeed if it were to be held that this aspect of the Regulation fell short of the guarantees in Article 6 of the European Convention on Human Rights.

Exceptions apply only where the lack of jurisdiction derived from the provisions on insurance contracts, consumer contracts, and exclusive jurisdiction regardless of domicile:[32] in these cases the particular jurisdictional rules enshrine policies which are so strong that they demand reinforcement by the recognizing court, though it is striking, and inexplicable, that this does not extend to the special rules on jurisdiction over employment contracts. Nor does it cover a case in which the adjudicating court has violated a jurisdiction agreement validated by Article 23. The further conclusions to be drawn from this are unclear. It may show Article 23 to occupy a relatively low position in the hierarchy of jurisdictional rules, so that to regard Article 23 as prevailing over the

---

[27] Art. 35; and it is expressly forbidden to find the jurisdictional rules of the court to be contrary to public policy: Art. 35(3).
[28] Jenard was open about it: [1979] OJ C59/20. He should be ashamed of himself.
[29] Recital 10.   [30] Fifth and Fourteenth Amendments.
[31] See, e.g., *Asahi Metal Industry Co. v. Superior Court of California*, 480 US 102, 108–9, 113–15 (1987).
[32] Art. 35(1). Breach of a jurisdiction agreement is not included.

remainder of the Regulation is inappropriate. On the other hand, if Article 35 does not allow for the non-recognition of a violating judgment, there may be all the more reason for an English court to give pre-emptive force to a jurisdiction agreement by means of an anti-suit injunction.

Those limited cases apart, the plea that the adjudicating court should have realized that it had no jurisdiction is inadmissible. The divergence from the approach of the common law at this point may seem sharp, for under the common law regime the first line of defence to a plea that a foreign judgment should be recognized is that the foreign court lacked jurisdiction. But this is an illusion. Under the Regulation, the defendant may actually make a submission to the adjudicating court that it does not have jurisdiction according to *English* rules: this is because its rules and those of English law are the same.[33] Outside the Member States, where the Regulation does not apply, such an argument cannot usefully be made to the foreign court, which has no concern with English jurisdictional rules, and therefore has its first opportunity for airing only at recognition. The schemes therefore agree that *this* argument, that the foreign court did not have jurisdiction according to English rules, may be made once, and that it must be made at the earliest sensible point. The divergence is only in the identification of this temporal point.

Procedural or substantive objections to recognition: Article 34

There are four procedural or substantive objections, exhaustively listed in Article 34,[34] which may be made to the recognition of a judgment. Compared to their predecessors in the Brussels Convention, which were frequently said to be narrow in scope,[35] those in the Regulation are designed to be narrower still, so as to make the circulation of judgments from and within the Member States even more free. In the Brussels and Lugano Conventions there was and still is a fifth ground, for the case where the foreign judgment was founded on a conclusion about status which conflicted with the law of the recognizing state. But as questions of marriage and status were excluded from the Convention by Article 1, it was always surprising that there was provision for the non-recognition of judgments which had taken a view on an issue which lay outside the domain of the Convention and was unaffected by it. It was best regarded as inept use of

---

[33] Apart from Art. 4 cases, where such concerns of due process are irrelevant.

[34] Cf Art. 27 BC.

[35] It appears that they are not supposed to overlap, at least where Art. 34(1) is concerned: Case C–78/95, *Hendrickman* v. *Magenta Druck & Verlag GmbH* [1996] ECR I–4943.

belt and braces,[36] and it has not been reproduced in the Regulation. Its omission makes no broader point.

Public policy: Article 34(1)

If recognition of the judgment would be manifestly contrary to public policy, recognition is precluded by Article 34(1). The content of public policy is a matter for English law, though operating within outer limits marked by the Regulation. Under the Brussels Convention it was held that where recognition of the judgment would infringe a law which was regarded as fundamental in the recognizing state, such as where the adjudicating court had failed to comply with the standards of the European Convention on Human Rights such as by refusing one party the right to be heard,[37] recognition could be considered to be contrary to public policy. But to recognize a judgment which contained a misapplication of European competition law could not be considered to be contrary to public policy, especially where the adjudicating court had a facility for securing the correct interpretation of European law.[38] The Regulation adds the word 'manifestly' to the corresponding provision of the Convention, which will presumably mean that the scope of Article 34(1) is intended to narrow rather than expand.

It has been held that the argument that the judgment was obtained by fraud will not prevent recognition if the state of origin has its own procedures for investigating such a plea;[39] and the jurisprudence of the Court of Justice appears to bear this out. Even so, as will be shown below, to impeach a judgment for fraud before the original court is more difficult— and seeks a more radical remedy—than using fraud to prevent recognition in England. In that sense the state of origin may not have a remedy which corresponds to the fraud doctrine of the common law; but the tide is running against the doctrine of fraud in foreign judgments, and this argument cannot really be expected to prevail. But if a foreign court has refused to give effect to a commercial arbitration agreement, recognition may well be contrary to English public policy as set out in the Civil Jurisdiction and Judgments Act 1982, section 32:[40] the wording of the Act certainly seems to support the view that this is regarded as a fundamental matter; and recognition of a judgment obtained in defiance of an English

---

[36] Art. 27(4) BC; Case 145/86 *Hoffmann v. Krieg* [1988] ECR 645.

[37] Case C–7/98 *Krombach v. Bamberski* [2000] ECR I–1935. See also *Re Enforcement of a Guarantee* [2001] ILPr. 425 (German Fed. Sup. Ct.).

[38] Case C–38/98 *Régie Nationale des Usines Renault SA v. Maxicar* [2000] ECR I–2973.

[39] *Interdesco SA v. Nullifire Ltd.* [1992] 1 Lloyd's Rep. 180.

[40] *Phillip Alexander Securities & Futures Ltd. v. Bamberger* [1997] ILPr. 73, 103 (CA).

anti-suit injunction must be contrary to public policy.[41] Were a court in a Member State ever to hand one down, recognition of a judgment for multiple damages, which violates the Protection of Trading Interests Act 1980, certainly would offend public policy.

Judgments in default of appearance: Article 34(2)
There has been a narrowing of the defence to recognition for certain judgments in default of appearance, as defined by Article 34(2). If as a matter of fact, and notwithstanding that the adjudicating court did not consider there to be such a default,[42] the judgment was in default of appearance, and either the document instituting the proceedings was not served in accordance with the law of the adjudicating state[43] or it was served but not, according to the assessment of the judge in the recognizing state, in sufficient time to allow the defendant to arrange for his defence,[44] recognition will in principle be denied. This provision is intended to reinforce[45] the legal protection of the defendant, by giving him the right to be properly and timeously summoned; though if the document was duly served,[46] the requirement is that it happen in time to allow him to forestall judgment in default of appearance. Whether there has been sufficient time is assessed in the light of the mode of service. Where service has been made on the defendant personally, a relatively short period is needed to forestall a default judgment. But where service was made on (say) the local Consul, or on the *parquet* for onward transmission to the defendant,[47] or by leaving it at the last known address, the time period may well need to be much longer. Likewise, orders obtained without notice to the respondent will be denied recognition,[48] so a

---

[41] *Phillip Alexander Securities & Futures Ltd.* v. *Bamberger* [1997] ILPr. 104, 115 (CA).

[42] This means that there must be an autonomous definition of the term: it essentially covers the case where the defendant was denied a proper right to be heard or represented: Case C–78/95, *Hendrickman* v. *Magenta Druck & Verlag GmbH* [1996] ECR I–4943.

[43] If irregularity in service was cured under the law of the state of origin, this presumably ceases to be a maintainable point.

[44] Case 228/81 *Pendy Plastic Products* v. *Pluspunkt* [1982] ECR 2723; Case 49/84 *Debaecker and Plouvier* v. *Bouwman* [1985] ECR 1779.

[45] Art. 26 will oblige the adjudicating court to check, in the case of an absent defendant, that the defendant has been served and has had time to arrange for his defence; the recognizing court must, however, make that assessment for itself.

[46] As it is the document of the adjudicating state, this is the law by which it must be served, though irregularities which may be cured by this law will obviously be curable: Case C–305/88 *Isabelle Lancray SA* v. *Peters und Sickert KG* [1990] ECR I–2725.

[47] A German court held this 'service' to be ineffective under the European Convention on Human Rights as discriminating against non-French defendants: *Re the Enforcement of a French Interlocutory Order* [2001] ILPr. 208 (Karlsrühe CA).

[48] Case 125/79 *Denilauler* v. *SNC Couchet Frères* [1980] ECR 1553.

freezing injunction obtained without notice will be denied recognition. But the order may lose its original default character if a subsequent application is made to set it aside but this is dismissed. The true answer should depend upon whether the respondent was disadvantaged by the fact that the order had already been made in proceedings in which he did not appear.[49] If he was, with the result that he faced an uphill struggle as a result of the default judgment, his application to set aside should not involve the loss of the shield of Article 34(2); but if his application had the effect of re-imposing the original burden of proof on the applicant, any new or confirmed order will not be vitiated. Moreover, and in contrast to the corresponding provision of the Brussels Convention,[50] the Regulation provides that the shield of Article 34(2) will be lost if the defendant had the opportunity of bringing proceedings to challenge the judgment but did not do so. It is submitted that this cannot be taken at face value, but must be interpreted as meaning that the defendant had a reasonable opportunity to bring proceedings in which he would have been under no appreciable disadvantage when compared to the defendant who did appear.

Irreconcilability with English judgment: Article 34(3)

If recognition of the foreign judgment produces consequences which are incompatible with an English judgment in a dispute between the same parties, whether this is handed down earlier or later than the foreign one, recognition will be denied by Article 34(3).[51] In principle, Article 27 should prevent parallel proceedings at the point when the second action is commenced, or the rules of *res judicata* should apply if the English judgment has not yet been given, so that the English court could therefore recognize the foreign judgment when handed down. If all goes according to the plan of the Regulation, there will be little practical space for Article 34(3) to occupy. But when this does not quite work, an English court is entitled to prefer its own judgment. Irreconcilability may involve a measure of evaluation. A judgment that a contract was lawfully rescinded is certainly irreconcilable with an order that damages be paid for its breach.[52] But a decision that A is liable to B for breach of warranty of quality may not be irreconcilable with a judgment that B was liable to pay the price of goods sold and delivered by A. Again, a decision that A is

---

[49] Cf Case C–474/93 *Hengst Import BV v. Campese* [1995] ECR I–2113.
[50] Art. 27(2) BC.
[51] Case 145/86 *Hoffmann v. Krieg* [1988] ECR 645.
[52] Case 144/86 *Gubisch Maschinenfabrik KG v. Palumbo* [1987] ECR 4861.

liable to B for damage to B's cargo is irreconcilable with one that B owes
no liability for damage to the cargo, but is not irreconcilable with a claim
for damages for short delivery.

Irreconcilability with prior foreign judgment: Article 34(4)
If a judgment from a member or non-member state was given in proceedings between the same parties and involving the same cause of action, and
satisfies the criteria for its own recognition in England, and was the first
to be handed down, and is irreconcilable with a later Member State
judgment, Article 34(4) provides that the later Member State judgment
will not be recognized. The text does not say that proceedings to secure
the enforcement of the non-member state judgment should have been
instituted: indeed, as that judgment may well be entitled to recognition
without any such proceedings, there would be no reason to impose such a
limitation.

Where there is irreconcilability between two different and foreign
Member State judgments, the Brussels and Lugano Conventions left it
unclear how a court was to proceed. The problem was notorious for years,
but the solution offered by Article 34(4) will not apply to the Conventions, where the better view probably is that a court will have to fall back
on its own rules of private international law; in England this would mean
that the first judgment in time prevails.[53]

Australian and Canadian defendants: Article 72
Article 59 of the Brussels and Lugano Conventions provided that a state
might enter a bilateral treaty with a non-contracting state, to stipulate for
the local non-recognition of judgments from other contracting states,
which judgments were founded on the national jurisdictional rules whose
use was authorized by Article 4, and which were given against nationals
or domiciliaries of the non-contracting state. The United Kingdom has
such arrangements with Australia[54] and Canada,[55] and Article 72 provides
that these remain in force. But there will be no new bilateral treaties, as
competence over external relations in the field of the Regulation now
reposes in the European Commission.

No other grounds for non-recognition
There is no other ground upon which it is permitted to impeach the

[53] *Showlag v. Mansour* [1995] 1 AC 431 (PC).
[54] Reciprocal Enforcement of Foreign Judgments (Australia) Order 1994, SI 1994/1901,
Sch., Art. 3.
[55] Reciprocal Enforcement of Foreign Judgments (Canada) Order 1987, SI 1987/468,
Sch., Art. IX.

judgment and deny it recognition. Article 35 precludes any further review of the jurisdiction of the foreign court, and explicitly provides[56] that public policy may not be invoked to launch a collateral attack on the jurisdiction of the adjudicating court. This is obviously aimed at judgments based on Article 4;[57] but it is submitted that it does not prevent the denial of recognition to judgments which disregard a valid and binding arbitration agreement, for in such a case it is not the jurisdiction, but the rejection of the arbitration defence, which is the basis for objection.

Article 36 absolutely prohibits any review of the merits of the judgment, though this must be permitted to the extent required to apply the provisions of Article 34.[58] What may appear to be an exception arises when a court is called upon to recognize a provisional or protective measure which was granted on the basis of Article 31, that is, not by the court with jurisdiction over the merits of the claim. The extent of the permitted review is to ascertain that the order is, as a matter of substance, a provisional or protective one; but if it is not, it will be denied recognition. This limitation appears to be necessary to counter the inherent weakness of Article 31, which simply abnegates any jurisdictional control over such measures. Accordingly, if a foreign court has made an order for an interim payment, but does not have jurisdiction over the merits of the claim (perhaps because the parties have agreed to arbitrate, with the result that no court has merits jurisdiction), an English court, called on to recognize and enforce the order, must check that it is provisional or protective: that is to say, limited to assets within the territory of the court which made the order,[59] and guaranteed to be reversible in the event that the applicant does not succeed in the substantive claim.[60]

Judgments under appeal: Article 37

If an 'ordinary appeal' is pending against the judgment in the state of its origin, Article 37 permits, though does not oblige, the recognizing court to stay any proceedings in which the issue of recognition will arise. An ordinary appeal is a term unknown to English law, but all English appeals

---

[56] Art. 35(3).

[57] But also Art. 5(4): Case C–7/98 *Krombach* v. *Bamberski* [2000] ECR I–1935.

[58] Case C–78/95 *Hendrickman* v. *Magenta Druck & Verlag GmbH* [1996] ECR I–4943.

[59] If that requirement is taken seriously, it may be very rare for such an order ever to be presented for recognition in another country. But in the case of an English freezing order, not made in relation to assets as distinct from being ordered against a defendant personally, this limitation may be an irrelevance, and the order more likely to be presented for recognition in another country.

[60] Case C–99/96 *Mietz* v. *Intership Yachting Sneek BV* [1999] ECR I–2277.

are ordinary appeals.[61] The sense of this is clear: a court must have the power to conclude that it is inappropriate to proceed in a case in which the foreign judgment upon which issues turn may be reversed on appeal. No doubt it will be necessary to make some form of assessment of how likely it is that the judgment will be reversed, and the degree of prejudice likely to be suffered if the application is or is not stayed.

Consequences of recognition under the Regulation

The main consequence of recognition will usually be to pave the way for the enforcement of the judgment, the procedure for which is examined below. But this is not the only effect the recognition of the judgment may bring about. To recognize a judgment means, in principle at least, to give it the effect it has under the law of the state in which it was given.[62] So if the judgment is in the nature of a provisional order, which would not be taken as binding or conclusive in subsequent proceedings in the adjudicating court, it should be given neither greater nor lesser effect in England. In certain cases a judgment may be regarded by the adjudicating court as impinging upon non-parties,[63] such as sureties for the defendant, or an insurer; but whether this must be respected and given effect to by an English court is unclear. The problems arise at a number of levels. First, it may be argued that, so far as the non-party was concerned, the judgment must have been given in default of his appearance, and so be denied recognition against him by reason of Article 34(2). Secondly, it may be contrary to public policy, as crystallized in the European Convention on Human Rights, for a person to be bound by a judgment in respect of which he had no right to be heard. Thirdly, it may be that once the judgment has been shown to qualify for recognition as between the parties to it, it is thereafter for English private international law, and not for the Regulation, to determine what further effects it may have.

ENFORCEMENT OF THE JUDGMENT: ARTICLES 38–52

Any judgment which is entitled to recognition and is enforceable in the state in which it was given[64] may, in principle, be enforced by the procedure set out in detail in Articles 38–52. In England, an application is made to the High Court[65] for an order that the judgment be registered under Council Regulation (EC) 44/2001, by producing an authenticated copy of the

---

[61] Art. 46(2).   [62] Case C–145/86 *Hoffmann* v. *Krieg* [1988] ECR 645.
[63] Cf the Schlosser Report [1979] OJ C59/71, 127–8.
[64] Art. 38.   [65] Annex II to the Reg.

judgment[66] and proof in standard form that it is enforceable under the law of the state in which it was given.[67] When registered for enforcement under the Regulation, Schedule 1, paragraph 1(3), of Civil Jurisdiction and Judgments Order 2001 provides that, the judgment has the same force and effect for the purposes of enforcement as if it were an English judgment. This is easy to understand when dealing with a money judgment, but enforcement under the Regulation applies also to non-money judgments. In the case of a foreign order of a type close or identical to an English equivalent, there is no difficulty in giving effect to paragraph 1(3). Where the order is rather different, it is unclear exactly what an English court is to do. The practice of the German courts apparently is to transmute the order into its nearest German equivalent,[68] and to use this as the template for enforcement. It is difficult to see that there is a better alternative.

Application without notice: Articles 39–42

The applicant produces a copy of the judgment and certain other specified documents, and applies to a High Court Master,[69] without notice to the respondent, for an order for registration; the respondent has no right to be heard at this stage.[70] By way of contrast with the position under the Brussels and Lugano Conventions, the Regulation denies any right to refer to Articles 34 and 35 to refuse to make the order for registration,[71] which change was made to overcome the prevarication and chauvinism occasionally encountered on an application for enforcement of a foreign judgment against a local. Even so, in an egregious case, for example where it is manifest that the judgment is not in a civil or commercial matter, there must still be a discretion to refuse to register, a conclusion which is reinforced by the fact that either side may appeal against the decision on the application.[72] But assuming that the court grants the order, it will notify the applicant and serve the order for registration on the respondent, who may learn about it for the first time.[73]

Appeal against the decision on the application: Article 43

If the application for registration was refused, Article 43 permits the applicant to appeal to a High Court judge.[74] If the application was

---

[66] Art. 53(1).   [67] In the form in Annex V to the Reg.; and see RSC O. 71 Pt. V.
[68] A. Zuckerman and J. Grunert [1996] *Zeitschrift für Zivilprozess International* 89.
[69] RSC O. 71 Pt. V.   [70] Art. 41.   [71] Art. 41.
[72] Art. 43(1).   [73] Art. 42(2).
[74] Annex III to the Reg. The more usual English usage may be to label this as an application to set aside the order for registration, rather than an appeal, but the terminology is established by the Reg.

granted, Article 43(5) gives the respondent one month if domiciled in the enforcing state, or two months if domiciled in a different Member State,[75] from the date of service, to appeal under Article 43 against the order for registration. This marks the stage in the procedure when, in practice, the arguments touching recognition will be raised. According to Article 45(1), the order for enforceability can be refused or revoked only on the grounds specified in Articles 34 and 35, but it is unintelligible. Suppose the court hearing the appeal considers that the judgment was not in a civil or commercial matter,[76] or was for a periodic payment which had not been quantified,[77] or was of a measure which should not have been granted under Article 31, or in respect of which there was a bilateral treaty:[78] Article 45 appears to provide that none of these matters is within the competence of the court, and for this reason it is submitted that Article 45(1) should be ignored.

Further appeal on a point of law: Article 44

The order made on the hearing of the Article 43 appeal may itself be further appealed, but only once, and on a point of law. The grounds on which the court hearing the further appeal may revoke or refuse registration are again defined by the unconvincing Article 45(1).

Procedural matters concerning enforcement: Articles 46 and 47

If an appeal has been lodged, or could still be lodged, against the judgment in the court of origin, Article 46 provides that the court hearing the appeal under Article 43 or the further appeal under Article 44[79] may, on the application of the respondent, stay the appeal proceedings; it is also, presumably as an alternative, empowered to authorize enforcement on the condition of provision of security. After the order for registration has been made, Article 47 permits the court to grant protective measures against the property of the respondent, but until the final determination of the appeal, only protective measures may be taken. The dominant principle in all these cases will be the need to strike a fair and proportionate balance between the interests of the applicant who, having won, should not be kept out of his money by a prevaricating respondent; and the respondent whose rights to appeal

---

[75] It is not said how long is allowed if he is not domiciled in a Member State, but the answer is presumably two months which can be extended.

[76] Art. 1.   [77] Art. 49.   [78] Art. 72.

[79] Thereby reversing the effect of the decision: Case C–439/93 *SISRO* v. *Ampersand Software BV* [1995] ECR I–2269.

are prescribed by law and should not be undercut by allowing irreversible measures of enforcement to take place in advance of its determination.

JUDGMENTS FROM DENMARK, ICELAND, NORWAY, SWITZERLAND, POLAND

Because the Brussels Convention is still the vehicle for the registration and enforcement of Danish judgments, and the Lugano Convention for judgments from Iceland, Norway, Switzerland, and Poland, applications for registration of these judgments, under section 4 of the 1982 Act, will continue to be governed by the provisions of those Conventions.[80] The rules of these Conventions are in most respects the same as those now in the Regulation, differing only in relative detail, some of which has been alluded to above, but which is of too little importance to justify its closer examination here.

JUDGMENTS FROM SCOTLAND, NORTHERN IRELAND, GIBRALTAR

Apart from providing the mechanism for the recognition and enforcement of judgments under the Conventions, the 1982 Act provides for the recognition and enforcement of judgments from Scotland and Northern Ireland, and Gibraltar. Judgments from other parts of the United Kingdom, whether for money or otherwise, may be registered for enforcement subject to only minor restrictions.[81] For the purpose of the Regulation,[82] Gibraltar is treated as part of the United Kingdom. In England, however, judgments from Gibraltar are recognized and enforced by reference to provisions which are modelled on the rules of the Brussels Convention.[83]

RECOGNITION AND ENFORCEMENT AT COMMON LAW

By contrast with the closed world of the Member States, whose judgments are recognized under the Regulation, the rules of the common law have to deal with the recognition of judgments from the courts of the rest

---

[80] Recital 10; Art. 71. [81] 1982 Act, s. 18; Schs. 6, 7.
[82] And by contrast with the position under the Brussels Convention.
[83] 1982 Act, s. 39; Civil Jurisdiction and Judgments Act 1982 (Gibraltar) Order 1997, SI 1997/2602.

of the world.[84] The basic scheme of common law recognition is that if the foreign court is adjudged to have been competent, as a matter of *English* law, to give a judgment by which the losing party was bound, this may, and if there is no other defence to the claim for recognition will, be recognized as making the cause of action or the issue *res judicata*. If all that a party requires is for the judgment to be recognized, it is sufficient to plead the effect of it as *res judicata*, but if the judgment creditor wishes to enforce the judgment in offensive fashion, he will need to bring an action on it at common law: the action is founded on the judgment and not on the underlying cause of action. In the case of an action to enforce it, the judgment must meet further criteria which determine its enforceability by action in the English courts.

RECOGNITION OF JUDGMENTS AT COMMON LAW

A judgment will be recognized at common law if it is the final and conclusive judgment of a court which, as a matter of English private international law, had 'international jurisdiction', and as long as there is no defence to its recognition. By contrast with some forms of statutory enforcement procedure, there is no requirement that the judgment be that of a superior court: any judicial tribunal will suffice for the common law. But the award of an arbitral tribunal is not sufficient,[85] nor is the decision of an administrative body.[86]

In principle, at least, only final and conclusive orders are recognized. The terminology is more commonly used than it is defined, but 'final' means that it cannot be re-opened in the court which made the ruling, even though it may be subject to appeal to a higher court; and 'conclusive' that it represents the court's settled conclusion on the merits of the point adjudicated.[87] For this reason, a foreign freezing order will not be recognized, as it is not predicated upon a final determination of the validity of the claim, nor is it usually incapable of review by the court which ordered it. Likewise, recognition will not be accorded to a decision that there is, for example, a good arguable case on a disputed point, jurisdictional or otherwise: the decision may be final, in that the court will not re-open the

---

[84] And to judgments from the Member States and of the contracting states if and in so far as these fall outside the scope of the Reg. or the Conventions, respectively.

[85] These do not give rise to issues of recognition; and their enforcement is regulated by specialist Convention and statute.

[86] *Midland International Trade Services Ltd.* v. *al-Sudairy*, 11 Apr. 1990, not yet reported (the Saudi Chamber for Settlement of Commercial Paper Disputes was held to be a court).

[87] Which may be the whole dispute or a single point: *The Sennar (No 2)* [1985] 1 WLR 490 (HL).

question, but is not conclusive if it would not tie the hands of the same court at a later stage when the merits are tried. By contrast, an order made on an interlocutory matter may be recognized if it represents the final decision of the court on the point in issue. An example may be an order dismissing an action on the ground that it was covered by a jurisdiction agreement for a specific court: if this represents the court's final decision, it is in principle entitled to recognition.[88] A difficulty therefore arises in relation to default judgments, which will often be capable of being re-opened in the court in which they were entered, at least on conditions, and not usually only within a fixed time limit. It appears to follow that these cannot be recognized as final, with the counter-intuitive result that if the defence is so hopeless that the defendant elects to allow judgment in default of appearance to be entered against him, the claimant may be left with a judgment of reduced effectiveness. It is generally assumed that this argument is unsound, but it is less easy to see the technical argument which will overcome it.

International jurisdiction

A foreign court has international jurisdiction, as this is defined and acknowledged by English private international law, if the party against whom the judgment was given submitted to the jurisdiction of the court, or was present or resident—either will suffice—within the jurisdiction of the court when the proceedings were instituted.[89] The occasional suggestion that the nationality of the defendant is sufficient[90] is discredited today. The grounds stated are exhaustive; at present English law does not acknowledge jurisdictional competence on the basis that the foreign court exercised a jurisdiction which mirrors that which English law would exercise itself,[91] nor that the foreign court was the natural forum for the trial of the action.

But this step has been taken by the Supreme Court of Canada, which has since embarked on a wide and radical re-examination of the law

---

[88] *The Sennar (No 2)* [1985] 1 WLR 490 (HL); cf *Desert Sun Loan Corp.* v. *Hill* [1996] 2 All ER 847 (CA).

[89] Which probably means when process was served on him: *Adams* v. *Cape Industries plc* [1990] Ch. 433, 518 (CA).

[90] *Emanuel* v. *Symon* [1908] 1 KB 302 (CA).

[91] Traditionally this proposition is supported by *Schibsby* v. *Westenholz* (1870) LR 6 QB 155. But the analogy is not perfect, for it took no account of the fact that an English court would not have exercised the jurisdiction invoked unless it was also the natural forum for the claim.

which connects the exercise of jurisdiction, the power to grant anti-suit injunctions, and the recognition of foreign judgments.[92] It has been prepared to recognize the judgments from courts having a real and substantial connection to the dispute,[93] and it will require only a short further step to refine this to denote a court which is the *forum conveniens*. The argument is clear: if the claimant has sued in the court which is, in Canadian eyes, the most proper and appropriate place for the claim to have been brought why should the judgment be denied recognition? The pragmatic answer may be that it makes life awkward for a defendant, who may face difficulty in deciding whether it is safe to allow judgment to be entered in default of appearance, or prudent to appear and defend. But the interests of the defendant are not necessarily paramount in the assertion of jurisdiction; and if the claimant has played by the rules of *forum conveniens*, it may be that the balance should be held to favour him. As a matter of English law, however, it appears that such a development would require legislation.

Submission

No injustice is done to a party who submits to the jurisdiction of a court if its adverse judgment is taken as binding him. So a defendant who voluntarily submits to the jurisdiction of a foreign court is, in principle, subject to its international jurisdiction. A claimant, or counterclaiming defendant also clearly submits to the jurisdiction; but whether a claimant is taken to submit to any and every counterclaim will depend on whether the counterclaim arises out of the same facts or transaction as his claim or out of facts which are reasonably connected: a test of broad common sense applies.[94]

If a defendant appears for the purpose only of contesting the jurisdiction of the court or to seek a stay in favour of another court or for arbitration or to protect property which is threatened with seizure in the proceedings, the Civil Jurisdiction and Judgments Act 1982, section 33(1), provides that the appearance will not be a submission. This represents a departure from the common law which had held[95]— extraordinarily, as it now seems—that to appear before a court to apply

---

[92] See in particular *Amchem Products Inc.* v. *British Columbia (Workers' Compensation Board)* [1993] 1 SCR 897, (1993) 102 DLR (4th) 96.
[93] *Morguard Investments Ltd.* v. *De Savoye* [1990] 3 SCR 1077, (1991) 76 DLR (4th) 256.
[94] *Murthy* v. *Sivasjothi* [1999] 1 WLR 467 (CA).
[95] *Henry* v. *Geoprosco International* [1976] QB 726 (CA).

for jurisdictional relief was voluntarily to submit to its jurisdiction.[96] It appears to follow that if the defendant is required, strictly or as a matter of good practice, to plead to the merits at the same time as making his jurisdictional challenge, or finds that he is compelled to participate in other interlocutory procedures in order to keep his jurisdictional challenge alive, the statutory protection is not lost.[97] To claim the protection of the statute, it is plausible that the challenge has to be to the international jurisdiction, rather than to the local or internal jurisdiction of the court, as the existence or non-existence of local or internal jurisdiction is generally of no relevance to the English law on recognition.[98] So if a defendant argues that he should be tried in another country, this will be protected from being counted as submission, but if he argues that he should be tried in one city rather than another, or in the High Court rather than a lower court, or in a state court rather than a federal court, these arguments will be less likely to secure the protection of the statute. On the other hand, if the defendant appears under protest, whatever that may mean, his unenthusiastic appearance is nevertheless voluntary.

A troublesome argument, which appears to have proved more attractive than it should have, proposes that if a party has made an application to a court for a particular form of relief, issue estoppel may arise out of the decision of the court adverse to the applicant. It follows, so the argument runs, that if a party applies to a foreign court for a stay or dismissal on the ground that the court has no jurisdiction, the decision of the foreign court that it does and any finding made in support of this decision may give rise to an estoppel, and be utilized by the opposite party in an attempt to secure recognition of the consequent judgment. At first sight this may appear sound: a party who has applied for an order ought to be bound by the court's decision on it. But this can be true only if he submitted to the jurisdiction of the foreign court in the first place, and if

[96] The reasoning being that if relief is applied for, the very making of the application involves accepting that the court has jurisdiction to grant it; and there is therefore a submission. A more sophisticated analysis would have been that to submit to the power of a court to rule on its jurisdiction is not the same thing as to submit to its power to rule on the merits: *Williams & Glyn's Bank* v. *Astro Dinamico* [1984] 1 WLR 438 (HL).

[97] *Marc Rich & Co AG* v. *Società Italiana Impianti PA (No 2)* [1992] 1 Lloyd's Rep. 624 (CA). In principle, if the foreign court does not characterize the defendant's participation as amounting to an appearance, an English court should not do so either: *Adams* v. *Cape Industries plc* [1990] Ch. 433, 461; *The Eastern Trader* [1996] 2 Lloyd's Rep. 585.

[98] *Pemberton* v. *Hughes* [1899] 1 Ch. 781. For a challenge to the existence of a power of attorney to accept service of process and whether this constitutes a challenge to the jurisdiction protected by s. 33, see the divergent analyses in *Desert Sun Loan Corp.* v. *Hill* [1996] 2 All ER 847 (CA).

he appeared for the purpose of contesting the jurisdiction, section 33(1) provides him with an answer to the contention that he submitted: it denatures and subverts section 33 to hold that an adverse decision on the motion to contest the jurisdiction is itself entitled to recognition. The conclusion must be that before any question of recognition as *res judicata* can arise by reason of a party's submission, there must actually be submission; and if section 33(1) provides that there is not, that is the end of the argument.

Submission may also be made by contractual agreement. The dispute and the particular court[99] in which the action is brought must fall within the four corners of the contractual term. To the extent that this raises a question of construction, the principles will be the same as those examined in relation to jurisdiction. The term itself must have remained valid and contractually enforceable at the date of the action.[100] It has been said that an implied agreement to submit will not suffice.[101] A better view may be that an implied agreement is possible, but will be found to have been made only in the clearest of cases.

Presence or residence
If the defendant was present within the territorial jurisdiction of the foreign court on the date on which the proceedings were commenced, he is considered to be subject to its international jurisdiction.[102] At one time the rule was taken to require residence rather than presence, but it is now tolerably clear that either presence or residence on the material date will suffice;[103] and even if the defendant satisfied neither condition on the day in question, but did appear to defend the proceedings, there will be a submission in any event. It has been held that the relevant territorial jurisdiction is defined by reference to the court, so that a defendant sued in a state court must be within the territorial jurisdiction of the state, but if sued in a federal court all that is required is that he be within the federation; but in so far as this ascribes an international relevance to rules of local jurisdiction it is to be questioned whether it is correct.

[99] There are cases where a court bears the same name as one contractually agreed to at an earlier date, but where revolutionary political change means that it is no longer to be seen as the 'same' court: *Carvalho v. Hull Blyth (Angola) Ltd.* [1979] 1 WLR 1228 (CA).
[100] *SA Consortium General Textiles v. Sun and Sand Agencies Ltd.* [1978] QB 279 (CA).
[101] *Vogel v. R.A. Kohnstamm Ltd.* [1973] 1 QB 133, not following *Blohn v. Desser* [1962] 2 QB 116.
[102] *Adams v. Cape Industries plc* [1990] Ch. 433 (CA).
[103] *State Bank of India v. Murjani Marketing Group Ltd.*, 27 Mar. 1991, not yet reported (CA).

It is striking that this rule acknowledges in a foreign court a jurisdiction effectively wider than English law claims for itself. On the existing state of the authorities, it is irrelevant that the foreign court was a *forum non conveniens* so that, if the roles were reversed, an English court would have stayed its proceedings and declined to adjudicate. It was explained above that the development of the law in the Supreme Court of Canada pointed to the widening of the grounds of recognized international jurisdiction; and that court has not seen fit to use the concept of the natural forum as a basis for narrowing, in this respect, the definition of jurisdictional competence. Of course, if a defendant submits by voluntary appearance, there will be no question of denying recognition to the judgment, any more than there will be of staying an English action in which the defendant submits. But in cases in which the foreign court has exercised a jurisdiction which is so wide that it has not observed comity, it may be argued that its judgment forfeits any right to be recognized in return.[104] Whether such a change can be made to English law without the need for legislation is doubtful, but it is unlikely that the current dissonance between adjudicatory jurisdiction and recognition jurisdiction can be regarded as stable.

The presence of a natural person is easy to ascertain, but the same rule applies also to corporate defendants. In their case, the rule requires a reasonably fixed and definite place of business, maintained by the corporation and from which its business is done.[105] So a peripatetic sales representative does not establish the presence of the company represented, even if the foreign court may regard it as sufficient for the purpose of its own jurisdictional rules. The same is true of a local representative who merely acts as a conduit for those wishing to transact business with the defendant who is otherwise out of the jurisdiction.[106] But if the local representative has been invested with power to make contracts which bind the defendant, it is probable that the test of corporate presence is satisfied.[107] Though a company may therefore be present if another company is doing its business as well as its own, there is no broader English doctrine which allows all the members of an economic group to be treated

---

[104] Cf *Amchem Products Inc.* v. *British Columbia (Workers' Compensation Board)* [1993] I SCR 897, (1993) 102 DLR (4th) 96.

[105] *Adams* v. *Cape*, above n. 102.

[106] Cf *Littauer Glove Corp.* v. *Millington (F.W.) (1920) Ltd.* (1928) 44 TLR 746.

[107] *Adams* v. *Cape Industries plc* [1990] Ch. 433, 531 (CA).

on the basis that if one is present all are present,[108] or that one member of
the group is the *alter ego* of the others.[109]

The recognition rule therefore mirrors the jurisdictional rule of the
common law that if a company is present within the jurisdiction it can be
sued, and nothing turns on whether the claim arises out of the conduct of
the company in the particular place: it is subject to the unlimited jurisdiction of the court or not at all; but there is no middle way. This contrasts
with the jurisdictional rule in Article 5(5) of the Regulation and may
explain why, given the dramatic consequences of finding that there is
corporate presence, the common law requirements are relatively
demanding.

Defences to recognition at common law

A judgment will be denied recognition as *res judicata*, and there can
therefore be no question of its enforcement, if any of the defences allowed
by English private international law is made out. But it is no defence that
the foreign court got the law or the facts, or both, wrong, or that it applied
the wrong choice of law rule, or that it tried to apply English law and got
that manifestly wrong.[110] The merits of the judgment are not reviewable,
so the allegation that the foreign court erred in its reasoning is irrelevant.
Were it otherwise, almost every judgment would be re-examinable, and
the advantage of the rule would be utterly lost. Even so, in a case where a
court has failed to give effect to an agreement on choice of law, there may
be room for a limited reconsideration of the rule. A judgment will be
denied recognition at common law if the adjudicating court failed to give
effect to a choice of court clause or arbitration agreement,[111] it may be
wondered whether the policy which this enshrines ought not to extend
this to disregard of an agreement on choice of law. The analogy lies in the
fact that all such provisions are designed to make dispute resolution clear
and predictable; and if the claimant elects to sue in a court which will pay
them no heed, there is something to be said for the view that he should
not profit from his breach. There is also some authority for the view that a
case will be allowed to proceed in England if the consequence of its being
heard in another country is that a choice of law clause will not be given

---

[108] *Adams* v. *Cape Industries plc* [1990] Ch. 433 532–9.

[109] P. Muchlinski, 'Corporations in International Litigation: Problems of Jurisdiction and
the United Kingdom Asbestos Case' (2001) 50 *ICLQ* 1.

[110] *Godard* v. *Gray* (1870) LR 6 QB 288.

[111] Civil Jurisdiction and Judgments Act 1982, s. 32 (unless the other party acquiesced in
the breach).

effect.[112] The argument awaits convincing approval. Subject to that, six possible defence arguments need to be examined.

Violation of arbitration or choice of court agreement

If the foreign court took jurisdiction in breach of a valid choice of court or arbitration agreement, its judgment may not be recognized at common law, even if the foreign court addressed the issue and concluded in accordance with its own law that there was no breach; it is otherwise if the complaining party acquiesced in the breach.[113] It follows that if the court rules against the claimant, it is not open to him to complain about the disregard of the agreement, because he brought it about.[114] The justification for this defence is the premium placed on the encouragement and support of these clauses; but the rule is one which operates only where recognition is governed by the common law: where the Regulation or Conventions govern recognition it has no application. Where the judgment comes from a court in a Member State, therefore, it is only the arbitration component of the rule which may be of relevance.

Absence of local jurisdiction

It is unclear whether or to what extent the fact that the court did not have jurisdiction under its local law may furnish a defence, for the authorities are old and inconclusive.[115] But in principle, if the foreign judgment is a complete nullity, and not just voidable, under the foreign law—a rare state of affairs—it would be unexpected for it to be recognized in England, particularly if the defendant had been locally well advised to ignore the proceedings. If the judgment is, however, voidable, it is valid and remains so unless and until proceedings are taken to set it aside. As an English court cannot assume that this will happen, the result must be that the judgment will be recognized notwithstanding the fragility of local jurisdiction.

Fraud

When it is alleged that the judgment was procured by fraud, the defences to recognition become more complicated. Though, as said above, the merits of the judgment may not be re-examined by an English court, a different approach prevails if there is a credible allegation that it was

---

[112] *Britannia Steamship Insurance Association v. Ausonia Assicurazioni SpA* [1984] 2 Lloyd's Rep. 98 (CA).
[113] 1982 Act, s. 32. And see *Marc Rich & Co. AG v. Società Italiana Impianti PA* [1992] 2 Lloyd's Rep. 624 (CA).
[114] *The Sennar (No 2)* [1985] 1 WLR 490 (HL).
[115] *Vanquelin v. Bouard* (1863) 15 CBNS 341; *Pemberton v. Hughes* [1899] 1 Ch. 781.

procured by fraud.[116] Both the definition of fraud and its effect are controversial. Fraud has been held to encompass any misleading or duping of
the foreign court, such as by the advancing of a claim known to be false,
fabrication of evidence, intimidation of witnesses, and so on: the fraud
will generally lie in the use of improper means to defeat justice and
prevail over the defendant.[117] Whether this covers the case where a claimant pleads a case to which he knows the defendant may have an answer
is unclear, but it cannot be expected that in adversary *inter partes* procedure the claimant has a duty to advance defences. On the other hand,
an English claim form must contain a declaration of the truth of its
contents,[118] and this may increase the likelihood of a pleading being
characterized as fraudulent.

The matters which support the allegation may be put forward, and if
credible will be investigated,[119] even though they were put before, and
specifically rejected by, the foreign court. In sharp contrast to what is
required to impeach an English judgment for fraud, the defendant need
show no new discovery of evidence which could not have been put forward at trial: he may recycle the very evidence which failed to persuade
the foreign court. But the position is not quite as stark as this may suggest. In order to have the allegation of fraud investigated, the defendant
will have to make a credible case that the foreign court was the victim of,
or party to, fraud. The evidence required to reach the standard of cred-
ibility will vary from court to court: it is reasonable to suppose that an
English court will take much more persuading that fraud deceived an
Australian or American court than where the judgment came from a
court with less of an international reputation for excellence. The standard
which must be met to trigger a review is, on this view of the matter,
contextual. Even so, the law is controversial, for it appears to suppose that
the foreign court is less skilled than the English court at the detection of
fraud; and as a new discovery of evidence is required to impeach an
English judgment for fraud,[120] it should, so the argument would run,
equally be required for a foreign judgment. Though this criticism has

[116] *Abouloff* v. *Oppenheimer* (1882) 10 QBD 295 (CA); *Vadala* v. *Lawes* (1890) 25 QBD 310
(CA); *Syal* v. *Heyward* [1948] 2 KB 443 (CA); *Jet Holdings Inc.* v. *Patel* [1990] 1 QB 335
(CA); *Owens Bank Ltd.* v. *Bracco* [1992] 2 AC 443.
[117] Though the defendant may also use fraud to support a defence which defeats the claim
and, if this happens, the claimant may seek to impeach the judgment which the defendant
seeks to have recognized in his favour.
[118] CPR, Pt. 22.   [119] *Jet Holdings Inc.* v. *Patel* [1990] 1 QB 335 (CA).
[120] *Hunter* v. *Chief Constable of the West Midlands* [1980] QB 283 (CA).

found a measure of judicial[121] and scholarly support, the fraud rule is soundly based and the criticism is less so. Two reasons may be given. First, it is dangerous for the law, in effect, to require a defendant to make his allegations in a court which may have been selected by the claimant *mala fide* and for reasons of his own illicit advantage: the proposition that the defendant is entitled to a hearing of a serious allegation in a court over which no suspicion may float is inherently attractive. Secondly, a finding of fraud in relation to a foreign judgment means only that the judgment may not be recognized in England, just as a finding that an arbitral award was contrary to English public policy means only that the award cannot be enforced in England. The finding of fraud does not purport to set aside the judgment or award *in toto* and *in rem* and prevent its recognition and enforcement outside England. It is much less dramatic, and much more domestic, a measure than is the setting aside for all international purposes of an English judgment; and the justification for intervention may, for this reason, properly be rather more modest.

However, if the allegation of fraud has already had an independent hearing in, and been rejected by, a court of the defendant's choosing, this may preclude its being raised *de novo* in England. Either the principles of *res judicata* will mean that the second judgment is binding on the party who brought the proceedings in which it was handed down, or it may be an abuse of the process of the English court for it to be advanced again.[122] Vigorous use of the abuse of process doctrine has the potential to overwhelm much of the fraud defence.[123] Even here, however, there is need for caution before the fraud defence is altogether swept away. If the defendant has chosen to make the allegation of fraud before another court but in the country of the original judgment, it may be that he did so because he faced the prospect of execution against assets which he had in that country. His choice to sue in the form of an action to set aside the judgment in the courts of that country will have meant that he faced a much stiffer task[124]—in all probability, needing a fresh discovery of evidence—than he

---

[121] See, e.g., *Owens Bank Ltd.* v. *Bracco* [1992] AC 443; *Owens Bank Ltd.* v. *Etoile Commerciale SA* [1995] 1 WLR 44 (PC).

[122] *House of Spring Gardens Ltd.* v. *Waite* [1991] 1 QB 241 (CA). There is no reason in principle why the findings against the judgment debtor in the second action should not give rise to an estoppel, but cf the 1982 Act, s. 33(1)(c).

[123] *Owens Bank Ltd.* v. *Etoile Commerciale SA* [1995] 1 WLR 44 (PC); *Desert Sun Loan Corp.* v. *Hill* [1996] 2 All ER 847 (CA).

[124] Which may also mean that it was a different cause of action, or issue, from that which arises before the English court in an enforcement context, and that *res judicata* is not applicable.

would have done if he had merely defended enforcement elsewhere; and though his choice to bring his action where he did was technically voluntary,[125] it will have been very much constrained by the prospect of execution. To say, against this background, that the raising of the issue for a second time is an abuse of process will require considerable care.

Want of natural or substantial justice

If the proceedings in the foreign court fell short of the standards set by the rules of natural justice such as the right to be notified, represented, and heard;[126] or if the procedure violated substantial justice such as by adopting a global and non-judicial assessment of damages,[127] it may be possible to deny recognition to the judgment. Such cases are historically rare, but the enactment of the Human Rights Act 1998 may well raise the profile of this defence. It is unclear whether the argument may be advanced in a case in which it has already been advanced in the foreign jurisdiction. The analogy from international arbitration suggests that it should not,[128] but it has been judicially suggested that, as with fraud, the view of the foreign court does not preclude the English court from making its own assessment.[129] But even if this is correct, one supposes that the court will not allow an argument to be advanced past the point where it becomes an abuse of process.

Public policy

If recognition of the judgment would offend English public policy, it is obvious that it will not be recognized. Judgments based on laws repellent to human rights, or producing a result which is equally repellent, for example, will be denied recognition. A judgment obtained in defiance of an English anti-suit injunction will be denied recognition on this ground;[130] it is much less likely that a judgment obtained in defiance of a foreign anti-suit injunction could be so stigmatized.

Res judicata *in England*

If the judgment is inconsistent with an English judgment, or with a foreign one handed down earlier in time, which is entitled to recognition

---

[125] Above, p. 135.
[126] Cf, from the context of judgments falling within the Reg., Case C–7/98 *Krombach* v. *Bamberski* [2000] ECR I–1935. And see *Society of Lloyd's* v. *Saunders* [2001] ILPr. 18 (Ont.).
[127] *Adams* v. *Cape Industries plc* [1990] Ch. 433 (CA).
[128] *Minmetals Germany GmbH* v. *Fercosteel Ltd.* [1999] CLC 647.
[129] *Jet Holdings Inc.* v. *Patel* [1990] 1 QB 335 (CA).
[130] *Phillip Alexander Securities and Futures Ltd.* v. *Bamberger* [1997] ILPr. 73, aff'd 104 (CA).

in England, it cannot be recognized, for there will have remained no issues to adjudicate.[131]

The effect of recognition at common law

The most usual reason to seek the recognition of a foreign judgment at common law will be to pave the way for an action to enforce it. If the party in whose favour it was given wishes to enforce it, he may bring an action to enforce the judgment, subject to the further limitations examined below. But there are two further consequences of recognition which may be of importance. First, if the party against whom the judgment was given was subject to the international jurisdiction of the foreign court— the claimant will necessarily[132] have been, the defendant may have been— and no defence applies, the cause of action or the issue, as the case may be, will be regarded as against him[133] as *res judicata*. This means that he may not contradict it in or by later English proceedings unless some exception to the application of the doctrine of *res judicata* applies.[134] But secondly, if the party in whose favour the judgment was given, and *against whom* there is no *res judicata*, had been hoping for a better outcome or seeks to rely on a claim which was not put forward the first time around, he may fail: Civil Jurisdiction and Judgments Act 1982, section 34, now generally precludes his suing for a second time on the same underlying cause of action in the hope of improving on the result obtained first time round.[135] In the interpretation of the 'same cause of action' it has been held that any claim which arises out of a single contract constitutes the same cause of action as any other, so that a failure to deliver part of a consignment of goods has the same cause of action as the failure to deliver the balance of the cargo. But a claim for damages for one's own injury is not the same cause of action as a claim for damages for a child's loss of dependency;[136] and it is uncertain whether a claim for damages for pecuniary loss resulting from personal injury has the same cause of action as a claim in respect of pain and suffering caused by the same injury, for in a

---

[131] *Showlag* v. *Mansour* [1995] 1 AC 431 (PC).

[132] Except in his capacity as defendant to a counterclaim which was not sufficiently within the penumbra of the claim he advanced.

[133] And against his privies: those with the same interest or title in the matter, especially if they have stood by, hoping to be regarded as strangers, while one with the same interest as them fights the case: *House of Spring Gardens Ltd.* v. *Waite* [1991] 1 QB 241 (CA).

[134] *Carl Zeiss Stiftung* v. *Rayner & Keeler Ltd. (No 2)* [1967] 1 AC 853.

[135] *Republic of India* v. *India Steamship Co. Ltd. (The Indian Grace)* [1993] AC 410; *Republic of India* v. *India Steamship Co. Ltd. (The Indian Grace) (No 2)* [1998] AC 878.

[136] *Black* v. *Yates* [1992] QB 526.

tort claim there is no liability without damage, and the two types of damage may indicate two causes of action. Even so, a claimant who manages to steer a careful course around section 34 may well find that his claim is considered to abuse the process of the court if it raises a matter which could and should have been advanced in the first action.[137]

ENFORCEMENT OF JUDGMENTS AT COMMON LAW

As a matter of theory, a foreign judgment which satisfies the criteria for its recognition creates an obligation which the judgment creditor may sue to enforce in an action, founded on the foreign judgment, at common law. The action is brought as one for debt; it follows that only final judgments for fixed sums of money can be enforced by such proceedings.[138] As for its being final and conclusive, a judgment which may be reviewed or revised by the court which gave it is not final,[139] but its being subject to appeal to a higher court is irrelevant. This is in fact the same requirement as will already have applied to its recognition in the first place, and though the requirement is always stated as an enforcement condition, this reflects only the tradition of seeing the law on foreign judgments as concerned with their enforcement rather than with recognition. As a debt claim must be based on a judgment for the payment of a fixed sum in money, if the sum is open to variation by the court which awarded it, it is not final and cannot be enforced.[140] If the judgment was final as regards liability but reviewable as regards damages, or led to the making of a non-money order, the finding of liability may be recognized as *res judicata* if and when an action is brought on the basis of the underlying cause of action.

But there is no jurisdiction to enforce a foreign penal, revenue, or analogous law; and if the action to enforce the judgment would have this effect it will be dismissed. So if a foreign taxing authority has obtained a judgment in its favour, enforcement of the judgment by action in England will necessarily fail.[141] Nor, by reason of the Protection of Trading Interests Act 1980, section 5, may an action be brought to recover any part of a foreign judgment for multiple damages, even—perhaps unexpectedly—for the unmultiplied compensatory element. By curious contrast, it appears that judgments for exemplary damages, unless truly extreme and

[137] *Henderson* v. *Henderson* (1843) 3 Hare 100.
[138] Or is the tail wagging the dog here?
[139] *Nouvion* v. *Freeman* (1889) 15 App. Cas. 1.
[140] Though if, e.g., instalments already due are now fixed and beyond review, enforcement of these by debt action is possible.
[141] *United States of America* v. *Harden* (1963) 41 DLR (2d) 721 (Can. Sup. Ct.).

on that account contrary to public policy, are not covered by the Act, and prevented from enforcement by the rule, as long as the judgment debt has not been calculated by 'doubling, trebling or otherwise multiplying' the sum fixed as compensation.[142] The logic of this is elusive, not only because the difference between multiplication and addition has not been generally thought of as having legal as well as arithmetical significance, but also because the recovery of such damages is often in partial compensation for the fact that costs are not recoverable.[143]

Enforcement procedure at common law

The claimant will plead that the judgment debt is due and owing, and may apply under the CPR, rule 24.2, for summary judgment on the ground that the defendant has no real prospect of successfully defending the claim. If the application succeeds judgment will be entered forthwith. But if it is shown on the hearing of the application for summary judgment that the defendant has a real prospect of defending the claim, the court will dismiss the application and the claim will proceed to trial in the usual way.

ENFORCEMENT OF JUDGMENTS BY STATUTORY REGISTRATION

As explained at the outset, there are some countries whose judgments are registered for enforcement pursuant to the provisions of two statutes. The terms of the statutes are very close to the common law, as this stood at the date of enactment, so in substance, though not in form, recognition will be according to the rules of the common law. As regards enforcement, the few further conditions are much the same as those of the common law. But instead of it being necessary to commence original proceedings by service of a claim form, proceeding from there to an application for summary judgment, these two statutes allow the applicant to register the judgment for enforcement, it being then of the same force and effect for enforcement as if it had been an English judgment. The respondent may apply to set aside the registration and the order for registration; and it is on the hearing of this application that the principal issues will emerge. The substantive grounds on which registration may be obtained or set aside closely reflect the common law.

---

[142] Protection of Trading Interests Act 1980, s. 5.
[143] And see, for the same proposition in the European context, *SA Consortium General Textiles SA v. Sun & Sand Agencies Ltd.* [1978] QB 279 (CA).

Administration of Justice Act 1920

Part II of the 1920 Act applies to many, but mostly smaller colonial and Commonwealth, territories: of the larger jurisdictions the Act applies to Malaysia, Singapore, and New Zealand.[144] It does not depend on any treaty with the foreign state; it applies to judgments from 'superior courts', which may be registered under the Act within twelve months of their delivery.[145] Upon an application to set aside the registration, the grounds which are stated to confer international jurisdiction and the permitted defences to recognition differ from those of the common law only in minor detail, but if the judgment is still subject to appeal it may not be registered.[146]

Foreign Judgments (Reciprocal Enforcement) Act 1933

The 1933 Act applies to judgments from Australia[147] and Canada;[148] also from Guernsey, Jersey, India, the Isle of Man, Israel, Pakistan, Surinam, and Tonga,[149] but it applies only to courts identified by name in the Order which implements the bilateral treaty: judgments from other courts in these countries may still be enforced by action at common law. The grounds of international jurisdiction and the defences to recognition[150] differ from those of the common law only in minor detail; if the judgment is subject to appeal the application for registration may be stayed.[151]

---

[144] Reciprocal Enforcement of Judgments (Administration of Justice Act 1920, Part II) (Consolidation) Order 1984, SI 1984/129, as amended by SI 1985/1994, SI 1994/1901, SI 1997/2601. The entry for Hong Kong has been of no effect since the cesser of sovereignty on 1 July 1997.
[145] S. 9.   [146] S. 9(2)(e).   [147] SI 1994/1901.
[148] SI 1987/468, 2211; SI 1988/1304, 1853; SI 1989/987; SI 1991/1724; SI 1992/1731; SI 1995/2708. Quebec is not included.
[149] The current list is published in *Civil Procedure* (Sweet & Maxwell, London, 2001), in the notes to RSC O. 71.
[150] S. 4.   [151] S. 5.

5

Contracts

GENERAL

Until 1991, the rules for choice of law in respect of contractual obligations were a matter of common law, but the question is now[1] substantially governed by the Rome Convention on the law applicable to contractual obligations 1980, as enacted by the Contracts (Applicable Law) Act 1990.[2] The Rome Convention serves to harmonize the choice of law rules for contractual obligations throughout the Member States of the European Union;[3] and it applies to contracts made after 1 April 1991.[4] If[5] there is a justification for the new uniform law it must be this: that the greater the predictability of choice of law rules, the less will legal uncertainty impede the free movement of persons, goods, and services throughout the Member States. Harmonization of choice of law on contractual matters is also only the first step in a more complete harmonization of rules for choice of law: a project to produce 'Rome II', to cover tort, delict, and possibly unjust enrichment, is under way and may come into effect within the lifetime of this book; and it is intended that the Rome Convention will be converted into a Council Regulation, though without substantial textual amendment.

It is sometimes claimed that the Rome Convention draws inspiration from the common law choice of law rules for contracts, but it would be unwise to place much weight on that assertion or to interpret the Convention by the twilight of authorities on the common law. Moreover, the

---

[1] See generally, Dicey & Morris, *The Conflict of Laws* (13th edn., Sweet & Maxwell, London, 2000), chap. 32; R. Plender, *European Contracts Convention* (2nd edn., Sweet & Maxwell, London, 2001); P. M. North (ed.), *Contract Conflicts* (North Holland, 1982). On the interpretation of the Rome Convention see in particular the Report of Giuliano and Lagarde [1980] OJ C282/1.

[2] Hereafter 'the 1990 Act'. A consolidated version of the text of the Convention, updated by new accessions, is printed at [1998] OJ C27/34.

[3] In the context of this chap., the Member States include Denmark; the states party only to the Lugano Convention (Iceland, Norway, Switzerland, and Poland) are not party to the Rome Convention and not affected by its terms.

[4] Art. 17; SI 1991/707. [5] Which is not universally admitted.

status of the Convention as an international text means that pressure for it to receive a uniform interpretation[6] will inevitably draw it away from any common law ancestry which it may have had. The Report of Professors Giuliano and Lagarde[7] is the authorized[8] aid to its interpretation. Though matters excluded from the Convention continue to be governed by the common law, these are relatively few and rather minor, and require mention of the rules of the common law only where this residual role persists.[9] But the occasional comparison of a rule in the Convention with its common law counterpart may allow for analytical insight into the benefits and shortcomings of each. We will therefore examine the common law rules for choice of law only within the framework of the Rome Convention.

So far as the operation of the Convention is concerned, it is irrelevant that none of the parties has any connection with England or, indeed, the European Union, or that the law which the Convention makes applicable is that of a country which is not a signatory to the Convention,[10] or that the choice of law lies only as between the parts of the United Kingdom.[11]

JURISDICTION OVER CONTRACTUAL CLAIMS

The majority of contractual claims will arise as civil or commercial matters, and jurisdiction over defendants in respect of them will therefore fall within the domain of Council Regulation (EC) 44/2001.[12] It is reasonable to suppose that the definition of 'contract' in the Rome Convention and the Regulation will be substantially the same, and there is authority for the view that these two European Instruments may be considered side-by-side in determining whether a particular cause of action (say for a payment of an agreed sum of money on the unilateral termination of a distribution agency) is contractual.[13] The scope of the term 'contract' in CPR rule 6.20 will, however, be different, and will be defined by the common law conflict of laws. Accordingly, a claim founded on the principle that a person who gives professional advice to one who relies on it may incur liability if he is negligent,[14] may yet[15] be held to be

---

[6] Art. 18.   [7] [1980] OJ C282/1.   [8] 1990 Act, s. 3(3).
[9] The rules of the common law are set out in detail in Dicey & Morris, *The Conflict of Laws* (11th edn., Sweet & Maxwell, London, 1987).
[10] Art. 2.   [11] Art. 19; 1990 Act, s. 2(3).
[12] [2001] OJ L12/1, Chap. 2, above.
[13] Case 9/87 *SPRL Arcado v. SA Haviland* [1988] ECR 1539.
[14] *Hedley Byrne & Co. Ltd. v. Heller & Partners Ltd.* [1964] AC 465.
[15] No case has yet held this to be so.

contractual if the question arises in the jurisdictional context of the Regulation, but will be tortious only if it arises in the context of service out with permission under rule 6.20.

CHOICE OF LAW

As will be seen, the general principle which underpins much of the choice of law, at common law and under the Rome Convention, is that parties have very substantial autonomy,[16] and that if they can choose to make any contract they wish, it follows that they can choose any law they wish to govern it. But this deceptively clear proposition almost immediately leads into a logical thicket. Which law will determine whether the parties have made an effective choice? Will that law make the assessment finally or provisionally? Can the law whose significance derives from the fact that it was chosen also be the law which determines whether a permissible choice was made? If the parties purport to alter the law they have chosen, which of the various interested laws determines whether they have made that choice lawfully and effectively? If the parties dispute whether a contract has been made, can the law which would govern it if it were assumed to be valid properly answer the question whether it *is* valid, or whether an alleged choice of law is effective? If the identification of a governing law depends on the terms of the contract, but the terms of the contract depend on the governing law, where does the analysis begin? The principle of party autonomy cannot be self-supporting: some external point of reference is required to explain why the recourse to autonomy is justified. The difficulties which can be spun out of such navel-gazing can often obscure the fact that the rules work satisfactorily, at least where there is no dispute whether the parties are contractually bound, and the only issue is as to the performance of their agreement. But, as will be seen, there are other places, especially where the very existence of the contract is a matter of dispute, in which the theoretical underpinnings of the law are not as firm as they might be.

THE ROME CONVENTION

The Rome Convention applies to contractual obligations entered into after 1 April 1991, except for the points and issues specifically excluded from its scope by Article 1: Article 1 therefore identifies the material scope of the Convention as an instrument which defines its own domain.

---

[16] P. Nygh, *Autonomy in International Contracts* (OUP, Oxford, 1999).

But even in the areas which are outside the domain of the Convention, there is no reason why the common law rules for choice of law, operating by default, may not refer some or all of the excluded issues to the governing law as identified by the Rome Convention for those issues which do fall within its scope. So, for example, arbitration agreements are excluded from the Convention by Article 1(2)(d); and the Rome Convention therefore makes no claim to apply its rules for choice of law to them. Nevertheless, the common law is free to provide that the law which governs an arbitration agreement is the law which governs the contract of which it is a term, and this will be identified by the Rome Convention. The process may be regarded as the inverse of what is done by Article 4 of the Council Regulation on jurisdiction. Article 4 serves to incorporate by reference the jurisdictional rules of the common law. In the context of the Rome Convention, the common law may be seen to incorporate the Convention for purposes which are, and remain, its own. There is a dynamic equilibrium at work.

The Rome Convention applies in principle to all such cases litigated before an English court and involving a choice between the laws of different countries.[17] It is in force throughout the European Union, and it is required to be construed with a view to securing uniformity of interpretation and application.[18] It follows that certain of its definitional terms will receive an independent or autonomous interpretation, and will not be read as if they were pieces of domestic English legislation. Protocols have been drafted to give the European Court competence to give preliminary rulings on interpretation,[19] but these have not come into force, and references under them to the European Court would be wholly permissive, and not mandatory. But if the Convention mutates into a Regulation, the common reference procedure under Article 234 EC will apply instead.

The material scope of the Convention is defined inclusively and exclusively: to determine whether an issue is subject to the choice of law rules of the Convention, it must be within the general scope of the Convention, and not specifically excluded from it.

Domain of the Convention

The Convention applies to identify the law applicable to 'contractual

---

[17] Art. 1(1). For this purpose the separate parts of the UK are treated as separate countries: Art. 19 provides that a state may do this, and by the Contracts (Applicable Law) Act 1990, s. 2(3), the UK did so.

[18] Art. 18.

[19] Brussels Protocol, which is in the 1990 Act, Sch. 3; Second Protocol [1989] OJ L48/17.

obligations' in agreements made after 1 April 1991. A critical first question is whether the meaning of this expression is defined according to national law, so that the definition of contractual obligation is, for an English court, exactly the same as in English domestic law or whether, on the other hand, it has an autonomous meaning, which will largely overlap, but which will not be congruent, with the meaning of the expression in English law. If examined in the detail which appears to be necessary, it is a question of the greatest complexity, for as soon as one abandons the characterization categories of English law, and the relationship between them, it becomes necessary to define the outline of the new category, and to explain whether it overlaps with, or overrides, those it cuts across. It would be so much easier to treat the Convention's expression 'contractual obligations' as if it operated only within the territory which English private international law would define as contractual; and it is doubtless true that in the majority of cases no difference would emerge between the various possible approaches. The reader who wants an easy life should consider skipping the remainder of this section. But categories have edges, and in the delineation of these it is unlikely that the simple solution is right.

The fact that the Convention is meant to be interpreted with regard to its uniform character, and that it will be less likely to achieve its aim if it is interpreted within the framework of national laws, must result in its being given an autonomous meaning. As a result, it is misleading to see the rules of the Rome Convention as being neatly slotted into the space defined but now vacated by the common law rules for choice of law, but necessary to define contractual obligations, for the purpose of defining the scope of the Rome Convention, without looking backward to the common law, whose detail but also whose definitions it has supplanted. The definition is an autonomous one.

'Contractual'

The autonomous definition of contractual obligations will encompass most obligations regarded as contractual in English law, and will exclude most which are not. If, as said earlier in this section, the definition of contractual obligations follows that used for special jurisdiction under Council Regulation (EC) 44/2001, the defining characteristic of a contractual obligation will be that it was freely entered into with regard to another. If this is correct, the question whether an obligation is regarded as contractual in national law is not decisive. On the basis of the jurisprudence of the Court of Justice, the obligations of a member to his trade association or of a shareholder to his company will be contractual even if national law categorizes them differently, because the relationship between the parties is one in which the obligations were freely undertaken in relation to an identified other. Conversely, the claim of a sub-buyer to enforce the manufacturer's warranties of quality will not be contractual, even though arguably so seen in national law, and even though the manufacturer's obligations were undertaken by him freely and voluntarily, because the party seeking to enforce them was not identifiable by the manufacturer. It seems probable that any obligation said to be contractual must satisfy both components of this definition.

That the obligation be freely and voluntarily assumed cannot mean that it must be one which was expressly agreed to, or one which could have been excluded by the choice of the parties. Were it otherwise, the obligations of a supplier in a consumer contract, which are often incapable of being excluded by contractual term, would not be contractual, nor would the implied terms and conditions in a contract for the sale of goods. It appears that it is the relationship created, rather than the individual terms within it, which needs to be voluntary. And it is probable that the relationship is still contractual even if it is alleged that the agreement was vitiated from the outset,[20] or even void *ab initio*:[21] it is a common usage in domestic law to talk of a void contract, and the Rome Convention, as we shall see, indicates which law is to be applied when it is alleged that a party did not consent,[22] and when dealing with the consequences of nullity.[23] It follows that a 'void contract' is still within the scope of the Convention. Moreover, the Convention will apply to obligations which were not created by the contract, but which arise before its creation or after its termination. Whether there is an obligation to negotiate in good faith, or to make disclosure of matters material to the agreement, or to refrain from taking advantage of a dominating position must all be tested by reference to the Convention, for all go to the question whether there was an obligation, freely entered into, or the material validity of that obligation.[24] Likewise, questions which arise after termination or rescission are within the scope of the Convention, so remedies

---

[20] Cf *Agnew* v. *Länsförsäkringsbolagens AB* [2001] 1 AC 223.

[21] But cf *Kleinwort Benson Ltd.* v. *Glasgow City Council* [1999] 1 AC 153.

[22] Art. 8.

[23] Though the specific provision which secures this—Art. 10(1)(e)—is not in force in England (1990 Act, s. 2(2)), this fact does not alter the scope of the Convention, just its effect in England.

[24] Art. 8(1).

consequent upon breach, or on rescission, of a contract will be within the choice of law rules of the Convention. The obligations which arise from the nullity of a contract are also within the framework of the Convention, though, as will be seen, with slight qualifications.

But obligations can be freely assumed outside the domestic law of contract, and it is these which are problematic. Liability for statements negligently made to someone who was expected to rely on them is sometimes explained as based on a voluntary assumption of liability,[25] which comes close to replicating the autonomous definition of contracts. Moreover, if liability under this principle of domestic law is said to arise from a relationship 'equivalent to contract', and which is not contractual only by reason of the absence of consideration,[26] it is plausible that these will be contractual obligations for the purpose of the Rome Convention. After all, English private international law long acknowledged that a promise unsupported by consideration counted as a contract,[27] and it may follow that the question whether the person who has agreed to provide a reference owes liability to the recipient will be governed by the law identified by the Rome Convention. Similarly, the obligations of someone who volunteers to assume fiduciary duties in relation to another may fall within the definition of obligations freely entered into, and the existence of these duties, their extent, and their consequences governed by the law identified by the Rome Convention. After all, the fact that such obligations are treated as equitable as a matter of domestic law is a historical and doctrinal accident which is unlikely to be echoed in the Rome Convention. The eventual answer in relation to the first part of the autonomous definition will be to ask whether the relationship out of which the liability is said to arise can be described as one in which the defendant freely assumed obligations in relation to another and, if he did, the law which governs the relationship will be that specified by the Rome Convention.

The second aspect of the definition of 'contractual' appears to require that the obligation be assumed in relation to another who can be identified, so that if the defendant has no idea who the other party is, the relationship is not contractual.[28] It is hard to avoid the conclusion that this lacks coherence and cannot form the basis of a workable definition. Were it taken at face value, the purchaser of the carbolic smoke ball,

[25] *Henderson v. Merrett Syndicates Ltd.* [1995] 2 AC 145.
[26] *Hedley Byrne & Co. Ltd. v. Heller & Partners Ltd.* [1964] AC 465.
[27] *Re Bonacina* [1912] 2 Ch. 394.
[28] Case C–26/91 *Soc. Jakob Handte v. Soc. Traîtements Mécano-chimiques des Surfaces* [1992] ECR I–3967; see above, p. 71.

through whom every first year student meets the law of contract,[29] could not be party to a contractual obligation: the Carbolic Smoke Ball Company neither knew nor cared who its customers were, any more than does anyone who advertises a reward, or the fire brigade which responds to a call for help, or the transport company which sells more than one ticket at once. Nor would an assignee ever have a contractual claim to enforce. In none of these cases is the identity of the other party known to, or probably even discoverable by, the supplier or advertiser; and that appears to place the obligations of the relationship outside the Rome Convention. The trouble is that these cases must be contractual, for the law has no other category into which it would be even remotely realistic to accommodate them. The better conclusion may therefore be that the requirement that there be an identified or identifiable 'other' is incorrect, and that an obligation is contractual if the defendant freely assumes a promissory obligation to another or to others, but that if the promisor does not know, or wish to know,[30] the identity of the other this is immaterial to its characterization as contractual. But it does entail the conclusion that the claim of the sub-buyer to enforce the original seller's obligations may sometimes be contractual. So also will be an obligation undertaken with the deliberate intention that it be enforceable by a non-party: there is no reason to suppose that after the partial abolition of the English doctrine of privity of contract,[31] consensual obligations enforceable by non-parties will be excluded.

'Obligations'

The Giuliano-Lagarde report states that gifts are included within the scope of the Convention where these are seen as contractual: a curious proposition for an English lawyer,[32] but one which underlines the different contours of the autonomous conception of contract. The sense in which they give rise to obligations is obscure, but there may be requirements of formal validity, or if there is a right to revoke a gift on account of ingratitude, perhaps this right (or the obligation to be grateful) is contractual.

Property rights are excluded. So intangible property, such as intellectual property rights, lies in principle outside the scope of the Convention, though contracts to create or transfer such rights will be within it,

---

[29] *Carlill v. Carbolic Smoke Ball Co.* [1893] 1 QB 256 (CA).
[30] Such as where an offer is made to the world for acceptance without the need for communication, or where the offer is made to a single promisee, but without restraint on assignment.
[31] Contracts (Rights of Third Parties) Act 1999.   [32] [1980] OJ C282/1, 10.

just as are contracts to transfer tangible moveable or immoveable property. A more troublesome question arises in connection with the assignment of intangible moveable property in general, such as shares, policies of insurance, contractual debts, and so forth. There is a view, respectable and ancient, that all these are property, and that their status as property is separate and distinct from the contract which created them: a contract may well be needed to give birth to the right, but once this act of creation has taken place what results is a right of property which can be bought, sold, mortgaged, pledged, assigned, alienated, bequeathed, confiscated, and obtained by deception. From this it follows, so the argument runs, that the relationships thus created are proprietary and are not contractual, and that the particular issue of what law governs dealings with these rights is therefore not governed by the Rome Convention.

The difficulties presented by this argument arise on two levels. True, transfers or assignments of some forms of intangibles, such as shares and intellectual property rights, are undeniably proprietary and distinct from any contract which created them, and assignments are not governed by the Rome Convention. And in English law, and perhaps in others, there are many contexts, of which insolvency is certainly one, where it is convenient for contractual debts to be regarded as property rights. But the view that there is a difference between owning a debt (which is a statement in proprietary language) and being owed a debt (which is in contractual language) requires the fiery certainty of faith, for it is an illusion: the question of who owns a debt is co-terminous with the question to whom the debt is owed, and there is no obvious way in which the two can be separated and no distinction between them. At a more general level, it is easy to see the distinction between contract and property where, in the real world, the conclusion of a contract will be followed by delivery or conveyance; but when dealing with simple contractual obligations there is no separate item to regard as 'intangible property': the whole of the question is contractual, there being neither need nor room for a separate property: after the contract has been concluded, nothing remains to be done.[33] There is difficulty in accepting the argument that these are things rather than obligations when the property is a simple contractual debt. But even if that were not so, Article 12 of the Rome Convention contains a rule to deal with choice of law for the voluntary assignment of contractual obligations. Though it extends only to the single question of

---

[33] *Raiffeisen Zentralbank Österreich AG* v. *Five Star Trading LLC* [2001] CA Civ. 68, [2001] 2 WLR 1344.

which law governs the assignment of such rights, it overrides any objection that a contractual choice of law rule is irrelevant to an issue which is not contractual. There is therefore no basis for excluding the assignment of contractual rights from the scope of the Rome Convention; the law which governs their assignment is that specified by Article 12 of the Convention.[34]

Concurrent liabilities
In some contexts—in the field of employment law[35] and in the provision of professional services,[36] for example—English domestic law permits a claimant to frame his claim concurrently in contract and in tort, or electively between them; and English private international law allowed this as well. But it is now unclear whether this approach, if persisting in private international law, would be consistent with the Convention. For if the claimant formulates in tort a claim which would otherwise fall within the four corners of the Convention—he alleges that his employer breached the common duty of care, rather than pleading a broken contractual promise to take care; he alleges negligent misstatement on the part of his investment adviser, rather than a breach of a contractual promise to use reasonable care and skill—it means that a claim between two contracting parties, falling within the material scope of the Convention, will be subjected to a law other than that specified by the Convention, and the apparently mandatory words of Article 1 will have been overcome. A similar argument could be advanced if a claimant were to elect to enforce fiduciary duties owed by his opponent, rather than the contract between them.[37] The dominant English view is that this traditional freedom of a claimant to elect how to frame the claim continues in full force and effect, and until abrogated by judicial decision, this procedural freedom represents the law.[38] Yet if judged by result, it is undeniable that the Convention will have failed, in this respect, to do what it set out to do; and this cannot be accepted without substantial reservation.

Excluded issues
The Convention eschews any claim to govern the matters set out in Article 1(2), and to these the appropriate choice of law rule will be

[34] The content of the rule is examined in Chap. 8.
[35] Cf *Coupland* v. *Arabian Gulf Oil Co.* [1983] 1 WLR 1151 (CA).
[36] *Henderson* v. *Merrett Syndicates Ltd.* [1995] 2 AC 145.
[37] Assuming for present purposes (but see Chap. 7, below) that there is a different choice of law rule for claims based on fiduciary duties.
[38] If it is seen as a procedural point, it is unaffected by the Rome Convention: Art. 1(2)(h).

supplied by English private international law. Many of these were not
seen as contractual as a matter of English private international law in the
first place, so Article 1(2) mainly confirms what was already known. They
are: status and the capacity of natural persons;[39] contractual rights relating to wills and succession and matrimonial property rights; and rights
and duties arising out of a family relationship;[40] obligations arising from
bills of exchange and promissory notes and other negotiable instruments
where these arise from their negotiable character;[41] questions governed by
the law of companies, such as creation, capacity, and winding-up;[42] the
power of an agent to bind a principal, or organ of a company to bind the
company, to a third party;[43] the constitution and internal relationships of
trusts;[44] evidence and procedure.[45] Also excluded is insurance where the
risk is situated in the territory of the European Union: in fact, in relation
to insurance a separate, and highly complex, system of rules deals with
choice of law.[46] Where any of these issues arise for decision in an English
court, common law conflict of law rules will continue to apply. As regards
these, and as explained in the chapters where they arise for examination,
the *lex domicilii* has a dominant role in relation to wills, succession, and
family matters; the *lex situs* in relation to negotiable instruments; the *lex
incorporationis* in relation to companies; the proper law of the trust in
relation to trusts; and the *lex fori* over issues of evidence and procedure:
none of these was traditionally seen as a contractual issue, and that has
not changed. In relation to the power of an agent to bind a principal to a
third party, the exclusion was probably brought about by the complexity
of the issue and the irreconcilable differences between the common law
and civilian analyses of agency; but it will remain open to the common
law conflict of law rules to provide that this issue is governed by the law
which governs the contract of agency, which will in turn be identified by
the Rome Convention. Though the Convention makes no claim to govern
this issue, it cannot and does not prevent a national law taking that same
decision, as a matter of its own legal authority.

[39] Art. 1(2)(a); though this is subject to Art. 11; see below.
[40] Art. 1(2)(b).
[41] Art. 1(2)(c). But contracts pursuant to which these instruments are issued are not
excluded: [1980] OJ C282/1, 10.
[42] Art. 1(2)(e).
[43] Art. 1(2)(f). But in so far as they are contractual, relations between principal and agent
and agent and third party are not excluded: [1980] OJ C282/1, 13.
[44] Art. 1(2)(g).
[45] Art. 1(2)(h).
[46] Art. 1(3). But the exclusion does not apply (so the Convention does apply) to
reinsurance: Art. 1(4).

In the same way, though Article 1(2)(d) excludes agreements on arbitration and choice of court from the domain of the Convention,[47] which is contrary to the view of English law that the validity of these is principally a matter for the law of the contract in which they were contained, which may be regarded as the 'proper law' of the agreement.[48] An agreement on jurisdiction or arbitration will generally be valid if effective under its proper law, and not if not. But the *lex fori* can in certain cases override this answer: by denying effect to an agreement valid under its proper law[49] or by regarding as valid an agreement invalid and ineffective under its proper law.[50] Indeed, the reason for this exclusion from the scope of the Convention is that under the laws of many countries, the validity of such agreements is seen as a procedural matter rather than a contractual one: a position which, in the light of Article 23 of Council Regulation (EC) 44/2001 is not so far removed from the English one. But again, the Convention presents no obstacle to English private international law deciding on its own authority to treat jurisdiction and arbitration agreements as being governed by the law which applies to the contract of which they are a part, and this therefore remains the position in England.

The status of a person is predominantly the concern of the law of the domicile, as is that person's capacity. Contractual capacity is governed by the common law conflict of laws, according to which an individual would be capable if he had capacity either by the law of the country with which the contract was most closely connected or by the law of his domicile.[51] But the Convention intrudes on this in one respect. Article 11 provides that where two individuals make a contract in the same country, and one later relies on a personal incapacity according to some other law to plead the invalidity of that contract, he may do so only if the other party was, or should have been, aware of it. For corporations, the existence and extent

---

[47] Though they may be taken into account in the determination of the governing law.

[48] See *Egon Oldendorff* v. *Libera Corp.* [1995] 2 Lloyd's Rep. 64. The 'proper law' is the term which was used at common law to signify the law by which the validity of the contract was tested, and is used in this context to acknowledge that the identification of the law which governs a jurisdiction or arbitration agreement is a matter for the common law rules of the conflict of laws.

[49] See *The Hollandia* [1983] 1 AC 565 (though it would be decided differently today) on the effect of the Carriage of Goods by Sea Act 1971; and the provisions of Council Reg. (EC) 44/2001 [2001] OJ L12/1 limiting the validity of jurisdiction agreements in insurance, consumer, and employment contracts.

[50] Cf Case 25/79 *Sanicentral GmbH* v. *Collin* [1979] ECR 3423, where Art. 17 BC, substantially re-enacted as Council Reg. (EC) 44/2001 [2001] OJ L12/1, Art. 23, overrode a rule of the proper law which denied effect to a jurisdiction agreement ousting the jurisdiction of the employment tribunals.

[51] *Charron* v. *Montreal Trust Co.* (1958) 15 DLR (2d) 240 (Ont. CA).

of contractual capacity is a matter for the *lex incorporationis*. But the legal effect of a contract made by a corporation without capacity to do so is a matter for the governing law of the contract.

The governing law: express choice or its equivalent

Article 3 of the Convention provides that a contract is governed by the law chosen by the parties, provided that this is express or may be demonstrated with reasonable certainty by the terms of the contract or the circumstances of the case. The parties are permitted to choose a law having no other connection to the facts of the contract. They may choose different laws for separate parts of the contract and, so far as the Convention is concerned, alter the governing law at any time. The Convention therefore broadly adopts the principle of party autonomy, allowing a choice to be decisive except only in relation to limited and clearly specified matters; but it requires two things: the choice to be made, and that choice to be expressed or demonstrable, and this will preclude the argument that the parties (as reasonable people) must have chosen a particular law but did not express that choice or suggest that they had made it.

A choice expressed in the form 'this contract shall be governed by the law of France' will therefore be effective to make French law the governing law; and a less artful choice, such as 'this contract shall be construed in accordance with French law', will probably be taken as a choice of governing law. In advising clients, one hopes that a legal adviser will recognize the freedom to choose, but also the responsibility to express that choice clearly, which is afforded by Article 3. But one could be forgiven for thinking that some draftsmen regard a clear expression of choice as being too easy, rejecting it for something more challenging. An expression of choice of the law of the United Kingdom, or of British law, for example, cannot be given literal effect, because there is no such law to be chosen; and to interpret this as an express choice of English law is to make an assumption which is probably factually correct[52] but politically incorrect. Again, a choice of the *lex mercatoria*, or of the law of Mars, not being the law of a country, cannot be upheld, because the Convention sanctions only the choice of the law of a country and in such a case Article 3 cannot apply.

Nor is it clear that Article 3 will always validate a purported choice which is expressed formulaically, such as where the contract is expressed to be governed 'by the law of the place where the carrier has its principal

---

[52] Cf *The Komninos S* [1991] 1 Lloyd's Rep. 370 (CA).

place of business'. If there is no dispute about these identifiers, the expression of choice will be effective. But what if there is genuine disagreement about who (shipowner, charterer) is the carrier, or which is the principal place (of day-to-day decision-taking, of supervisory direction) of business?[53] In principle, the governing law will be charged with answering these questions, for they go to the construction of a term of the contract. The trouble is, the answers to these questions are required in order to identify the governing law in the first place. Though the Court of Justice has held, in the jurisdictional context, that a provision in such terms may be effective as an agreement on jurisdiction,[54] this presupposes that the choice of law rules of the court seised have served to identify the geographical place which is referred to. But if one asks the simple question whether these words choose a law, expressly or as may be identified with reasonable certainty from the terms of the contract or the circumstances of the case, the answer is no. It is no help to say that, as a matter of English law, the carrier will be regarded as the charterer, or the principal place of business that from which day-to-day control is exercised: the Rome Convention is meant to operate independently of English law, and to be a full, complete, and sufficient code for the identification of the governing law. From that point of view, some forms of words, though superficially intelligible, do not achieve it.

As a matter of common law choice of law, if the parties did not choose a law but selected English jurisdiction, this was not taken as an unequivocal and express choice of English law to govern the contract, but it was probably conclusive unless substantially all the other factors coincided in pointing to another law.[55] Under the Rome Convention this will not be taken to fall within Article 3 as an express choice of English law, or, at least not certainly, as a case where the choice of English law can be deduced with reasonable certainty from the contract; but it will certainly be effective within the framework of Article 4, in default of an Article 3 choice. But if the parties contract on the basis of a standard form, which is known in the trade as being founded on English law, this may be a case in which the parties' actual choice may be deduced from the terms of the contract or the circumstances of the case.[56]

---

[53] *The Rewia* [1991] 2 Lloyd's Rep. 325 (CA).

[54] Case C–387/98 *Coreck Maritime GmbH* v. *Handelsveem BV* [2000] ECR I–9337.

[55] *Compagnie Tunisienne de Navigation SA* v. *Compagnie d'Armement Maritime SA* [1971] AC 572.

[56] Giuliano-Lagarde Report [1980] OJ C282/1, 17.

Split choice, deferred choice, altered choice
Although it allowed for freedom to choose the proper law of a contract, the common law was reluctant to permit two laws to govern separate parts of the contract, no doubt to avoid the untidiness and possible irreconcilability which might well arise from allowing it. And it denied the validity of an agreement to defer the actual choice of law to a date in the future: it was not open to the parties to specify that no choice of law was to be made until, at some point after the formation of the contract, one party nominated the proper law.[57] Such a 'floating' choice of law was axiomatically precluded, for a contract must be a source of obligation from its inception, and in the absence of a governing law it would have no mechanism to impose any obligations. But as a matter of common law, there appeared to be nothing in principle to prevent the parties changing the original proper law: if it was open to them to vary the contract, it must also have been open to vary this provision as well.[58] As a matter of logic, if not clear authority, however, the alteration to the proper law would need to comply with, or be permitted by, the original proper law as well as being permitted by English law: the contract would be and remain a source of obligations governed by its original proper law unless and until this proper law recognized the validity and effectiveness of a change.

The position under the Convention is at once simpler and more complex. Proceeding from the view that the parties are permitted to exercise freedom of choice, it is provided that they may agree to have separate parts of the contract governed by different laws.[59] They may agree to alter the governing law at any time,[60] but it is not clear which law determines whether a purported variation was effective, or conformed to any conditions which the parties may have imposed on the exercise of this choice. As a matter of logic, if the parties expressly choose the law of Ruritania to govern the contract, according to which law no subsequent variation of governing law is permitted, it is hard to see why the Rome Convention should authorize the making of a change which the parties have bound themselves not to make: if this is correct, a rule of double reference would also be applicable here: the Rome Convention will allow the change as a matter of English private international law, but to avoid being a breach of contract the change of law must be permitted by the law which governed

[57] *Armar Shipping Co. Ltd.* v. *Caisse Algérienne d'Assurance* [1981] 1 WLR 207 (CA).
[58] *Whitworth Street Estates (Manchester) Ltd.* v. *James Miller & Partners Ltd.* [1970] AC 583.
[59] Art. 3(1).   [60] Art. 3(2).

the contract as the source of the parties' rights and duties.[61] Any other solution appears to degrade the law chosen by the parties to govern the contract they agreed to make.

It is not clear from the Convention whether the parties may choose not to have a law at the outset. Logic suggests that the answer is that this is impossible, for a contract without a law makes no more sense under the Convention than it did under the common law;[62] but does the original governing law, supplied as it presumably will be by Article 4, also need to approve the making of a later choice? Here again, it is one thing to provide that the parties may agree to, or choose to, alter the governing law, but another to say that every purported (or disputed) choice is actually effective; and if this question is put in issue, there has to be a law by reference to which the issue can be resolved; and the comments in the previous paragraph apply.

The meaning of 'law'

According to the Convention, 'law' means the domestic law of the country chosen by the rules of the Convention: *renvoi* to another law is excluded by Article 15. The general justification for this lies in the pragmatic argument that if the parties went to the trouble of choosing a law it would be unlikely to the point of perversity for them to have chosen anything other than the domestic law of the nominated country. Where they have not chosen, they may have been perfectly content to accept the default option provided by the law; and for this factual variant to lead to a difference in the meaning of 'law' would be unacceptable. One might question the wisdom of the exclusion of *renvoi* for the case where the parties have not chosen a law but have chosen a forum for adjudication. The common law orthodoxy, which carried into the Convention,[63] that this is a pretty powerful indicator of choice for the domestic law of the court chosen looks very odd: it is a clear and unambiguous choice for whatever law the court at the place of trial would itself have applied. But this pattern of reasoning is apparently precluded by Article 15, so indirect and unreliable means will have to be used to achieve what cannot be done directly.

---

[61] But in *Aeolian Shipping SA* v. *ISS Machinery Services Ltd.* [2001] CA Civ. 1162, 20 July 2001, the court appeared to treat the question as one of simple fact, not dependent upon satisfaction of any additional condition.

[62] *Amin Rasheed Shipping Corp.* v. *Kuwait Insurance Co.* [1984] AC 50.

[63] Giuliano–Lagarde Report [1980] OJ C282/1, 17.

Absence of express choice

Save for the case of consumer contracts, Article 4 provides that, if not chosen in accordance with Article 3, the governing law is that of the country with which the contract is most closely connected. The looked-for connection is therefore to a country, rather than to a legal system; once the connection to a country has been ascertained, the law of that country applies to govern the contract.[64] This may mean that though a contract is most closely connected to English law, it may still be governed by the law of a different country; and if this were so, the Rome Convention departs from the approach of the common law. This would be unfortunate, for any interpretation of the Convention which produces a result which conflicts with what rational commercial men would have expected does not deserve support. For example, there may be a set of connected contracts: a bill of lading and contracts made in accordance with it,[65] or letters of credit or of comfort, issued as part of a larger financial transaction,[66] or contracts of reinsurance made back-to-back with contracts of insurance,[67] in which an express choice of law is made in some but not all contracts. Common sense would say that all were intended to be governed by the same law, to prevent the dislocation which would otherwise be risked. But in the absence of an express choice of law, recourse to Article 4 may make it difficult to give effect to the sensible implied intention as regards governing law if the balance of factual connections points to a different country.

It is not clear how the degrees of connection are to be assessed. Under the common law there had been an informal hierarchy of connection, so that the place of arbitration was seen as a strong connection, the place of domicile of the parties as a weak one, and the others ranged between the two. This was probably based on a crude reflection of how far, if at all, each allowed the court to read the parties' minds as regards intended proper law; and if this is correct, it will be inapplicable in the context of Article 4, where the search is not for clues to intention as to law, but for connections to a country, where intention is irrelevant.

Presumptions,[68] of debatable utility, provide that the country most closely connected to the contract is that of habitual residence (but for a

[64] *Crédit Lyonnais* v. *New Hampshire Insurance Co.* [1997] 2 Lloyd's Rep. 1 (CA).
[65] *The Mahkutai* [1996] AC 650 (PC).
[66] *Bank of Baroda* v. *Vysya Bank Ltd.* [1994] 2 Lloyd's Rep. 87.
[67] Cf *Forsikringsaktieselskapet Vesta* v. *Butcher* [1989] AC 852, where the contracts were governed by different laws.
[68] Art. 4(2)–(4).

corporation, its central administration) of the party whose performance is
characteristic of the contract, unless the contract is made in the course of
that party's trade or profession, in which case the country presumed is
that of the principal place of business; for contracts concerning an
immoveable it is the country where the immoveable is situated; different
and complex presumptions apply to contracts for the carriage of goods.
The technique of providing presumptions was alien to the common law,
and it will take a while to discover how useful these presumptions are. But
it is important to observe that the focus is not on the place of characteristic performance, but on the residence of the party who is to make it.[69] The
characteristic performance referred to is usually taken to be the performance for which the payment is made; but if a contract does not conform to
the model of sale and purchase (ironically, the mutual exchange of money
or of options on money, the basis of the economy of the western world,
will not easily fit the template), Article 4(5) concedes that the presumptions may be inapplicable. That said, however, the seller or supplier or
reinsurer who undertakes performance for payment, will tend to be seen
as the characteristic performer. Moreover, if the contract appears to be
more closely connected to another country, Article 4(5) also provides that
that country's law will apply in any event.[70]

One might wonder whether Article 4(5) has not scuppered the entire
system of presumptions: either the country identified has the closest
connection, in which case the presumption added nothing, or it does not
and another country does, in which case the presumption will not apply.
Either way, the answer would be found by the direct application of the
Article 4(5) test, but without the hoop-jumping which will have preceded
it. In the absence of a ruling from the Court of Justice, practice may vary
from court to national court, but the English approach appears likely to
involve liberal recourse to Article 4(5).

At common law it was occasionally proposed that a presumption of
validity meant that where the issues were finely balanced, a contract
should be governed by a law under which it would be valid.[71] The legitimacy of such a presumption was debatable, but was defended as reflecting the presumed intention of the parties. There is therefore no obvious
basis for including such a presumption where Article 4 of the Convention
identifies the governing law, and party intention has no formal role.

[69] Presumably he will be the dominant party, most likely to have dictated the terms of the
contract, and most likely to have wanted his own law to be applied.
[70] See generally *Bank of Baroda* v. *Vysya Bank Ltd.* [1994] 2 Lloyd's Rep. 87.
[71] e.g., *Coast Lines Ltd.* v. *Hudig and Veder Chartering NV* [1972] 2 QB 34, 44, 48 (CA).

Modification of choice of law: certain consumer contracts

Article 5 modifies the general provisions of Articles 3 and 4 in respect of certain consumer contracts. Article 5 applies where the contract is for sale or supply (or for credit for the purpose) to a person for a purpose outside his trade or profession;[72] and does apply to a package holiday. It does not apply to a contract of carriage, or where the services are to be supplied wholly outside the country of the consumer's habitual residence. But where the contract falls within this definition, an express choice of law under Article 3 cannot deprive the consumer of the protection afforded to him by mandatory rules[73] of law of the country of his habitual residence if either (1) in that country the conclusion of the contract was preceded by a specific invitation addressed to him, or by advertising, and he had taken in that country all the necessary steps for his conclusion of the contract, or (2) the supplier or his agent received the consumer's order in that country, or (3) the contract was for the sale of goods and the consumer travelled from that country to another and there placed his order, the journey having been arranged by the seller for the purpose of inducing the consumer to buy. In the absence of express choice under Article 3, a consumer contract is governed by the law of the country of the consumer's habitual residence.[74] The fragmented state of Article 5 is presumably attributable to the history of its negotiation, but its protective intent is clear. Its application to contracts made by computer is yet to be explored.[75]

Modification of choice of law: individual employment contracts

Article 6 modifies the applicable law for contracts of employment. An express choice of law is effective, but only subject to the mandatory protective laws of the country whose law would have applied in the absence of an express choice. If there is no express choice of law under Article 3, the contract will be governed by the law of the country where the employee habitually carried out his work[76] or, if there is no such single country, by the law of the country where is situated the place of business

---

[72] It is not specified whether the supplier must be acting in the course of his trade or profession.

[73] As regards this expression, see under 'Modification of Choice of Law: mandatory rules', below.

[74] Art. 5(4).   [75] See pp. 30–2, above.

[76] Where the duties of the employment are carried out in more than one country see Case C–125/92 *Mulox IBC* v. *Geels* [1993] ECR I–4075; Case C–383/95 *Rutten* v. *Cross Medical Ltd.* [1997] ECR I–51.

which engaged him, unless (in either case) the contract appears to be more closely connected to another country.[77]

Modification of choice of law: mandatory rules

Apart from the special contracts just mentioned, there are four further, general, instances in which the hegemony of the governing law is limited. The Convention identifies the first three of these as 'mandatory laws': a rather unhelpful expression whose meaning varies according to the context in which it appears. In these cases, choice of the governing law is not set aside, but its operation is in certain respects overridden and subordinated to the rules of another system of law; the same applies to a governing law identified by Article 4.

First, Article 3(3) provides that an express choice of law is still subject to those laws of another country which may not be derogated from by contractual agreement, but only if all the relevant elements at the time of choice are connected with that country. The intent is that where a contract is entirely connected only to one country, freedom of choice of law should not extend to those issues which that law regards as applicable regardless of choice. In England, an example is the requirement of consideration, so that if a contract is wholly connected to England, a choice of Scots law will be effective, but consideration will still be required for the promise to be enforceable, even though this is not required under Scots law. There is obvious room for disagreement about which elements are 'relevant' for the purpose of this rule.

Secondly, Article 7(2) provides that laws of the forum which are mandatory and must be applied by a judge regardless of choice of law will continue to be applicable. The operation of this provision is therefore entirely dependent upon the court in which the trial takes place, and provides, notwithstanding the uniformity in choice of law created by the Convention, a possible incentive to forum-shop. In the context of a trial in England, examples may include legislation controlling contract terms which purport to limit or exclude liability,[78] the Carriage of Goods by Sea Act 1971, giving the force of law to the Hague-Visby Rules,[79] or those provisions of the Financial Services and Markets Act 2000 which make unenforceable an investment agreement made through an unauthorized

---

[77] For cases in which the duties are carried on outside the jurisdiction of any state (such as on an oil rig) see [1980] OJ C282/1, 26.

[78] Unfair Contract Terms Act 1977, s. 27(2); Unfair Terms in Consumer Contract Regs. 1999, SI 1999/2083 (though Art. 20 expressly provides for the application of such rules as these which derive from Dir. 93/13/EC [1993] OJ L95/29).

[79] Cf *The Hollandia* [1983] 1 AC 565.

person,[80] and which are not to be sidelined by the simple expedient of choosing a law other than English to govern the contract.

Thirdly, Article 7(1) of the Convention[81] would have permitted the application by a court of the mandatory laws of a third country (that is, neither the country whose law is the applicable law, nor the law of the country whose courts are hearing the case) which had a close connection with the contract. But as this would have been a dangerous novelty for judges, and a source of uncertainty for litigants, the provision was deleted from the the Convention as enacted in England.[82] The legislative technique involved may have an impact on the analysis of contracts which are illegal under the law of the place of performance when this is neither the governing law nor the law of the forum. It appears from the structure of Article 7 in general that the manner in which the law in question must be mandatory is that which applies under Article 7(2), but as there is no possibility of an English court being called on to apply such a rule, it need not be examined any further.

Fourthly, a rule of the governing law will not apply where this would be manifestly contrary to public policy.[83] The relationship between this and Article 7 may not be immediately clear, but whereas Article 7 provides for the governing law to be overlaid by another law, Article 16 proceeds by the blanking out of a rule of the governing law, with the result that the answer appears by default. So if the governing law allows damages to be claimed for breach of a contract to sell slaves or narcotics, Article 16 will prevent its application in English proceedings; such a case will fit less easily into Article 7(2), for no substantive rule of English law—as opposed to the principles of public policy—demands application in such a case.

Domain of the governing law

Subject to those reservations, the Convention variously provides that the governing law, ascertained as above, applies to the interpretation and performance of the contract; also to the consequences of its breach and the extinction of its obligations.[84] In relation to formal validity, compliance with the governing law is sufficient; otherwise compliance with the law or laws of the place where the parties were when they made the contract will also suffice.[85] The effect is that, subject to what follows,

[80] Financial Services and Markets Act 2000, ss. 26, 27.
[81] Cf *The Torni* [1932] P 78 (CA).
[82] Contracts (Applicable Law) Act 1990, s. 2(2).
[83] Art. 16.   [84] Art. 10.   [85] Art. 9.

almost all points of construction, interpretation, and discharge (by performance, frustration, and breach) are within the domain of the governing law as, in principle,[86] is the availability of remedies for breach. The
Convention provides that the consequences of nullity are governed by the
governing law, but it does not insist on this; and the United Kingdom did
not enact Article 10(1)(e).[87] This contractual issue is therefore examined
under choice of law for restitutionary obligations but, as indicated above,
many cases of nullity should be regarded as contractual and resolved in
accordance with the governing law.[88]

Disputes about contractual validity

Subject to the fact that the formal validity of a contract is, by Article 9,
assessed by a rule of alternative validating reference, the governing law
will in general determine whether the contract is valid. But the concept
of 'validity' covers a range of possible objections, ranging from break-
downs in formation to the effect of a change in the law making performance illegal. Nevertheless, the point of departure is that the contention
that there was, or is now, no binding contract is one which will be
resolved by the law which would govern the contract if it were taken to be
valid. This is the effect of Articles 3(4) and 8(1),[89] and is broadly in line
with what some[90] took to be the solution given by the common law.
References to the putative governing law (or the governing law of the
putative contract) are to this law. But the methodology involved in this
approach is obviously flawed. If we suppose that one party will be contending that there was a valid and binding contract, while the opposite
party argues that there never was any such thing, it is unprincipled to
proceed by assuming, conditionally but still decisively, that the first
party's submission is correct and that the appropriate tool of decision is
the law which would have governed the contract if it were valid. The
reverse proposition appears equally convincing. The opposite party will
say that the remedies lie in the law of restitution or not at all, so one
should assume the contract to be invalid, and look to the law which would

---

[86] Remedies not known to English law cannot be granted: Art. 1(2)(h). It is uncertain
whether specific performance must be ordered in a case in which it would be available under
the *lex contractus* but not, in these circumstances, under English domestic law.

[87] 1990 Act, s. 2(2).   [88] P. 152, above.

[89] Which also provides that whether a particular term is valid is determined by the law
which would govern it on the footing that it was valid: a proposition which is particularly
unrealistic where each party has proposed a contract term, including a choice of law, which
contradicts that of the opposite party.

[90] Though not all: A. Briggs, 'The Formation of International Contracts' [1990]
LMCLQ 192.

govern the restitutionary claim. If that law considers that there was indeed no valid contract, and that the claim is for restitution, the choice of law will be the restitutionary one. If instead it considers that there was a contract, and no cause for restitution, the *lex causae* will be the contractual one. Why should one of these be preferred to the other? If this is an intelligible question, the answer will be that there is no reason, and the solution must lie elsewhere.

But alternative solutions are not immediately attractive, either. One possibility might be to characterize the facts to see whether they disclose an issue falling within a broad conception of contract; but this is uncertain in its operation. Another might be to apply the *lex fori* to decide whether there is a contract and, if there is, to use the proper law which it must necessarily[91] have to decide whether there was a valid contract; if according to the *lex fori* there is no contract, that would be an end of it. Yet another might be to apply the putative governing law, but with a saving provision for people whose own laws would have reassured them that there was no contract and that they were not bound.[92] In effect, this is the solution adopted by the Convention. Accordingly Article 8(2) allows the party arguing that he should not be bound to rely on the law of his habitual residence 'to establish that he did not consent' if it would be unreasonable to apply the governing law to the question. But if he has dealt by reference to the foreign law before, or maybe simply because he was prepared to make an international contract, he may be found to have forfeited a protection designed for the innocent abroad.[93] What precisely is encompassed by the argument that 'he did not consent' is uncertain. As a matter of first impression, an argument which has at its root the proposition that X did not in law consent to bind himself to Y seems to be comprehended, and therefore any assault on the legal effectiveness of the alleged consent is within the material scope of Article 8(2). Giuliano–Lagarde express a different view,[94] claiming that the scope of Article 8(2) is narrower than this, and is confined to the existence, as distinct from the validity, of consent. It is unclear whether this is tenable; it remains to be seen whether Article 8(2) will be confined to the limited role proposed by Giuliano–Lagarde.

---

[91] *Amin Rasheed Shipping Corp.* v. *Kuwait Insurance Co.* [1984] AC 50.

[92] Foreshadowed by A. Jaffey, 'Offer and Acceptance and Related Questions in the English Conflict of Laws' (1975) 24 *ICLQ* 603.

[93] Cf *Egon Oldendorff* v. *Libera Corp.* [1995] 2 Lloyd's Rep. 64.

[94] [1980] OJ C282/1, 28.

The Rome Convention in contractual litigation

One of the curious things about the private international law of contract
is that whilst the domestic law of contract divides its subject up into
familiar and everyday pieces—offer and acceptance, consideration, mistake, misrepresentation, and so on—the rules of private international law
use categories and address concerns which cut across these more practical
issues, or make disproportionate provision for issues (such as formal
validity) which are of only occasional practical importance. As a result, it
is instructive to look at the issues which might be raised in a simple
contract action in an English court, and to examine how and where these
points are accommodated by the Rome Convention. We will proceed on
the assumption that C is suing D, a defendant habitually resident in
England, for breach of contract, and examine the elements of the law of
contract as if raised by D as a defence to the claim. We will also assume
that by the governing law, which will be ascertained on the basis that the
contract is, for this purpose at least, assumed to be valid, the contract
would be valid and enforceable, and all the defences raised by D would
fail; but that as a matter of English domestic law, the several defences
raised by D would be well founded and that, also on the facts, D would
satisfy the requirement of its being reasonable for him to rely on his own
law.

If D argues that he is not bound and cannot be liable because there was
no *offer and acceptance*, this plea is a matter for the governing law, for it
goes to the validity of the contract; but D may rely on his own, English,
law to demonstrate that he did not consent, by reason of Article 8(2). If D
argues that there was no *intention to create legal relations*, the effect of this
plea will be a matter for the governing law. But if D formulates the
argument to say he did not consent to, nor had any reason to suppose that
he was, entering into legal relations at all, because under English law such
an agreement would not be legally enforceable, Article 8(2) may avail
him. If D argues that the alleged contract cannot be enforced because the
price was never agreed, and there was therefore no *certainty of contractual
terms*, the governing law may again be displaced by the argument that D
cannot be held to have consented to something which, as a matter of his
own law, he could never have been bound by; and if this is so, Article 8(2)
is in principle available to him. All these issues go to the existence of
consent to bind oneself to enforceable obligations.

If D argues that he is not bound because there was no *consideration* for
the promise, and that he knew that if he asked for nothing of value in

return for C's promise, then he could not be said to have given his consent to be legally bound to C, it seems arguable that Article 8(2) will apply here also, even though the governing law would not regard this as a necessity for the formation of a contract. If C argues that he contracted to benefit C2, who was not a party to the contract, nor known about by D, and that under the governing law C2 may sue in his own name, D may say that under the English doctrine of *privity*[95] he would not be bound to, and did not consent to be bound by, C2. Likewise, if C argues that he contracted with D2 and the effect of their contract under its governing law was that D was bound by an obligation in it, D may argue that under the English doctrine of privity he is not taken to consent to be bound to an obligation in a contract to which he was a stranger. Article 8(2) may preserve his right to argue that he did not consent to be bound by the obligation created by the contract. These issues may not go to the question whether D agreed something with somebody, but if D submits that he did not consent to an agreement which would have legal effect or that he never consented to be bound to C2 or by D2, it is arguable, despite the apparent view of Giuliano-Lagarde, that these arguments go to the existence of the consent which C asserts and D denies.

If C argues that D is bound despite the fact that there was a *limitation or exclusion clause* in the contract, the validity of this defence will be a matter for the governing law to assess. But if the governing law would regard the limitation clause as valid, it may still be struck down as a matter of English law by reference to Article 7(2), assuming that the provision of English law relied on is one which must be applied by a judge whatever the governing law.

If D argues that his agreement was procured by *fraud*, or *negligent or innocent misstatement*, or by *material non-disclosure*, or by *duress*, or by the exercise of *undue influence*, the legal effect of his plea is that his consent was vitiated and, subject to conditions, is capable of being wiped away. If the governing law would nevertheless regard these pleas as insufficient to ground relief, may D rely on Article 8(2) to establish that he did not consent? Perhaps not: unlike issues relating to offer and acceptance, these are not factors where D will have known or believed at the time, or if asked at the time would have said that his own law provided that he was not bound to the other. Yet D may know that he has been the victim of what may be duress or undue influence; he may know that as matter of

---

[95] But cf Contracts (Rights of Third Parties) Act 1999 for modification of English common law.

English law he has no need to check the accuracy of representations made by another, or that he was entitled to rely on C to make disclosure in a contract made in the utmost good faith, so that he will not be bound if he relies on misrepresentations; and he may rely on the security of his own law accordingly, just as he does when he throws away an offer letter, knowing that he cannot be bound by it. Seen in those terms it is plausible that Article 8(2) should be relevant here too, for an alleged consent which does not bind D, and which D is right to assume does not bind D, is no consent at all. If D argues that the alleged contract was void on the basis of a mutual *mistake*, or his own unilateral mistake, this is, in effect, a confusion which prevents the parties coming to an agreement, and Article 8(2) is applicable in principle. If he argues that the alleged contract was void on the basis of fundamental common mistake or should be set aside on the basis of less fundamental common mistake, D is arguing that he did not consent to the terms of the contract alleged by C, because there was nothing to consent about.

If D argues that he cannot be made to perform because the contract was one which required him to perform an act which would be *illegal* under the law of the place where performance was called for, the validity of the contract is in principle a matter for the governing law, and if under that law the illegality renders the contract unenforceable there is no more to be said.[96] But the governing law may not accept this as an excuse for non-performance and, on that basis, would stand at odds with the common law, which probably held that illegality under the law of the place where the contract was to be performed rendered the contract unenforceable, whatever its proper law: an English court could hardly make an order on the basis that D was required to commit a crime in the place of performance. It is correct to point out that it was never completely clear whether this was a rule of private international law, or just the application of English domestic law: the reported cases all concerned contracts whose proper law was English, though the width of the language used did not give the impression of being restricted to English contracts,[97] and it may be suggested that the answer depends on the magnitude of the illegality, and on the awareness of the party prepared to commit it.[98] Had it been

---

[96] Art. 10.

[97] *Ralli Bros.* v. *Compania Naviera Sota y Aznar* [1920] 2 KB 287 (CA); *Foster* v. *Driscoll* [1929] 1 KB 470 (CA); *Regazzoni* v. *K. C. Sethia (1944) Ltd.* [1958] AC 301; *Lemenda Trading Co. Ltd.* v. *African Middle East Petroleum Co. Ltd.* [1989] QB 728; *Euro-Diam Ltd.* v. *Bathurst* [1990] 1 QB 30 (CA); *Soleimany* v. *Soleimany* [1999] QB 785, 803 (CA).

[98] Cf *Royal Boskalis Westminster NV* v. *Mountain* [1999] QB 674 (CA).

possible to have recourse to Article 7(1), an English court might have been permitted to apply the law of the place of performance, but this provision is not part of English law, and it may be that its exclusion has killed off a rule about illegality under the law of the place of performance. But there are two alternatives. First, to apply the provision of the governing law which required performance of a criminal act, or an act tainted with illegality, may be manifestly contrary to public policy, and therefore precluded by Article 16. Secondly, however, the rule of the common law, whatever it was, may still shine through the gap in the fabric of the Convention created by the excision of Article 7(1). In other words, the question whether and when the mandatory rules of a third country (not that whose law governs the contract or that of the courts hearing the case) may be applied is a matter for the common law to answer as the Convention does not; and according to the common law, it is only laws of the place of performance, rendering performance illegal, which can be picked up and applied by the English court.

If D argues that he cannot be sued because C's action is barred by *limitation* or prescription, this plea will be determined by the governing law. Article 10(1)(d) so provides, but the Foreign Limitation Periods Act 1984 had already brought English private international law into line with this.

If D argues that the contract was *discharged by performance* or by C's *breach*, or by *frustration*, the plea will be dealt with by the governing law, according to Article 10. If D denies that C is entitled to the particular *remedy* claimed, the answer will come from the governing law. The extent to which an English court is required to grant remedies available under the governing law but which an English court would not grant is uncertain, but an English court will probably be expected to follow and apply the remedial provisions of the governing law unless this is too inconvenient to be practicable, or would contravene some fundamental policy of English law.

6

Torts

GENERAL

After its century of tranquil slumber, during which hardly any cases were reported and the law underwent neither development nor degeneration, the rules for choice of law in tort now seem to be in a state of continual revolution.[1] In 1971 the House of Lords charted a new course for the private international law of torts, and subsequent decisions refined and polished it. In the 1990s the Law Commission, and then Parliament, thought to show they could do better; and some idiosyncratic legislation was enacted. To mark the new millennium, the European Commission pretends to consider that the completion of the internal market cannot be achieved without uniform choice of law rules for torts; and a Council Regulation is proposed to be settled and adopted within the next few years.

The choice of law rules for tort claims divide into two parts. For torts which occurred before 1 May 1996, and for claims whenever occurring alleging defamation, malicious falsehood, and similar complaints, the choice of rules of the common law remains in force by grace of the Private International Law (Miscellaneous Provisions) Act 1995.[2] For all other tort claims, the 1995 Act imposes new choice of law rules which, if destined to become clear and coherent with the benefit of much judicial and scholastic effort, nevertheless begin life as damaged goods. Moreover, as they are in places defined by reference to the rules of the common law, an understanding of these is a prerequisite to application of the 1995 Act. The scheme of this chapter is therefore to examine the rules of the common law, then those of the 1995 Act.

---

[1] See generally Dicey & Morris, *The Conflict of Laws* (13th edn., Sweet & Maxwell, London, 2000) chap. 35. For the background to the 1995 Act see Law Commission, *Private International Law: Choice of Law in Tort and Delict* (Law Com No 193, HMSO, London, 1990); *Proceedings of the Special Public Bill Committee* (HL Paper (1995) no 36). For comment on the 1995 Act, see A. Briggs, 'Choice of Law in Tort and Delict' [1995] *LMCLQ* 519.

[2] Hereafter 'the 1995 Act'.

JURISDICTION OVER TORT CLAIMS

Tort claims will usually arise as civil or commercial matters, and jurisdiction over defendants alleged to have committed them will fall within the domain of Council Regulation (EC) 44/2001, the details of which have been discussed above.[3] If a tort raises an issue of title to foreign land, or involves the enforcement of foreign intellectual property rights, there is, as a matter of common law, no subject matter jurisdiction.[4] In relation to foreign land, the common law rule was modified by the Civil Jurisdiction and Judgments Act 1982, section 30, with the result that the court will not lack jurisdiction unless the tort claim is *principally* concerned with title to foreign land;[5] and it has been said,[6] if unconvincingly,[7] that the corresponding rule about foreign intellectual property rights, which was not affected by section 30 of the 1982 Act, was never well founded. In any event, where personal jurisdiction over the defendant can be derived from the Regulation, these common law limitations are held by many to be inapplicable, even though they are concerned with subject matter jurisdiction, rather than personal jurisdiction over defendants. Where jurisdiction has to be established by service out of the jurisdiction with the permission of the court, CPR rule 6.20(8) is the applicable paragraph.[8]

CHOICE OF LAW IN TORT

Despite the fact that it appeared to generate little judicial interest in England until the end of the twentieth century, choice of law in tort claims produced an enormous amount of academic examination and, particularly in the lush litigational grasslands of the United States, a considerable amount of creative judicial thinking. A contract is an agreement, and the law which will be applied will often be that which the parties chose or, if not, will be deduced from points of connection which were known to the parties from the start. Torts, by contrast, are the law's accidents: essentially messy and unplanned, and covering a much more diverse set of interests and duties. It is arguable that a single choice of law rule is being stretched beyond its proper limits when it has to encompass

---

[3] [2001] OJ L12/1; Chap. 2, above. [4] Pp. 48–50, above.
[5] As to which see *Re Polly Peck International plc (No 2)* [1998] 3 All ER 812 (CA).
[6] *Pearce v. Ove Arup Partnership Ltd.* [2000] Ch. 403 (CA).
[7] Because the authorities on the common law position, though predominantly Australian, left little room for doubt.
[8] Above, p. 103.

claims which may include personal injury, liability for animals, defamation, nuisance, unfair competition, and conspiracy; but when causes of
action arising under foreign laws of tort and delict are added in, a single
and reliable choice of law rule, whether very flexible or very inflexible,
will be difficult to devise. Not only that, but the parties to a contract know
of each other, and the range of persons with a potential claim will therefore be limited and predictable; the parties to a tort claim, often thrown
together or strewn about by the tort, are only occasionally knowable in
advance. In devising choice of law rules this has to be borne in mind.

As a matter of history, choice of law rules in tort tended to rigidity, and
to centre on the *lex fori* or the *lex loci delicti commissi*. The justification for
the *lex fori* was sometimes said to lie in the similarity between torts and
crimes, but this was never really convincing, and a better view was that
the imposition of legal duties and civil obligations without regard to the
will of the parties was a matter on which each court was entitled to prefer
the standards of its own law. The justification for the *lex loci delicti commissi* was the homely advice that when in Rome, one should do as Romans
do. Even at this level of generality each has an attraction, and maybe this
was the reason English law blended the two into a rule of double actionability. But the objection that either could result in the application of a
law which had little genuine or durable connection with the parties, or the
facts of the claim, does not need illustration. This led to suggestions that,
in the same way that a contract was governed by a proper law, so should a
tort be.[9] The objection that it was one thing to subject a consensual, pre-
litigation, relationship to a proper law, but quite another to subject an
unplanned or non-relationship to the same process was obvious, but the
sense that only the proper law could guarantee that the law eventually
applied was the 'right' law was also strong. This sense manifested itself in
different ways. In England, it led to the development of a flexible exception to the erstwhile rigid rule of double actionability, thus resulting in a
high degree of predictability which could nevertheless yield in the face of
unusual facts. In the United States it led to a more fundamental re-
casting of the choice of law rule, to abandon the hegemony of the *lex loci
delicti commissi* in favour of a variety of alternative techniques. These
alternative approaches to choice of law flourished in the United States,
mainly because it was considered that the application of the law of the
place of the tort is less attractive within a federation in which each of the

[9] The suggestion is traceable back to J. H. C. Morris, 'The Proper Law of a Tort' (1951)
64 *Harv. LR* 881.

states is legally foreign but not noticeably geographically so: whereas it may be plain within Europe that one is in Rome, it may not be so obvious in the United States that one is not in Kansas any more. Inter-state trade and traffic are such that a rigid preference for the law of the place where the tort occurred has an appreciable chance of choosing a law which was accidental in both senses. So a variety of alternatives was developed to seek the elusive goal of an intuitively right answer derived nevertheless from scientific theory. In the first case to breach the dam,[10] the New York Court of Appeals experimented with a test of closest connection, and with a more complex approach which asked (and sought to answer) which state or states had laws which were intended, or interested, to apply to the particular issue before the court for decision: an approach puzzlingly entitled 'governmental interest analysis'.[11] The debate later extended to inquire which state's law would be the most impaired if not applied;[12] to the use of a 'better law' approach,[13] a technique liable to make it difficult for a court not to apply its own domestic law; and the result cannot be said to promote the goal of legal certainty, whatever else it may do.[14]

An English lawyer may recoil from the thought that a clear rule, with provision for an exception to serve as a pressure valve, should be abandoned in favour of a more individual approach. After all, though torts may be accidental and unplanned, the taking of insurance against liability for torts is a public good; and an approach which makes it uncertain which law will govern a claim is one which is difficult to insure against. But if the American jurisprudence demonstrates that one size of choice of law rule does not fit all, it has done a valuable job.

In Canada and Australia, by striking contrast, the fact that many torts take place in sister states has moved the courts in precisely the opposite direction from that which drew support in the United States. Faced with the need to fashion a choice of law rule for torts committed in another Canadian province, the Supreme Court of Canada opted for a rigid *lex loci delicti* rule,[15] on the footing that this was both correct and in step with Canada's sense and understanding of sovereignty. Faced with similar facts in relation to intra-Australian torts, the High Court of Australia also

---

[10] *Babcock* v. *Jackson*, 191 NE 2d 279 (1963), [1963] 2 Lloyd's Rep. 286 (NY CA).

[11] B. Currie, *Selected Essays on the Conflict of Laws* (Duke University Press, Durham, NC, 1963).

[12] *Bernard* v. *Harrah's Club*, 546 P 2d 719 (1976).

[13] *Cipolla* v. *Shaposka*, 262 A 2d 854 (1970); *Clark* v. *Clark*, 222 A 2d 205 (1966).

[14] For an annual survey of choice of law in the American courts see S. Symeonides in the *American Journal of Comparative Law* from vol. 36 (1988) to the present.

[15] *Tolofson* v. *Jensen* [1994] 3 SCR 1022, (1994) 120 DLR (4th) 299.

opted for a rigid and inflexible *lex loci delicti* rule,[16] also spurning the path taken in the United States, and going out of its way to express disapproval of the pragmatic English common law amalgam of rules and exceptions. Whether it will adopt precisely the same approach in relation to an over-seas tort is unknown,[17] but it has been the experience of other jurisdic-tions that the need to make an exception in the interests of flexibility becomes irresistible when the facts are sufficiently unusual. In Canada and Australia, the influence of constitutional theory, and respect for the sovereignty of sister states and provinces, had a significant impact on the development of the choice of law rule. If something similar were to emerge in England, the most likely engine of change would be an analogous developing sense of federation within Europe. And all this modern questioning of received choice of law rules does raise the ques-tion whether there are, in the conflict of laws in general but in tort in particular, differing degrees of foreignness, which in turn suggest that the law should develop choice of law rules which vary according to their context. After all, it is striking to see an English court treating a tort committed in Scotland or Ireland in precisely the same way as it would one committed in China or Peru, and it may yet come to be accepted that a tort committed within the territory of the European Union is less foreign than one committed outside, so that the approaches to choice of law may differ. The American, and Canadian and Australian, re-examinations of choice of law may in fact be symptoms of that emerging distinction.

Be that as it may, the outcome is that the private international law of tort has been the testing ground for the development of alternatives to the traditional view of a single choice of law rule which can be applied to all causes of action within a single and broad characterization category. As a matter of fact, this development is now unlikely to take place in Europe, as English and European legislation substitutes bureaucratic dogmatism for the probing analytical techniques of common law sophistication.

COMMON LAW CHOICE OF LAW AND THE PLACE OF THE TORT

The choice of law rules of the common law drew a fundamental distinc-tion according to where the tort was committed, and the location of the

[16] *John Pfeiffer Pty. Ltd.* v. *Rogerson* (2000) 172 ALR 625, modifying *Breavington* v. *Godleman* (1988) 169 CLR 41 and *McKain* v. *R. W. Miller & Co. (South Australia) Pty. Ltd.* (1991) 174 CLR 1.

[17] *Zhang* v. *Régie Nationale des Usines Renault SA*, 27 July 2000, not yet reported (NSW CA); under appeal to the High Court of Australia.

tort was therefore the starting point for analysis of choice of law. These choice of law rules continue to be applicable to torts in which the acts or omissions were committed before 1 May 1996, and to defamation whether committed before or after that date.[18]

The location of a tort was not problematic where all the elements comprising the claim were concentrated in one place. But where they were not, any test of location was bound to be imperfect. Some courts preferred the view that it was the place of the damage, for until there is damage there is no tort; but the illogic[19] and arbitrariness of this were easy to see, and it was soon abandoned. The test which came to prevail was to ask where in substance the cause of action arose,[20] and the answer was given by English law as the law which defines the connecting factor. For example, if a dangerous pharmaceutical product was sold and ingested in one place, this was where the cause of action arose, at least if the damage manifested itself in the same place, even though it had been engineered and manufactured elsewhere.[21] If negligent professional advice was received and acted on in one place, this was where the cause of action arose, even though the information grew out of work done elsewhere or the economic consequences were felt elsewhere.[22] If a defamatory statement was transmitted into a place where it was heard and the reputation of the victim injured, this was where the cause of action arose, even though the statement originated elsewhere.[23] Though occasionally rough and ready, and open to some manipulation by a court, the test was hallowed by usage. And even though it leaves a margin of appreciation to the judge, it is as workable as any 'place' rule could be. This is especially true when, as was found in almost every instance, the court was able to assemble the facts so that damage and the act complained of were located in a single place. In the one case where this alignment was not possible, the acts (a conspiracy) could have taken place anywhere, but the intended damage could have happened only in England: the place of the damage was taken as the indicative element.[24]

---

[18] 1995 Act, s. 13 (defamation), s. 14(1) (date).
[19] After all, there is no tort without a tortfeasor either.
[20] *Metall und Rohstoff AG* v. *Donaldson Lufkin & Jenrette Inc.* [1990] 1 QB 391 (CA).
[21] *Distillers & Co. Ltd.* v. *Thompson* [1971] AC 458 (PC).
[22] *Diamond* v. *Bank of London and Montreal* [1979] QB 333 (CA). But for a different view in relation to negligent advice from an accountant see *Voth* v. *Manildra Flour Mills Pty. Ltd.* (1990) 171 CLR 538, 568–9 (Aust. HC).
[23] *Bata* v. *Bata* [1948] WN 366 (CA); cf *Shevill* v. *Presse Alliance SA* [1992] 2 WLR 1 (CA), and as Case C–68/93 *Shevill* v. *Presse Alliance SA* [1995] ECR I–415.
[24] *Metall & Rohstoff AG* v. *Donaldson Lufkin & Jenrette Inc.* [1990] 1 QB 391 (CA).

The 1995 Act, proceeding from the need to protect free speech by reference to English standards, preserves the common law rules and defences for defamation, malicious falsehood, and torts (which must arise under foreign law) of a similar nature,[25] and so for these it may well be necessary to determine where the cause of action arose. But it is the privilege of the claimant to specify and to plead the facts and matters upon which he relies: if, as increasingly seems to happen,[26] he chooses to sue only in respect of publication of the statement in England, England will be where the cause of action arose.[27] By contrast, if the complaint is extended to multi-national publication of defamatory material, it is probable that each substantial national publication must be taken, and the law chosen for it, separately. The reason for this inconvenient result is that as a matter of English law, and in fact, each publication is a separate and distinct tort, and this principle has been relied on in the context of international defamation.[28] Even so, the choice of law rule for defamation contains a flexible exception, and it may be that this would be taken to permit a marshalling of international publications into a single choice of law.

Choice of law for English torts

Where the cause of action arose in England, English domestic law applies, alone and exclusively, and without any exception to reflect the fact that neither the parties nor the facts may have any measurable connection with England, but are wholly associated with another country.[29] True, the resultant application of English law could have been produced by the application of the double-actionability choice of law rule for foreign torts, but woven into that rule is a flexible exception, and it is this which is therefore specifically excluded from application to English torts. One can see how this is inconvenient: a defamatory statement made, for example, within a delegation of visitors will have no discernible impact on the English legal order, but may be enormously significant in the country of origin. If the trial nevertheless takes place in England,[30] the case for the

---

[25] 1995 Act, s. 13.

[26] Ironically, it appears that this shows English defamation law to be attractive to claimants, and a matter of concern to defendants who have exercised a freedom to speak. If this is so, the law appears to appeal at one and the same time to potential litigants with opposite interests, which is a remarkable state of affairs.

[27] *Berezovsky* v. *Michaels* [2000] 1 WLR 1004 (HL).   [28] Ibid.

[29] *Metall und Rohstoff AG* v. *Donaldson Lufkin & Jenrette Inc.* [1990] 1 QB 391 (CA).

[30] This may seem implausible, but *Berezovsky* v. *Michaels* [2000] 1 WLR 1004 (HL) suggests that England may be an attractive place for a claimant to sue.

non-application of English domestic law could hardly be higher, but on the authorities it will not succeed. A defendant applying in such a case for a stay of proceedings on the ground of *forum non conveniens* may be thought to have some chance of success, but the natural forum for an English tort is unlikely to be overseas;[31] and the defendant may have little to gain in any event from giving up the right to defend in England.

Choice of law for overseas torts

Where the cause of action arose in a foreign country, a claimant is required to show two things: that the facts would give rise to liability as a tort as a matter of English domestic law as *lex fori*, and also give[32] rise to civil[33] liability, though not necessarily in tort, under the domestic *lex loci delicti*, the law of the place where the tort occurred. This is a rule of 'double actionability'.[34] It follows from the *lex fori* limb[35] that the only claims which can succeed are those in respect of torts known to English domestic law. Though this rule came in for criticism, and was latterly modified by the incorporation of a flexible exception,[36] it achieved two significant advantages. First, it ensured that there was a limit to the claims which could be brought before an English court. The law of tort generally imposes liability without regard to the will or intentions of the defendant, and is in this respect the dark side of the law of civil liberties. It is not altogether unreasonable to regard English civil liberties as the benchmark for the reception of claims otherwise arising under foreign law, especially where there is room for flexibility.[37] Secondly, the use of English tort law gave a foundation for the question where the tort occurred: 'the' tort must have meant the cause of action as understood and defined by English domestic law. The *lex loci delicti commissi* limb was originally stated in terms of the acts not being justifiable[38] under the foreign law; this came to be understood as asking whether the facts gave rise to civil liability under the foreign law.[39] Taken in its two parts, the

---

[31] Cf *Berezovsky* v. *Michaels* [2000] 1 WLR 1004 (HL).

[32] Not 'gave': limitation under the *lex loci delicti commissi* will bar the claim: Foreign Limitation Periods Act 1984, s. 1(2).

[33] So established by *Boys* v. *Chaplin* [1971] AC 356, and on this point overruling *Machado* v. *Fontes* [1897] 2 QB 231 (CA), which had accepted criminal liability as sufficient to allow the action to proceed.

[34] *Boys* v. *Chaplin* [1971] AC 356.   [35] *The Halley* (1868) LR 2 PC 193.

[36] *Red Sea Insurance Co. Ltd.* v. *Bouygues SA* [1995] 1 AC 190 (PC).

[37] Though free recourse to public policy might have been a sufficient alternative role for the *lex fori*.

[38] *Phillips* v. *Eyre* (1870) LR 6 QB 1.   [39] *Boys* v. *Chaplin*, above n. 14.

rule serves to identify which defendant is liable, to establish which defences are available, and to limit heads of damage recoverable, to the more restrictive of English tort law and the civil law of the *locus delicti*. Unless the claimant can show that he is entitled to recover under both systems he will lose. So in a defamation claim, a defence of truth or privilege or fair comment, made out under English law, will answer a claim even though it would not do so under the civil law of the place where the cause of action arose; a defence under the foreign law, say of political free speech, though unknown as such to English law,[40] will similarly prevail to defeat the claim.

By way of exception, if the law of some other country is more closely connected to an issue, or even to the whole dispute, than is the *lex loci delicti*, that law may displace the reference made to the *lex loci delicti*. It is not clear whether this is exactly the same thing as saying that the particular law will not be applied if it has no interest in being applied to the particular facts, but both propositions have been advanced, without apparent recognition of their difference.[41] So where two English servicemen were involved in a traffic accident in Malta, English law displaced Maltese law for defining the heads of recoverable damage;[42] where an English employment agency sent a labourer to work on a German site, English law displaced German law on the nature and extent of the duty of care owed by the agency.[43] Building on this principle, it was later held that in an appropriate case, the reference to English law as *lex fori* may be displaced in favour of a law having a much closer connection to the dispute than the *lex fori*.[44] As a result the choice of law rule may be summarized as 'double actionability with double flexibility'. But the curious thing about the exception, especially in the formulation which asks whether the foreign law has any interest in being applied to the facts, is that it is asked at all. In the Maltese case just mentioned, the view was[45] that the Maltese legislature had not intended its law to apply to the facts of such a case, and it was disapplied. The imprecise science involved in coming to any such conclusion, however, would have been unnecessary if

---

[40] *Reynolds* v. *Times Newspapers Ltd.* [2001] 2 AC 127.

[41] *Boys* v. *Chaplin* [1971] AC 356: the 'closest connection' test may point to the application of the law of a third state, that is, neither the country of the forum nor of the place of the tort; the 'no interest in being applied' test will simply disconnect the foreign law, leaving English law to apply by default.

[42] *Boys* v. *Chaplin* [1971] AC 356.

[43] *Johnson* v. *Coventry Churchill International Ltd.* [1992] 3 All ER 14.

[44] *Red Sea Insurance Co. Ltd.* v. *Bouygues SA* [1995] 1 AC 190 (PC).

[45] *Boys* v. *Chaplin*, above n. 42, at 391–2 (Lord Wilberforce).

the *lex* of the *locus delicti* were interpreted as meaning the law *including its conflicts rules*. On that basis, it would be perfectly clear whether the Maltese rule was intended to apply: one would simply ask whether the Maltese judge would have applied it had he been trying the case. The inclusion of *renvoi* in the *lex loci delicti commissi* would have achieved, at a stroke, what the exception sought to do by unreliable means. An opportunity was lost.[46]

Despite the fact that double actionability means that the claimant must be able to win under both systems of law, it has sometimes been said that under the common law choice of law, the English law of tort applies, subject only to a condition in relation to the foreign law. This is misleading if it is meant to indicate that one of the two limbs is stronger than the other,[47] but this analysis has gained a tenacious foothold.[48] Even so, if the proposition could be reversed and still be equally accurate it serves no purpose. It does not help to contend that one co-equal limb of the test dominates the other.

STATUTORY CHOICE OF LAW: PART III OF THE 1995 ACT

Part III of the 1995 Act establishes a new choice of law rule which applies to all other torts. The Act is expressed to apply to all issues which were, prior to 1 May 1996, governed by the common law rule of double actionability with exceptions.[49] It is necessary to identify the material scope of the Act, and then its choice of law rule.

Material scope

The 1995 Act applies to torts, but without offering a definition of the term.[50] It cannot be restricted to causes of action which are regarded as torts under English domestic law, for this is one half of the very rule which section 10 of the Act was enacted to abolish, so it must extend to causes of action which are in some more general sense characterized as torts. This is easier to state than to accomplish. One effect of the rule of double actionability was that the common law conflict of laws was never called upon to characterize a claim which was not a tort as a matter of English domestic law, for the double actionability rule ensured that every

[46] See A. Briggs, 'In Praise and Defence of Renvoi' (1998) 47 *ICLQ* 877.
[47] Since *Red Sea Insurance* v. *Bouygues*, above n. 44, which allowed for either limb of the test to be disapplied, it cannot be said that one rather than another has the stronger hold on the case.
[48] *Boys* v. *Chaplin*, above n. 45, at 389; *Coupland* v. *Arabian Gulf Oil Co.* [1983] 1 WLR 1151 (CA).
[49] 1995 Act, s. 10.   [50] Ibid. s. 9.

such claim simply failed. But with that benchmark gone, it is necessary to draw some lines. Claims based on the violation of privacy, or insult, unless seen as akin to defamation;[51] claims for pure economic loss resulting from negligence, or alleging the wrongful infliction of economic loss, or based on a general *actio injuriarum* and so on should fall within the scope of the Act, on the ground that they were technically covered (not that it did the claimant any good) by the rule on double actionability. But claims for damages as a result of the breach of a statutory duty, and especially those which lie closer to public or regulatory law, may fall outside the category of torts by reason of their public law character. So claims founded on the violation of competition law, or for payments in respect of damage caused by environmental pollution, will lie much closer to the edges of the rule. On the other hand, claims for treble damages under the Racketeer Influenced and Corrupt Organizations Act, and the Clayton and Sherman Acts, of US law are considered to be torts, and subject to the argument that their application is contrary to English public policy, such claims will now be possible in the English courts. It is debatable whether this is a change for the benefit of the law and litigants, for the reliable assessment of some of these foreign rights may be difficult for an English court.

But problems abound, for it appears that the dismantling of the common law was not as simple as it appeared. In seeking to ascertain the scope of the Act, three particular difficulties may be observed. First, section 10 states that the Act repeals the rules on double actionability plus exceptions; and section 14(2) provides in express terms that the Act does not affect any matter which was not previously governed by these section 10 rules. It follows from this form of words that the Act has no application to torts committed in England. This would be an odd, and probably unintended, result, but it will take some rather muscular statutory construction to circumvent the plain language of the Act. True, section 9(6) provides that the Act will still apply even though events took place in England, but that is very different from establishing that the tort was committed in England; and it is in any event expressed to be subject to section 14. If the authority which established the irrelevance of double actionability to English torts were to be overruled, section 9(6) might be given the wider effect which would allow the Act to apply to English torts. The legislative methodology is incomprehensible, but it would have required little ingenuity to

---

[51] 1995 Act, s. 13.

enact that the Act applies to torts committed in England if that had been intended.

Secondly, as will be seen, the Act[52] directs attention to, and selects, the law of the place where the events constituting the tort occurred. This is not as easy as it seems. It is, in fact, unintelligible unless it has already been decided which law, and hence which law's identification of the elements which make up the tort, is applicable. Yet this is what the statutory test is meant to determine in the first place: one might say that the chicken and the egg have come home to roost. The point is best made by illustration. Suppose an Italian claimant, in possession of promissory notes, has these impounded by an English bank, on suspicion of impropriety, the notes not being returned despite its being accepted that the seizure was unwarranted.[53] If this were looked at from the standpoint of English law, there would be a claim against the bank for conversion, most of the elements of which took place in England. But from the standpoint of Italian law, the elements of the delict of *injuria* committed by the bank, by which the patrimonial estate of the claimant was diminished, were mostly located in Italy. The two torts are constructed differently, and to choose the law of the place where the elements of 'the' tort occurred is irrational. It cannot be right to frame the answer in terms of the English tort, for when there is none, the claimant would necessarily lose, and it would be found that the first limb of the double actionability rule had risen from the deep. Equally, there is no particular reason to prefer the Italian over the English analysis, because Italy may not be the place where the elements of the tort occurred. This may not be crucial if both ways of formulating the claim would lead to recovery in the same measure, but if the claimant would win in one but not the other, what is the outcome to be? Is the claimant entitled to cast around for whichever of the possible formulations would benefit him, and rely on that law alone? It seems unsatisfactory, but the best answer is not clear. Authority is of no assistance: this difficulty could not have arisen when the first limb of the double actionability rule defined recovery in terms of English torts. The most practical solution may be to identify the elements in the drama, as distinct from the events which make up the as yet undefined tort, and to ask where these in substance occurred. Some heavy-duty sticking plaster is needed to repair the Act.

Thirdly, it is unclear to what extent the Act will apply to claims which

---

[52] 1995 Act, s. 11.
[53] Cf Case C–364/93 *Marinari* v. *Lloyd's Bank plc* [1995] ECR I–2719.

may be regarded as tortious under some systems of law, but which have been characterized differently as a matter of English private international law. There is authority for the view that claims alleging the wrongs of breach of confidence or dishonest assistance in another's breach of trust, and other breaches of equitable duty were not governed by the rule of double actionability,[54] even though they resembled torts; nor were claims for contribution, nor restitutionary claims, such as for knowing receipt of trust property, which did not look like torts.[55] If these may nevertheless be torts under a potentially-applicable foreign law, it is unclear whether their prior or potential non-tortious characterization under common law renders the 1995 Act inapplicable to them, leaving them governed by common law choice of law rules. Maybe they did not appear to have fallen under the rules set out in section 10, not being actionable as torts, and followed an alternative path to choice of law. But they may have been governed by the rule of double actionability, in the sense that they were never pursued by a claimant who was well aware that he would fail if he tried. The best answer may be that if the claim is formulated as a non-contractual wrong, it should be governed by the choice of law rules of the 1995 Act. This is a strange way to go about law reform.

Choice of law: general rule

According to section 11, if all the events constituting the tort occur in one country, the law of that country applies to the claim. But if the events are less conveniently grouped, a claim in respect of death or personal injury (including disease, or impairment of physical or mental condition) is in the first instance governed by the law of the place where the victim was when killed or injured;[56] a claim in respect of property damage by the law of the place where the property was when damaged;[57] and any other case by the law of the country in which the most significant element or elements of the events constituting the tort occurred.[58]

Personal injury appears to cover psychiatric trauma or nervous shock; but a cause of action for bereavement on death appears to be governed by the law of the place where the deceased was killed, rather than the place

---

[54] In so far as they were characterized as equitable or restitutionary obligations they had their own choice of law rule: and see below, Chap. 7.

[55] Though *Arab Monetary Fund* v. *Hashim (No 9)* [1994] TLR 502 made some use of the rule of double actionability in relation to a claim for dishonestly assisting a breach of trust, this was not on the basis that the claim was one in tort. It is not therefore affected by the 1995 Act.

[56] 1995 Act, s. 11(2)(a).   [57] Ibid., s. 11(2)(b).

[58] Ibid., s. 11(2)(c), which was examined in the previous section above.

where the claimant was when bereaved. Where the damage manifests itself long after and far away from the place where the rot originally set in, such as where asbestosis is diagnosed decades after the inhalation of fibres, it appears that a claim for personal injury will generally be governed by the law of the place of inhalation, but a claim brought in respect of death will be governed by the law of the place where the victim died. If either of these leads to an arbitrary or unsatisfactory result, the rule of displacement in section 12 will be available as a corrective. Damage to property appears to exclude the loss of property, for example by theft or conversion; it works well for tangible property, but less clearly for intangibles. It does not appear to extend to cases of pure economic loss, unless this can be seen as damage to intangible property, which does not seem likely; though if a foreign law takes the view that the gist of the tort is one of damage to the patrimony of the claimant, the position is less clear. The infringement of intellectual property rights, though regarded as a tort, is not usually thought of as resulting in property damage, though it may be argued that this is exactly what an infringer does to the intellectual property of the claimant. And it is outside the cases of personal injury and property damage that the problems of definition of 'tort', examined above, will most usually arise, where the analysis for choice of law requires the elements of the events constituting the tort to be identified before it is possible to identify the applicable law by which they will be defined.

It has been said by some that section 11 enacts a *lex loci delicti* choice of law rule.[59] It does no such thing. Had the Act sought to apply the *lex loci delicti commissi* as the choice of law rule, the point of departure would have been to ask where in substance the cause of action arose. Section 11 does not go down this path. Where all elements of the tort are grouped in the one place, any rational test for the general choice of law will give the same answer; it is no more a *lex loci delicti* rule than it is a place of damage rule, or a place of the act rule, or even a proper law of the tort rule. But where the events are not concentrated in that one place, it is neither necessary nor helpful to inquire into the place of the tort. The Law Commission, whose Report and draft Bill provided the basis for the 1995 Act, was explicit in its view that the *locus delicti* is too often artificial, a legal fiction, to be defensible as the basis for a choice of law rule.[60] Instead, the methodology adopted by the Act was to provide a simple,

[59] Dicey & Morris, above n. 1, para. 35–013.
[60] Law Commission, *Private International Law: Choice of Law in Tort and Delict* (Law Com No 193, HMSO, London, 1990), paras. 3.6, 3.10.

though sometimes arbitrary, rule; and to allow its displacement whenever necessary. If follows that old authorities which seek to define the place of the tort should really be of no assistance in the application of the general rule provided by the 1995 Act; and the result is that England has now departed from the choice of law rule which operates throughout almost the whole of the world. It is unlikely to be an export earner.

Choice of law: displacement of the general rule

Following the tradition of the common law, section 12 invites the making of a comparison between the factors which connect the tort with the country whose law was ascertained by the general rule in section 11 and the factors which connect it with another country. If it is substantially more appropriate to apply the law of the latter, this will displace the former law in relation to the claim or in relation to any individual issue, as the case may be: the points of connection are to countries, but the question of appropriateness is answered in terms of a law. So in the case of the two servicemen mentioned above[61] it would be substantially more appropriate to apply English law, and not Maltese law, to the particular issue of the recovery of general damages, for this issue is closely connected to England, where the injured party will be living, and it has no impact at all on the state of Malta. It would be different if the defendant were Maltese, not least because any insurance which he may have taken out will presumably have been undertaken with an eye to Maltese law and levels of liability. More problematic is the case in which the facts are just as unconnected to Malta, but the parties are from different countries, the law of each differing from Maltese law and allowing the recovery of damages for pain and suffering. On the face of it, section 12 works on the basis of a bipolar comparison only, and does not allow a more complex analysis to indicate the irrelevance of the law applicable by virtue of the general rule; in this respect it follows the pattern of the geographical 'centre of gravity' exception of the common law, and does not apparently support the interest analysis reasoning.

Section 12 allows displacement where it is not just an issue, but the whole question of liability, which is more closely connected to another country. In fact, the distinction between the case of liability in general and a head of damages in particular is more apparent than real, for the issue in the Maltese case is really whether there is any civil liability for

---

[61] P. 182, above; *Edmunds* v. *Simmonds* [2001] 1 WLR 1003 (two English friends, accident in Spain in a hired car; English displaces Spanish as the applicable law).

negligently inflicting pain and suffering on another, Maltese law answering that there was not. In the case of the contract labourer discussed above,[62] it would be substantially more appropriate to apply English law, and not to apply German law, to the entire question of liability, namely whether the English agency was liable for failing to provide a safe system of work, not least because no matter how close the factual connections were with Germany, the intentions of the parties may well have pointed to England as chosen governing law for the contract. But this does risk detaching appropriateness of laws from the geographical closeness of connection.

Choice of law: exclusion of certain laws

Section 14 makes clear that the Act does not authorize the enforcement of foreign penal or revenue or other public laws, nor of any foreign law whose enforcement would conflict with public policy, nor of any foreign law which would prevent a matter of procedure[63] being governed by English law; and it does not override the application of a rule of English law which is otherwise mandatory. In this respect it enacts what the common law had always provided, but the reference to other public laws is a novelty, and if at some later stage it is held that there is no such category of exclusion at common law, the legislation will be to that extent ineffective.

Contractual defences to tort claims

Where a defendant relies on a contractual promise that the claimant will not bring the action, a preliminary distinction must be drawn.[64] The question whether a valid contractual promise may be admitted as a defence to a claim in tort will be governed by the *lex delicti* as this has been identified by the 1995 Act. After all, a defence of *volenti* is governed by the *lex delicti*, and *volenti* and a contractual promise not to sue are two species of the same genus. But whether a contractual promise was validly made and binds the promisor, as distinct from whether it is effective as a defence if intrinsically valid, is a matter for the law which governs the contract. Quite apart from the common law logic of this, the answer is dictated by the 1995 Act: the validity of a contract has its own choice of law rule and was not, on the coming into force of the 1995 Act, governed

---

[62] Page 32, above.
[63] Such as quantification of damages: *Edmunds* v. *Simmonds* [2001] 1 WLR 1003.
[64] For the common law see *Sayers* v. *International Drilling Co. NV* [1971] 1 WLR 1176 (CA).

by the rule of double actionability.[65] Take the example of a workplace injury, the contract of employment containing an undertaking not to sue the employer but to participate in a scheme of insurance. Suppose the contract was governed by Saudi law, and that both the contract in general and the insurance provision in particular were valid and enforceable under Saudi law. This, subject to one proviso, establishes the intrinsic validity of the contractual defence (if it is not valid by its governing law, it will be disregarded). The proviso is that if a mandatory rule of English law strikes down such a term even in a foreign contract, this will be applied by virtue of the Rome Convention, Article 7(2).

But assuming the promise is validated by the contract choice of law rules, whether it will be admitted as a defence to the claim in tort is a matter for the law governing the tort. This will mean the law identified by section 11, subject to the possibility that the admissibility of a contractual promise not to sue may be more appropriately referred by section 12 to the law governing the contract. This is not a compelling argument, but it is one which has remote support at common law.[66] On the other hand, it may be contended that where the claim is brought between parties to a contract (say) of employment, the entire issue of liability and defence to liability may be contractual, with the result that the defence is one to a contractual action. The reasoning to support this would be that the entire claim is within the scope of the Rome Convention, as it seeks to enforce obligations freely entered into in relation to another, and the Convention provides that the *lex contractus* shall apply to all such obligations. In an unexpected way, this echoes a view of Lord Denning MR, to the effect that it was not appropriate to have a choice of law rule for claim and another for defence; it was preferable to have a unitary choice of law rule for such cases.[67] It is not yet supported by authority, but it is not unprincipled. Alternatively, section 12 of the 1995 Act could produce this result, on the footing that where a tort is committed within the context of a contractual relationship, it is substantially more appropriate—not least because this may be what the parties would have intended,[68] and may have insured against—to apply the law governing the contract, to the entire question of liability.

---

[65] 1995 Act, s. 14(2).
[66] *Sayers* v. *International Drilling Co. NV* [1971] 1 WLR 1176 (CA).
[67] Ibid.   [68] Especially where the choice of law has been expressed.

7

Other Obligations

GENERAL

As a matter of English domestic law, there are more sources of obligation than contracts and torts: two more need to be considered. Restitutionary obligations are now generally acknowledged to have an independent juridical basis, resting on the slightly shaky foundation of the principle against getting away with unjust enrichment. Though there is considerable uncertainty about what falls within it, it is not now disputed that there is a choice of law rule, or rules, for restitutionary claims, or that there is an appropriate characterization category. As a matter of domestic law, equitable obligations spring from a distinct historical origin, and remnants of this history have an uncertain impact on the plane of private international law. It is unclear whether this distinctiveness—domestic, jurisdictional, and historical—is also reflected in English private international law. Moreover, there is doubt about the methodology which is employed when equity meets the conflict of laws. For rather than characterize issues and choose a law, some cases simply allow a claimant to rely on domestic English equity, albeit tweaked to make some allowance for the foreign connections in the case; and if this is indeed the way to proceed, there appears to be little chance of relying on a foreign cause of action framed along similar lines. Despite the pervasive character of equity, and despite the fact that the Chancery Division and Commercial Court appear to spend much of their time handling litigation against international frauds and fraudsters, the case law is strikingly under-developed; and where it exists, it can be very difficult to comprehend.

The difficulty is compounded by the fact that courts and scholars have failed to reach a consensus on the fundamental nature of these two areas as part of English domestic law. Within restitution, a state of continual intellectual revolution appears to prevail, and domestic law causes of action are regarded and disregarded as restitutionary with unsettling rapidity. There appears to be some overlap with the domains of contract and tort, which is not itself unprecedented in the common law,[1] but which will tend only to increase as remedies for breach of contract stray further from the limiting principle of compensation for loss and share with the law of restitution the task of divesting of ill-gotten gains.[2] But there is also unease in relation to the law of property, as the development and use of the constructive trust continue to blur the line of demarcation which separates, or ought to separate, vindication of one's property from remedial awards against another's property. This domestic instability is reflected in the emerging rules of private international law. Not that the fault is entirely that of the domestic law, though: a clear and principled approach to characterization is required to get the ground rules straight, and characterization is not a notable strength of the English conflict of laws.[3]

When one turns to equity, the problems are similar but worse. For whereas restitution may overlap a little with contract and tort and property, equity pervades all three. Equity does provide distinctive remedies in aid of other causes of action when acting in its 'auxiliary jurisdiction', that is, when it acts in aid of legal rights. But it also fashions causes of action in its 'exclusive jurisdiction', that is, where no legal right is involved, but using material and scientific concepts which are also used, if not in identical ways, by the common law. If all equity could be regarded as being no more than remedial law, or as procedural law, it could be fitted, *holus bolus*, into an existing characterization category. But this is not possible, for most of equity is substantive and not remedial. A variant upon this would be to develop a new characterization category for equitable issues. But it would need to be internally coherent, and to have a rational choice of law rule attached to it. It is very doubtful indeed that the bare common and ancient origin in the Court of Chancery suffices to make modern equity a coherent characterization category to which private international law can properly attach a uniform choice of law rule. Yet another suggestion might be that equity should be regarded as a meaningless expression within the conflict of laws (rather as is the arcane domestic law distinction between realty and personalty[4]), and the issues

---

[1] The existence of overlapping causes of action in contract and tort is permissible and not uncommon: see, e.g., *Henderson* v. *Merrett Syndicates Ltd.* [1995] 2 AC 145; and it is contrary to common law principle to suppose that this is not also reflected in the relationship between restitution and other common law causes of action.

[2] *Att.-Gen.* v. *Blake* [2001] 1 AC 268.

[3] Though *Raiffeisien Zentralbank Österreich AG* v. *Five Star Trading LLC* [2001] CA Civ. 68, [2001] 2 WLR 1344, is a step in the right direction.

[4] *Re Berchtold* [1923] 1 Ch. 112; *Re Cutcliffe* [1940] Ch. 565.

which make up an equity textbook be split up and parcelled out between existing characterization categories. This would be a manageable solution, but it has not happened yet. The analysis which is put forward here is therefore one which will try to make sense of such sparse material as exists, and which attempts to propose a simple and pragmatic framework for the development of private international law. But it is not the only view which may legitimately be held.

RESTITUTIONARY CLAIMS

Despite what was said above about the possibility that restitutionary claims will overlap with contract or tort,[5] the characterization category for the restitutionary choice of law rule must still be mapped, by using positive and negative indicators. As with all characterization categories, the point of departure is that of restitution as a term of art in English domestic law. Despite the observation[6] that 'the receipt-based restitutionary claim' may not be appropriate for use in the construction of a characterization category, it is thought that it does identify the essence of claims which are based on unjust or unjustified enrichment, *enrichissement sans cause*, and so on. That the cause of action in English domestic law is not precisely the same as its foreign law counterparts is not significant; the task is to construct a characterization category, not to elevate domestic law, whole and unchanged, onto the plane of private international law. At this general level, restitution is identified by a receipt which unjustly enriches the defendant at the expense of the claimant: the cause of action focuses on the enrichment or gain rather than on any measure of loss; and if the enrichment is justified by the laws of contract or of property, there is no basis for advancing a claim. In other words, it is enrichment *ex injusta causa* which provides the basis for recovery.

An attempt to describe the relationship to other causes of action can now be made. There may well be points of overlap. The correct reponse to this is not to seek to define those characterization categories so as to prevent there being any overlap between them, but to develop choice of law rules which ensure that a single choice of law applies in the area of overlap, no matter how the claim is characterized. As regards contract, if the contract rules lead to the conclusion that a supposed contract was

---

[5] Whether it overlaps with equity is best left until choice of law for equitable claims has been examined.

[6] Auld LJ in *Macmillan Inc.* v. *Bishopsgate Investment Trust plc (No 3)* [1996] 1 WLR 387 (CA).

void or otherwise ineffective, any recovery action brought as a consequence cannot be derived from the contract and must therefore be restitutionary. As regards tort, if the victim of a tort elects not to sue for damages on account of the loss he sustained, but 'waives the tort' and pursues the profit made by the tortfeasor, the claim is restitutionary, because it is gain-based, not loss-based.[7] As regards trusts, if the claimant is a beneficiary of a completely constituted trust, a claim to enforce his rights will be governed by the rules on trusts. But a claim to have the defendant placed under fiduciary obligations as a response to his unjust enrichment is restitutionary. As regards property, a claim to vindicate that which one owns is governed by the choice of law rules for the particular type of property. But if the claimant seeks to have the defendant dealt with as if he were holding the property of the claimant, the claim may be restitutionary. And in general, if the claim is founded on an obligation owed to the claimant which is neither contractual nor tortious, in the conflicts sense, nor is founded on an existing proprietary right— always bearing in mind that these terms are given a broad construction for the purposes of characterization—it should, *faute de mieux* if not otherwise, be regarded as restitutionary. So a claim for reimbursement for intervening in another's affairs, say by putting out a fire on his land or for discharging another's debt by paying his creditor, would be regarded as restitutionary. This may not be the most intellectually satisfying of definitions (indeed, it may not even be a definition at all), but it appears to describe much of the territory which is considered to fall within the scope of the characterization category and rule.

CHOICE OF LAW

As a matter of legal history, many proposals have been made for the choice of law rule to govern restitutionary claims, but none has been found to be wholly convincing. All agree that in general the proper law of the obligation to make restitution is the umbrella rule, but there is less agreement whether one can go further than this.[8] The balance of academic authority[9] suggests that where there was a contract between the parties, its law should govern any obligation to make restitution, but that

[7] This view focuses on the remedy rather than on the absence of fault, for tort claims founded on strict liability are also independent of fault.
[8] See generally J. Bird, 'Choice of Law' in F. D. Rose (ed.), *Restitution and the Conflict of Laws* (Mansfield Press, Oxford, 1995).
[9] Dicey & Morris, *The Conflict of Laws* (13th edn., Sweet & Maxwell, London, 2000) Rule 200. But Cheshire & North, *Private International Law* (13th edn., Butterworths, London, 2000), chap. 20, expresses a different view, favouring unrestricted flexibility.

outside this context[10] the most frequent contender is the law of the place where the enrichment[11] occurred. As an alternative, it can be suggested that the issue should be governed by the law which established that the enrichment was unjust: the law under which the contract was shown to be invalid; the law which established that there was a tort; the law which established that the defendant had behaved unconscionably; and so on. This is more promising, for it accepts that there may be different laws to be applied in different types of case, and that one rule does not necessarily fit all claims. But this too can be criticized: the law which establishes the invalidity of a contract may be the law of the defendant's habitual residence,[12] which may have a small connection to the facts of the case; or there may be several laws which invalidate the contract, such as where there is a failure to comply with the formalities required by any of the available laws,[13] or a combination of laws which determined that there was a tort.[14] The law which establishes that the defendant has behaved unconscionably is, all too frequently, the *lex fori*, and there is little reason to make a bad rule bigger.

As indicated at the beginning of this section above, the answer supported by academic authority is the proper law of the obligation to make restitution.[15] It is certainly faithful to the tradition of English private international law to accept that the right to reverse an unjust enrichment is governed by the law with which the duty to make restitution has its closest and most real connection: so loose and general a formulation can hardly ever generate a solution which is wrong in principle.[16] Dicey & Morris states the rule in this way, and it has been accepted as a correct statement of general principle.[17] There is some support for a tripartite

---

[10] And disregarding restitution in relation to land, which will be governed by the *lex situs* of the land.

[11] There is also some academic support for the place of the impoverishment, presumably on the basis that this is even closer to the law which applies in the case of torts. But it has not been promoted in England, and may well be very hard to apply in practice.

[12] Contracts (Applicable Law) Act 1990, Sch. 1, Art. 11.

[13] Ibid., Art. 9.

[14] The *lex deliciti*, and the governing law of the contract in which it was alleged that there was a promise not to sue, will be a frequent pairing.

[15] Dicey & Morris, above n. 9, Rule 200.

[16] The analogy is therefore with the approach taken to contracts, transfers of intangibles, where the proper law was dominant. If an analogy were sought with the law of tort it would be more oriented towards the law of the place where the obligation to make restitution arose and this, perhaps, supports the case for the law of the place where the enrichment occurred, and (presumably) should have been reversed.

[17] *Arab Monetary Fund* v. *Hashim* [1996] 1 Lloyd's Rep. 589 (CA); *Macmillan Inc.* v. *Bishopsgate Investment Trust plc (No 3)* [1996] 1 WLR 387 (CA).

sub-division, into cases connected to a contract (the *lex contractus*), cases connected with land (the *lex situs*), and all others (the law of the place of the enrichment).[18] The last of these may be justified on the footing that the event which gives rise to the obligation to make restitution is the receipt or the enrichment, and the law of the place where this happened is best placed to determine whether and on what terms it should be reversed. But there are formidable drawbacks to adopting a rule drawn in such terms. The private international law of contract abandoned a 'law of the place where . . .' rule almost 140 years ago,[19] presumably on the basis that it was simply not up to the task of providing a rational solution. The law of the place of an event is more prominent in the tort choice of law rule, but the facts which make up the commission of a tort are more physically connected to the place of its occurrence than the facts making up the enrichment ever are to theirs. This is all the more true when enrichment may take the form of electronic debiting and crediting of bank accounts, which process lacks a significant location. The law of the place of enrichment is insupportable. Instead there is wisdom in making a sub-division within the general curtilege of the proper law rule, but along different lines. This would separate cases where there was between the parties a prior legal relationship having its own choice of law rule from cases where there was not. The rightness of this cannot be derived from the few decided cases, but it is not contradicted by them either and, as it is hoped, may be shown to have inherent advantages over a rule expressed in more general or abstract terms. It is also inevitable, in the present stage of the law's development, that it should be expressed as a general rule, and not as a rigid one.

Restitution within prior relationships

Where there was a prior relationship between claimant and defendant, which has its own choice of law rule, and from or in connection with which the claim arose, the law governing the restitutionary obligation (relational restitution) to restore the benefit will be overshadowed, and will usually[20] be governed, by the law which applied to this prior relationship. So if the restitutionary obligation arises upon the failure of a real or supposed contract, or from the commission of a tort, the law which governed the contract or the tort will have a strong claim also to govern

---

[18] Dicey & Morris, above n. 9, Rule 200(2).

[19] *P&O Steam Navigation Co.* v. *Shand* (1865) 12 LT 808.

[20] It seems right in principle that the rule which is primarily pragmatic should make implicit provision for exceptions on the same basis.

the restitutionary claim.[21] This is not because the restitutionary obligation is itself contractual or tortious—it is plainly neither—but because it arises from and by reason of a prior relationship which is the *causa sine qua non* of the present claim, and because it is simply unreal to regard the consequential obligation as free-floating, independent of and uncoloured by its history. Quite apart from that, consistency of result may be enhanced by a choice of law rule according to which the laws applicable to history, claim, and remedy dovetail one with another. So the law governing the alleged obligation to repay sums paid over under a contract found to be void will probably be the same as that which applied to the supposed contract, and if the parties' supposed contract had an expressly chosen governing law, this law will probably govern the restitutionary obligation;[22] the law governing the alleged obligation to account to one's employer for a bribe corruptly received from another will probably be the law of the contract of employment;[23] the law governing the obligation to account for profits made from the commission of a tort will probably be the law applicable to the tort.[24]

If this is not accepted, there will remain problems for which a workable solution will still have to be found. If the *lex contractus* provides that the supposed contract was void, a claim for the repayment of money or reimbursement for services or other benefits conferred will be restitutionary. If this is not governed by the *lex contractus* but by another law, that law may independently conclude that restitution is not available because it sees no unjust enrichment, on the ground that, as far as it is concerned, there is a valid contract which insulates the enrichment from the allegation of injustice. This combination of answer may be possible in theory, but it is most unattractive. Again, the *lex delicti* may show that there was a tort, but the claimant eschews compensation in favour of a claim against the tortfeasor for the profit generated by his wrongdoing. But if that restitutionary claim is governed by something other than the *lex delicti*, it may be that under this other law recovery is denied on the ground that, according to it, there is no wrong. At some point it has to be recognized that the law needs to provide a reasonable solution to litigants'

---

[21] Cf *Baring Bros. & Co.* v. *Cunninghame DC* [1997] CLC 108 (Outer House).

[22] In *Dimskal Shipping Co. SA* v. *International Transport Workers' Federation (The Evia Luck)* [1992] 2 AC 152 a contract was avoided for duress by reference to its English proper law, and it appears to have been accepted without argument that restitution of money paid would be governed by English law.

[23] *Arab Monetary Fund* v. *Hashim* [1996] 1 Lloyd's Rep. 589 (CA).

[24] If the issue is characterized as one in tort under the Private International Law (Miscellaneous Provisions) Act 1995, s. 9(2), the statutory choice of law rule will in any event apply.

claims, not a construct of unimpeachable theoretical perfection. The claim of pragmatism is that if the application of the *lex contractus* or the *lex delicti*, or analogous rules in the case of other prior relationships, paves the way for a restitutionary claim, the choice of law rule for that restitutionary claim should be co-ordinated with one which was applied at the earlier stage, and should not contradict it. And no better solution is apparent.

Restitution outside prior relationships

Where there was no prior relationship between claimant and defendant (non-relational restitution), Dicey & Morris proposes that the proper law of the obligation to make restitution is the law of the place where the enrichment occurred.[25] Though in default of a better connected law there is some small justification for the place of enrichment, which may provide a fixed point of sorts in a rootless set of facts, it is submitted that it should not be accepted, even as an easily rebuttable presumption. Several reasons may be given. For one, in cases where there has been a passing of funds, or of electronic data notionally representing funds, through sundry hands (both clean and unclean), accounts, and jurisdictions, there may be several places which could be regarded as that of the enrichment, all artificial or casual.[26] For another, it should not be possible for a calculating defendant to protect himself by arranging receipt of his enrichment in a country whose law is favourable to him. For a third, it will often be debatable whether it is the ultimate receipt or the first unjustified receipt which is critical: a rule which is based on this matter of happenstance is hard to promote. In these cases, therefore, a flexible proper law rule is inevitable and correct, and the answer should be the law which has the closest and most real connection with the alleged obligation to make restitution, without embellishment. Any attempt to specify in advance what this means does not seem sensible.

Contribution claims as restitutionary issues

Contribution claims may be brought between parties pursuant to a contract or between wrongdoers, and, in a broader context, the same issue may extend to all cases in which A has made a payment or performed a service which benefits him and B, and now seeks an *ex post facto*

---

[25] Dicey & Morris, above n. 9, Rule 201(2)(c). Cf the arguable distinction between where enrichment occurs and where it is sustained.

[26] Cf *Hong Kong and Shanghai Banking Corp. Ltd.* v. *United Overseas Bank Ltd.* [1992] Sing. LR 495 (Sing. HC); *Thahir* v. *Pertamina* [1994] 3 Sing. LR 257 (Sing. CA).

adjustment of their responsibilities. Where such a claim for contribution or indemnity from another is advanced on the ground that he has, by paying a claimant,[27] discharged a liability[28] owed by both, the claim can be seen as being restitutionary in nature.[29] If this analysis were correct, it would follow that the choice of law would be derived from the principles outlined above. Where there was a prior relationship—a contractual obligation to indemnify or contribute, for example—between the two, the law governing this prior relationship would in those cases deal with the claim;[30] if not—in England, where statute[31] or equity[32] undertakes the task—the law of closest connection would apply. There is some judicial support for this, at least to the extent of seeing the claim as restitutionary. But it has also been held that where the claim for contribution falls within the statutory wording of the Civil Liability (Contribution) Act 1978, this regime applies without regard to choice of law.[33] As a matter of statutory construction this is questionable, for there is no particular reason—either deduced from the wording of the Act or from the policy involved—to consider that Parliament intended English contribution rules to be applied to each and every respondent brought before the English courts, any more than it intended English rules on contributory negligence to be applied with equally indiscriminate effect. The correct analysis ought to be that such a claim is restitutionary, and that choice of law is well within the framework of that for restitutionary claims.

EQUITABLE OBLIGATIONS

As indicated above, difficulty surrounds any attempt to show how domestic equity coexists with the rules of conflict of laws. Various possibilities exist.

---

[27] Actual or potential.   [28] Actual or potential.

[29] e.g., Law Commission, *Private International Law: Choice of Law in Tort and Delict* (Law Com No 193, 1990) paras. 3.47–3.48.

[30] It would not matter whether the claim were seen as restitutionary but most closely connected to the *lex contractus*, or contractual and governed by the *lex contractus*.

[31] Most prominently the Civil Liability (Contribution) Act 1978.

[32] Via the principles on subrogation, though as regards these Art. 13 of the Rome Convention (Contracts) (Applicable Law) Act 1990, Sch. 1, provides a partial statutory choice of law rule.

[33] *Arab Monetary Fund* v. *Hashim (No 9)* [1994] TLR 502. The judge admitted that in a case falling outside the statutory scheme, the proper law of the obligation to contribute would probably be applicable.

CHOICE OF LAW: ASSIMILATIONIST APPROACH

One suggestion would stake out the position that the domestic law distinction between common law and equity is irrelevant to the conflict of laws, and that claims founded on obligations in or analogous[34] to those found in English equity are to be fitted into existing characterization categories. According to this, some would be regarded as torts, or wrongs, to be dealt with by the *lex delicti*: examples may include misuse of confidential information or breach of confidence, and dishonest assistance of or participation in another's breach of trust. These impose remedies[35] for dishonesty, fault, wrongdoing: the remedies may differ[36] from those generally awarded for torts at common law, but this may not be decisive. Moreover, if the definition of 'tort' for the purpose of the statutory choice of law rule in the Private International Law (Miscellaneous Provisions) Act 1995 is taken to be wider than its meaning in English domestic law, the new choice of law rules for torts may already have supervened to encompass equitable claims which nevertheless fall within its scope. Other forms of claim may be regarded as contractual, or agreement-based; examples may be the breach by an agent of his fiduciary duty, or breach of the duty not to act unconscionably in relation to contractual rights or the holding of an office. The basis for liability is disloyalty to or unconscionable dealing with another with whom one had an agreement, and the difference between the remedies will diminish if an account of profits may be ordered for a breach of contract. Yet others may be restitutionary, because the aim is to ensure that its victim is not depleted, even if what is handed over is technically the property of the defendant: an example would be the knowing[37] receipt of trust property; and the choice of law will therefore reflect the distinction between relational and non-relational restitution.[38] Equity's rules on remedies would apply as part of the procedural *lex fori*; and the overall result would be the denial of a separate characterization category for equity, and the disappearance of a distinct choice of law rule.

---

[34] This form of words is meant to denote causes of action arising under a foreign law but which are analogous to those found in English equity.

[35] It is probably irrelevant whether this is assessed by reference to the claimant's loss or the defendant's gain, but if this *is* critical, loss-based recovery would be a wrong, and gain-based recovery would be restitutionary.

[36] Though the difference between equitable compensation and common law damages is not substantial.

[37] On the footing that liability does not depend on (dis)honesty, but knowledge.

[38] There is some basis for this distinction: *Kuwait Oil Tanker SAK* v. *Al Bader* [2000] 2 All ER (Comm.) 271 (CA).

The advantages of this approach are obvious: there would be a simplification of the law, the echoes of historical irrelevancies[39] would be played down, and a basis would also have been established for dealing with claims based on foreign laws but which are claimed to be enforceable in an English court. But there is another, more compelling, advantage. The account just given proceeds by taking English equitable causes of action and asking how they fit within the characterization categories. But this places the cart before the horse. It is the characterization category which identifies the choice of law rule, and thus which identifies the cause of action: if it points to English law it may also point to English equity. But not until this point is reached should there be any mention of equity. If the price to be paid is a measure of dissonance between domestic and private international law, it is worth the expense.

CHOICE OF LAW: FORUM-CENTRIC APPROACH

An alternative view of the matter proceeds from the proposition that operation of equity is, in effect, dependent only upon the court's having personal jurisdiction over the defendant and his conscience, and that choice of law is not material to the application of English equity by an English court. The extreme, ultramontane, form of the argument maintains just that: when a claimant formulates a claim by reference to English[40] equity—that is, any claim which would be brought in equity's exclusive jurisdiction if all the facts were domestic—he may rely on English equity even though some or all of the facts are foreign. Or, to put the same point another way, the equitable obligations contained in English domestic law are applicable as part of the *lex fori*, binding on and applicable to anyone subject to the personal jurisdiction of the court.[41] If equitable obligations were seen as a crystallisation of English public policy, this might, just possibly, be acceptable, but this would be an ambitious claim to make for the whole of equity.[42] After all, equity enforces

---

[39] In the sense that whatever the doctrinal history of equity may impose in other areas, it has no relevance in this context.

[40] As *lex fori*. In fact, the most significant cases in this line are decisions of the Australian courts.

[41] *National Commercial Bank* v. *Wimborne* (1978) 5 Butterworths Property Reports 11958 (NSW SC); *United States Surgical Corporation* v. *Hospital Products International Pty. Ltd.* [1982] 2 NSWLR 766, 797–8, aff'd [1983] 2 NSWLR 157 (NSW CA), rev'd on different grounds (1984) 156 CLR 41; *Paramasivam* v. *Flynn* (1998–9) 160 ALR 203, 214–18 (Aust. Fed. Ct.); cf *Macmillan Inc.* v. *Bishopsgate Investment Trust plc (No 3)* [1995] 1 WLR 976, 989, aff'd without reference to this point [1996] 1 WLR 387 (CA).

[42] Cf S. Lee, 'Restitution, Public Policy and the Conflict of Laws' (1998) 20 *U Qd LJ* 1.

standards of good faith and acts against fraud; the common law enforces duties of care and acts against deceit: it is unrealistic to regard the one but not the other as manifesting English public policy. That one but not the other should operate without regard to choice of law is incredible. Both should depend on the *lex causae* being English to begin with.

A slightly less extreme version of this approach recognizes that there may be cases when an undiluted dose of English equity would be a little too harsh. On this view, notice will be taken of a foreign law if it has a significant connection to the case.[43] But on this view, the maximum role of the foreign law will be to contribute data for the purpose of helping decide what English equity requires—if it requires proof of dishonesty, standards prevailing in the place where the defendant acted will assist in evaluating his conduct as honest or dishonest—or expects of a defendant in a given case. If this is correct, the availability to a claimant of English equitable obligations would again depend not upon the prior application of choice of law rules, but only upon the existence of personal jurisdiction. So far as can be deduced from cases on dishonest assistance, in particular,[44] this is approximately the basis of liability as it is currently understood: as long as the foreign law (usually in practice the place where the defendant acted) imposes a form of liability resembling the nature of the English action, the claim will proceed on the basis of English law; were it to be shown that under the foreign law there was no ground for even arguing that there would be liability, this would be a weighty factor in denying that there was dishonesty for the purposes of the English claim. In other words, English equity applies, without regard to choice of law, but with notice taken of foreign law.

In the context of anti-suit injunctions, however, there is a subtle difference. An applicant may obtain an anti-suit injunction by relying exclusively on English equity and its law on vexation and oppression: no observable part is played by the law of any other country in deciding whether the applicant has made out the cause of action which justifies the relief. But the court will not use English equity to adjudicate on the application unless England is the natural forum for the underlying claim.[45] In other words, the precondition to the application of English equity is not one cast in terms of choice of law, but the closeness of

---

[43] *Grupo Torras SA v. Al Sabah* [2001] CLC 221 (CA); *Kuwait Oil Tanker SAK v. Al Bader* [2000] 2 All ER (Comm.) 271 (CA).

[44] Ibid.

[45] *Airbus Industrie GIE v. Patel* [1999] 1 AC 119.

connection of the underlying dispute with England.[46] It is perhaps surprising that whereas this may be true for anti-suit injunctions, there is no
trace of it as a limitation when claims have been brought, say alleging
dishonest assistance of a breach of trust. In other words, in the context of
anti-suit injunctions, English equity applies as long as, but only if,
England is the natural forum for the claim.

CONCLUSION

Though the forum-centric approach probably represents the present
state of the law, it is difficult to look on it as being satisfactory. In particular, it seems strange that when equity enforces common law rights, such
as under contracts, choice of law first decides whether there is a legal
right on which to base the remedy, but where a remedy is sought on the
basis of an equitable obligation there is no similar process: it is as if equity
sits above choice of law, as if choice of law were a creature of the common
law alone. Whilst the restrictions on the application of English equity in
its pure and undiluted form, described above, are better than nothing,
they are not a lot better than nothing; and it is very hard indeed to explain
why English equity should not, like English common law and English
legislation, generally depend on choice of law pointing to English
domestic law as the *lex causae*. And if that is so, the assimilationist
approach probably represents the way ahead. It would certainly be wrong
to regard all equitable claims and obligations as restitutionary, for many
are not; but it would be equally strange to say that they are above and
beyond the reach of choice of law. The approach which assimilates them
into the characterization categories of contract, tort, and restitution does
no real damage to the law; and it removes the suggestion of characterization being unnecessary where the claimant relies on an equitable claim.
The approach to anti-suit injunctions can be explained and justified as a
procedural, remedial, issue, governed by the *lex fori*. But until this happens, the role of equity in the conflict of laws will be anomalous and
unstable.

JURISDICTION OVER RESTITUTIONARY AND EQUITABLE CLAIMS

The difficulty which shrouds the choice of law issues makes it appropriate to mention jurisdictional issues only as the end of the account. For

---

[46] As a country, not with English as a law, or so it seems.

restitutionary claims, those which arise in civil or commercial matters and fall within the domain of Council Regulation (EC) 44/2001,[47] the main question is whether any basis for special jurisdiction is provided by Article 5, for if not, a claimant may well be confined to suing where the defendant is domiciled. If the restitutionary claim arises out of a contract, that is to say, there was, or is alleged to be, an obligation freely entered into with regard to another, the fact that the court finds the alleged contract to be ineffective will not mean that the consequential restitutionary claim falls outside Article 5(1).[48] But if at the outset the parties agree that there was no enforceable agreement of any kind, and that this is why the claim now arises, it may not fall within Article 5(1).[49] If the claim arises out of a wrong, it will fall within Article 5(3), and it should not matter whether the relief sought is assessed by reference to losses or gains as long as the legal basis for liability is wrongdoing. And cases which do not fall within these loose definitions will not be eligible for special jurisdiction under Article 5. The same principles will apply to equitable claims. In cases which fall to be dealt with under traditional jurisdictional rules, CPR Part 6 makes particular provision for some restitutionary claims, but otherwise such actions will have to be accommodated within a paragraph which is not specifically dedicated to them.

[47] [2001] OJ L12/1.
[48] *Agnew* v. *Länsförsäkringsbolagens AB* [2001] 1 AC 223.
[49] *Kleinwort Benson plc* v. *Glasgow City Council* [1999] 1 AC 153.

8

Property

The private international law of property is a large topic, covering transactions *inter vivos* and transmission of property upon death. It can raise difficult questions about the relationship between jurisdiction and choice of law, and between property and the law of obligations. In most cases in which a court is called upon to adjudicate it is asked to settle a dispute about title, and to make an order which is good and reliable against the world, not just as between the parties to the action. As a result, a court will generally be entitled[1] to apply foreign law in its *renvoi* sense, that is, as the law would be applied by a judge sitting in the foreign country and hearing the case himself.[2] Though judges sometimes observe that parties have placed no reliance on the principle of *renvoi*, this cannot be taken as a decision that the doctrine is inadmissible in the context of property law.

The law of property divides into immoveable and moveable property, and moveables sub-divide into tangible and intangible property. Whether a thing is an immoveable is determined by the law of the place where it is, the *lex situs*.[3] It may be thought that this offends against the principle that characterization is a matter for the *lex fori*, and that in cases of potential disagreement, such as where the property is an oil rig, a pontoon bridge, the interest of a mortgagee in the property mortgaged, an interest under an old-style settlement of land, and so on, this question should be answered by the law of the forum. But in a context in which, as will be seen, the *lex situs* is broadly applicable, and *renvoi* applies also, it would be self-defeating to distort the very law which a court is seeking to apply with particular faithfulness. The result is that the question whether property is moveable or immoveable is determined by the *lex situs*.

---

[1] If the rules of foreign law are pleaded and proved to the satisfaction of the court.
[2] P. 14 above.
[3] Dicey & Morris, *The Conflict of Laws* (13th edn., Sweet & Maxwell, London, 2000), chap. 22; *Re Hoyles* [1911] 1 Ch. 179, 185.

IMMOVEABLE PROPERTY

At common law an English court had no subject matter jurisdiction to determine questions of title to immoveable property situated outside England, nor to entertain tort claims in which such an issue would arise for decision.[4] So where a claim was brought which alleged trespass to a hotel, and to chattels in the hotel, in the northern part of the island of Cyprus by defendants claiming authorization by the authorities of the *soi-disant* and illegal 'Turkish Republic of Northern Cyprus', the court had no jurisdiction to entertain the action concerning the land, but did have jurisdiction over the claim alleging conversion of the chattels. The decision shows the width of the rule, for according to the *lex situs*, a connecting factor defined by English law and which acknowledged only the laws of the Republic of Cyprus, there was no dispute about title: the illegal ordinances of the non-state were without effect. But the exclusionary rule still operated to deny jurisdiction. The rule was later amended to confer jurisdiction over tort claims where the issue of title is not a principal one[5] but otherwise the jurisdictional preclusion prevails.[6] So a claim alleging trespass can be defeated on jurisdictional grounds if the defendant pleads that the land was his. It is probably correct to read the reference to 'title' as being broad: if the same defendant alleged a licence to enter or remain, this too should be seen to raise a dispute about title. The historical basis of the rule lay in the common law principle that such actions were 'local', and had to be tried in the place where the land was situated, but a more compelling reason is that most laws impose the same limitation for reasons of public policy. Moreover, as titles to land are increasingly recorded on a register, only the court with personal jurisdiction over the registrar has any sensible basis for accepting jurisdiction. It follows that disputes about title to foreign immoveables must be tried in the courts of the *situs*, no matter how inconvenient this is, and notwithstanding that the parties are willing to submit to the personal jurisdiction of the court. By parity of reasoning, foreign judgments which purport to adjudicate title to English immoveables will not be recognized in England.

Moreover, if the land is in another Member State of the European Union to which Council Regulation (EC) 44/2001[7] applies Article 22(1)

---

[4] *British South Africa Co.* v. *Companhia de Moçambique* [1893] AC 602; *Hesperides Hotels Ltd.* v. *Aegean Turkish Holidays Ltd.* [1979] AC 508.

[5] *Re Polly Peck International plc (in administration) (No 2)* [1998] 3 All ER 812, 828 (CA).

[6] Civil Jurisdiction and Judgments Act 1982, s. 30.

[7] [2001] OJ L12/1. Or in a state to which the Brussels or Lugano Convention applies, where the corresponding provision is Art. 16(1).

denies jurisdiction to the English court where the proceedings have as their object a right *in rem* in, or a tenancy of, that land.[8] A different issue arises where the land is in a non-member state but the court has personal jurisdiction over the defendant under the Regulation. One view is that it may not have recourse to its national conflicts rules to decline to exercise it, on the basis that this common law jurisdictional principle would, in effect, negate a provision of the Regulation.[9] An alternative view would be that the absence of subject matter jurisdiction is unaffected by the Regulation, or that a court should be able to exercise a procedural discretion to stay proceedings which would be incompetent if the land were in a Member State.[10] Given the state of the national laws, this seems by far the better solution.

A common law exception to the exclusionary rule exists. As a matter of common law, if the claim may be reformulated as one to enforce a personal obligation, albeit one concerned with a foreign immoveable, there is no jurisdictional impediment to the action, even though it may appear that the court is doing indirectly what it cannot do directly. The exception derives from the ancient case of *Penn* v. *Baltimore*,[11] concerning an agreement to demarcate the boundary of two American proto-states, and which the court was able to enforce. Despite its unlikely origins, the principle is plain enough: if the claim is brought to enforce a contract or in respect of a pre-existing equitable obligation between the parties, the court does not lack jurisdiction even if the obligation derives from, or is created by, a transaction relating to land;[12] a similar principle applies if a court is administering an estate which includes foreign land. So if the claim is that the defendant vendor has failed to perform his contract for sale of land, or as bare trustee should convey title to the claimant beneficiary, the court has jurisdiction to make an order against the vendor or trustee in person, capable of being backed up by the court's considerable coercive powers, requiring the conveyance of the land; or awarding damages for the breach. Likewise, a court should have jurisdiction to assess shares in the equitable ownership of foreign land to the purchase of which

---

[8] See above; and Chap. III of the Reg. requires the non-recognition of judgments which conflict with this.

[9] See Report on the Convention on the Accession of Spain and Portugal [1990] OJ C189/6 at 47, 76; cf *Pearce* v. *Ove Arup Partnership Ltd.* [2000] Ch. 403 (CA).

[10] Cf *Re Harrods (Buenos Aires) Ltd.* [1992] Ch. 72 (CA); and see above, p. 86.

[11] (1750) 1 Ves. Sen. 444.

[12] Cf Case C-294/92 *Webb* v. *Webb* [1994] ECR I-1717 (a case on what is now Art. 22(1) of the Reg.).

the parties have contributed, and to decree the performance of the duties of any trust.

As regards choice of law in those cases in which the court does have jurisdiction, the inevitable choice is the *lex situs* as this would be applied in a court at the *situs* to any question concerning immoveable property: this may, of course, result in the application of the domestic law of country other than that of the *situs*. The usual justification for this is the futility of doing otherwise than what a local judge would do, for he alone has control of the immoveable, and his view on the correct answer is inevitably destined to prevail. This is oddly unconvincing. The real question for the foreign judge (as, were the roles reversed, it would be for an English judge) is whether he should acknowledge that a judge in another country had jurisdiction to make any order concerning local land at all, rather than whether that judge got the right substantive answer: he may still refuse to recognize a foreign judgment, even though the reasoning and the result appear to be unimpeachable; and the recognition of a judgment does not usually depend on the conclusion that the adjudicating judge decided correctly. But, that said, it is impossible to maintain a rational argument for the application of anything other than the *lex situs* where the question is properly one concerning title to the land.[13] Where the court has jurisdiction under the *Penn* v. *Baltimore* exception, it is possible that in a case concerned with a contractual obligation, the law governing the contractual issue will not be the *lex situs* of the land. But this will be the presumed governing law for contracts concerning land;[14] and only on issues of formality or personal capacity, for example, is there any real prospect of applying a law other than the *lex situs*.

TANGIBLE MOVEABLE PROPERTY

The reason for the application of the *lex situs* in the case of immoveables is that, because the land cannot be moved, the *lex situs* combines expectation with reality. But moveables move. True as this is, it does not affect the choice of law, only the justification for it. Disputes concerning title to, or the right to possession of, tangible moveable property are generally governed by the *lex situs* of the moveable at the date of the event which is alleged to have affected title to it.[15] It is accepted that certainty and

---

[13] *Bank of Africa* v. *Cohen* [1909] 2 Ch. 129 (CA). But the paucity of authority reflects the fact that jurisdiction will be rare.

[14] Contracts (Applicable Law) Act 1990, Sch. 1, Art. 4(3).

[15] *Cammell* v. *Sewell* (1860) 5 H & N 728; *Winkworth* v. *Christie Manson & Woods* [1980] Ch. 496.

security of title are paramount, and these aims are best achieved by the general application of the *lex situs*. Recognizing this, the courts have resisted the invitation to develop even limited exceptions to add to those established by authority. So if the parties are together in one place, but the thing is elsewhere the law of the place of the transaction, the *lex loci actus*, will not be applied, but the *lex situs* will.[16] True, if the parties have made a contract which specifies when property will pass, this may be effective, but only if its validity and effect are acknowledged by the *lex situs* applying (one presumes[17]) its own choice of law rule to appraise the contract. The *lex situs* prevails.

But by way of difference from dealings with land, there are many cases in which a succession of transfers of, or other dealings with, a moveable takes place, and in a series of countries with conflicting laws. There are two basic possibilities which may have been used to underpin the law. Suppose that X delivers a car to Y on hire purchase, according to which X remains owner during the period of hire, but that Y drives the car to a second country where he sells the car to Z. Let us also suppose that under the law of the second country, a person in possession of a chattel with apparent ownership of it can confer a good title on a buyer in good faith, but that under the law of the first country, the governing principle of *nemo dat quod non habet* would mean that Y had no title to give, nor capacity to confer the same. Under the law of the first country X had an indefeasible title, which could not be affected by a purported sale by a non-owner, Y. Under the law of the second country, the principle of indefeasible titles does not prevail, and a buyer in good faith, Z, may acquire a title which was not the vendor's to give. If one were to adopt a strictly chronological view, and regard each *lex situs* as having sole control over the issues as arose within its territory, one might say that the transaction in the first country reserved to X an indefeasible title to the car; and that when it was taken to the second country, that second law must have taken the indefeasibility of X's title as given, with the result that Y will have been unable to defeat the indefeasible by conferring title on Z: anything else allows the law of the second country to trespass on the role of the first country's law.

It is obvious that the analysis can be stood on its head, by pointing out that the law of the first country is purporting to dictate to the second in

---

[16] *Glencore International AG* v. *Metro Trading Inc.* [2001] 1 Lloyd's Rep. 283.

[17] The argument to the contrary is that the Rome Convention, Art. 15, does not allow for this. The response should be that as the Convention does not apply to proprietary issues, it does not infect the operation of the *lex situs* in its full, *renvoi*, sense.

relation to a transaction taking place in the second. An alternative analysis would be that the eventual question, who owns the car, is as to the legal effect of the second transaction; that this is exclusively governed by the law of the second country, and any anterior questions are answered by looking through the eyes of this eventual *lex situs*, leaving it to the law of obligations to remedy, as best it may, any losses sustained along the way. This is the solution adopted by the English conflict of laws. It therefore follows that the main question will be answered by the *lex situs* of the final disposition, and any earlier issues will be regarded as incidental, and resolved by looking at them through the lens of the law governing the main question.

As a result, the question whether A obtained good title to a camera which he bought in Ruritania is governed by Ruritanian law, even if the camera was delivered on hire purchase terms or under a conditional sale to A's vendor in England; whether B lost his title to a painting stolen from him in England and sold by auction in Italy is governed by Italian law, even though the theft took place in England;[18] whether C succeeded in reserving and retaining title to steel after its use or on-sale by D is answered by the *lex situs* at the time of D's dealing with it, which law will also decide whether it is still steel or is a completely different thing.[19]

The rule as it applies to transfers allows for one exception. If the goods are in transit and[20] their *situs* unknown there is a case for applying instead the law which governs the transaction which is alleged to have affected title.[21] By contrast, where a disposition of goods is effected by document, it is not yet established that the *lex situs* of the goods can be by-passed by the application of (say) the law of the place of the documents. In principle, the answer should be that if the *lex situs* of the goods accepts the purported disposition by transfer of documents as effective, that will be conclusive; but that if it does not, that is conclusive also.[22] Any uncertainty in the minds of those involved will presumably be reflected in the price or in the taking of insurance.

Though the rule was established in the context of derivative titles, that is, transfers, it will in principle also apply to original modes of

[18] *Winkworth* v. *Christie, Manson & Woods Ltd.* [1980] Ch. 496.

[19] *Re Interview Ltd.* [1975] IR 382, *Armour* v. *Thyssen Edelstahlwerke AG* [1991] 2 AC 339; but both cases are weak authority for the proposition advanced in the text.

[20] In its established form, this is conjunctive, not disjunctive. Though there is a case for restating the exception in disjunctive form, the increased scope for uncertainty which this would create will make it unlikely to be adopted.

[21] Dicey & Morris, above n. 3, Rule 118, exception.

[22] There will be consequential contractual claims.

acquisition, to establish the claim of title to things found (*occupatio*), new things made (*specificatio*), things incorporated into something else (*accessio*); and to mixing and blending (*commixtio* and *confusio*).[23] But the mere moving of a chattel from one country to another will not have any effect upon its title; to hold otherwise would be most inconvenient. So if goods are transported by train across several countries, and under the law of one of them an existing title is not recognized, it would be unhelpful for the thing thereafter to be regarded as ownerless and as available for *occupatio*. It may be necessary to adapt the exception, described in the last paragraph, to produce this result.

The choice of law rules for tangible moveables apply also to negotiable instruments.[24] As the instrument, being negotiable, is as good as the right to which it is the key, transfers of the document are, in effect, transfers of the thing. The same principle applies to bearer shares, which are treated as tangible things, and where transfer of the instrument is effective to transfer all rights or property inherent in it.

INTANGIBLE MOVEABLE PROPERTY

Choice of law in relation to intangible property—the debt owed by a bank to an account-holder, the rights under a policy of insurance, the rights of an investor in a unit trust, and so forth—raises issues of some complexity, for three among many reasons. First, it is sometimes difficult to see why or on what basis intangibles are characterized under the common law as property at all, as distinct from their being the simple contractual or analogous rights which they almost always are: the question of who is now entitled to an intangible, and who may therefore enforce the obligation against the debtor or obliged party, may really be asking no more than who stands in a relationship equivalent to privity with the debtor or obliged party, so that there is no intelligible distinction between owning a debt and being owed a debt. This suggests that the issues which may arise are neither more nor less than facets of the law of contract, albeit with a particular gloss supplied by laws regulating security and insolvency, but which may be got up to look like something else. Secondly, the universe of intangible things may be too wide for a uniform choice of law rule to be applied to them all. A rule developed in the nineteenth century for the

---

[23] *Glencore International AG v. Metro Trading Inc.* [2001] 1 Lloyd's Rep. 283. The *situs* rule also applies to seizure by way of nationalization or confiscation of property by governments.

[24] Whether the document is negotiable is determined by its *situs* at the time of its purported negotiation.

assignment of insurance policies and interests under private trusts and dynastic settlements was not designed for, and may not adapt to, dealings with interests in financial instruments held in indirect holding systems, or for delocalized or dematerialized securities of the sort which now serve to underpin the global financial market. Either a choice of law rule has to allow for pragmatic exceptions, so that mindless dogmatism does not defeat the expectations of commerce, or there have to develop new (sub-)rules for choice of law.

Thirdly, when dealing with choice of law for the assignment of intangibles, the common law authorities were remarkably opaque. But it was probably accepted that the law governing the underlying obligation would determine the effect of any purported assignment of it. Article 12 of the Rome Convention now provides a statutory rule for choice of law in voluntary assignments.[25] Article 12(2) states that the law governing the right assigned determines its assignability, the relationship between assignee and debtor, the conditions for invoking the assignment against the debtor, and the discharge of the debtor; and Article 12(1) that the mutual obligations of assignor and assignee are governed by the law applicable to the contract between them. In other words, issues involving the debtor and enforcement against him are governed by the law which governs the thing assigned; any residual or consequential issues between the creditors, or between those trading in the debt, are for the law governing their relationship. This has the basic elements of good sense about it, for it accords the greatest weight to the law which created the thing being dealt with; defends the expectation of the parties who created the obligation that it has all, but has only, the characteristics with which they endowed it, thereby reflecting the essentially contractual nature of the thing assigned; and invites the conclusion that, as Article 12 embraces these matters within the Rome Convention as matters relating to contractual obligations in the autonomous sense, it precludes any argument that they are, in any exclusionary sense, proprietary. Some writers had proposed to read down Article 12, by contending that it regulated contractual issues, but was irrelevant to the proprietary aspects of intangibles.[26] The difficulties with this argument were always many, but for reasons set out in the discussion of the meaning of contractual obligations, it is not tenable today.[27]

---

[25] Contracts (Applicable Law) Act 1990, Sch. 1.

[26] See especially R. M. Goode, *Commercial Law* (2nd edn., Penguin Books, London, 1995), 1128; M. Moshinsky, 'Assignment of Debts in the Conflict of Laws' (1992) 109 *LQR* 591.

[27] *Raiffeisen Zentralbank Österreich AG* v. *Five Star Trading LLC* [2001] CA Civ. 68, [2001] 2 WLR 1344.

If Article 12 is inapplicable, which will be the case where the right assigned is not contractual,[28] the Convention does not preclude the common law reflecting the basic structure of Article 12 as the basis of the law on assignment; and as Article 12 is probably a reflection of the state of the common law as it was best understood, in the rare cases where the common law rules on assignment of intangibles apply, they may well be indistinguishable from Article 12.

SPECIAL CASES

Assignments of registered shares are governed by the *lex incorporationis* for the pragmatic reason that any solution which departs from the law of the place of the share register is futile. In such cases, the general rule in Article 12 of the Rome Convention is inapplicable.[29] This may be deduced from the exclusion in Article 1(2)(e), or from the argument that it is inaccurate to say that shares are ever assigned: they being a bundle of duties and obligations as well as rights, assignment of them is impossible, and the process mis-described as 'share transfer' is in fact the surrender and re-grant of rights in the company. If this is accepted, then the nomenclature of 'share transfer' should be abandoned. For shares and other instruments held in holding systems, according to the terms of which a 'shareowner' in fact has only an interest as investor in a pool of similar assets registered in the name of someone else (a process which may be replicated upwards through several levels of holding), it seems reasonable to accept that a mechanical solution derived from a rule intended for cases of much less complexity is inappropriate, especially where this would, for no obviously good reason, defeat the expectations of all those who participate in the system.[30] But private international legal science has not yet settled on the best means of achieving this aim.

In relation to intellectual property rights, to the extent that a question is not governed by convention or statute, and is not outside the jurisdiction of an English court, patents, copyright, and trade mark rights are governed by the law of the place of the right of protection (*lex protectionis*), and that law will determine whether and on what terms they are assignable.

---

[28] Such as the right to sue a defendant in respect of a tort.

[29] *Macmillan Inc.* v. *Bishopsgate Investment Trust plc (No 3)* [1996] 1 WLR 387 (CA).

[30] For support for the development of an appropriate, tailor-made, characterization category and choice of law rule see Dicey & Morris, above n. 3, para. 24–049; *Raiffeisen Zentralbank Österreich AG* v. *Five Star Trading LLC* [2001] CA Civ. 68, [2001] 2 WLR 1344, at para. [27].

SEIZURE AND CONFISCATION OF PROPERTY

The treatment of nationalization or other expropriation or seizure of property by governments requires little more than an application of the general *lex situs* rule set out above. If the property is within the territorial jurisdiction of the state, the *lex situs* rule will lead to the recognition of the title acquired by this legislative act by reference to local law.[31] There is no question of an English court being called upon to 'enforce' the foreign law: once that law, the *lex causae* according to the rules of the English conflict of laws, has done what it set out to do, there is nothing left in it to require enforcing.[32] Accordingly, if property is seized by a state pursuant to a confiscatory decree, and is then sold by state authorities to a purchaser who gets good title under that law and who then brings the property to England, the former and dispossessed owner has no maintainable claim for its return, for the transfer of ownership and loss of the right to possession were both completed under the *lex situs* of the property at the time of the act. Likewise, if a government passes a decree to acquire ownership of shares in a company incorporated and registered under its law, it may, as controlling shareholder, direct the management of the company to recover debts and property abroad.[33] But, by contrast, had the law provided that overseas property vested in the state, the ordinary application of the *lex situs* rule would mean that title to the property in England, at least, would be unaffected or changed by this legislative act, and that any action in the English courts would be founded on an irrelevant law, not part of the *lex situs* at the time of the relevant act. Not only that, but the action would in such a case be for the enforcement of a penal, revenue, or other public law, and prohibited from enforcement on that ground too. The result is less clear where the property lies outside the territory of the legislating state, but the law of the *situs*, the (to it) foreign legislation would be regarded as effective in the particular case:[34] where the *lex situs* rule collides with the rule against the enforcement of penal laws, one has to give way. It may be said that if the *lex situs* accepts that the legislative decree has operated to alter the ownership, there is nothing left to enforce, and nothing to which enforcement can be denied. But on another, nannyish, view, English law should refuse even to recog-

---

[31] *Luther v. Sagor* [1921] 3 KB 532 (CA); *Princess Paley Olga v. Weisz* [1929] 1 KB 718 (CA).
[32] *Williams & Humbert* v. *W. & H. Trade Marks (Jersey) Ltd.* [1986] AC 368.
[33] Ibid.
[34] Such as where the law is accepted as effective in relation to nationals of the expropriating state.

nize such a law, whatever the *lex situs* may say, for were it to do otherwise this might encourage states to misbehave themselves in this way.[35]

Only if the law under which the seizure was made is so abhorrent to English standards will it be possible to deny even recognition to the law, and hence to the title acquired under it.[36] It is possible that this category of case, historically narrow, will be forced wider open as the standards of the European Convention on Human Rights come to pervade the reasoning of courts. But unless the Convention is interpreted as giving rise to one, there is no rule of English private international law which withholds recognition from an expropriatory law unless compensation is paid for the acquisition;[37] the fact that there may be such an obligation in public international law is of no general relevance in private law.

It is sometimes suggested that the answer is more complicated if the property is removed from the territory of the seizing state before it has been taken into the possession of the authorities. In cases where the *lex situs* requires possession to be taken as a precondition to the acquisition of title under it, this is uncontroversial.[38] But there seems to be no sufficient justification for imposing this as a requirement in cases where the *lex situs* makes no stipulation to this effect.[39] If it is argued that possession is required for procedural reasons—because the action in the English courts must be for conversion, which is a claim which pleads and relies on possession, rather than ownership—this may be to allow procedural matters to dominate matters of substance to an undue extent. There should be no rule of English private international law which provides that until possession has been taken, any action brought in consequence of the foreign law must be regarded as an enforcement as opposed to a recognition.

The rules about seizure apply to immoveable property, and to tangible property. In relation to intangible property it plainly applies to shares situated where the company is incorporated.[40] It is less obvious how it will apply to simple contractual intangibles, but the *situs* of a debt is in general the place of residence of the debtor,[40a] for it is there that he may be sued as a

---

[35] *Kuwait Airways Corp.* v. *Iraqi Airways Co.* [2001] 1 Lloyd's Rep. 161 (CA), at para. 370.
[36] *Oppenheimer* v. *Cattermole* [1976] AC 249; *Kuwait Airways Corp.* v. *Iraqi Airways Co.* [2001] 1 Lloyd's Rep. 161 (CA).
[37] *Williams & Humbert Ltd.* v. *W. & H. Trade Marks (Jersey) Ltd.* [1986] AC 368.
[38] *Att.-Gen. for New Zealand* v. *Ortiz* [1984] AC 1.
[39] *Brokaw* v. *Seatrain UK Ltd.* [1971] 2 QB 476 (CA); *Att.-Gen. for New Zealand* v. *Ortiz* [1984] AC 1, 20 (CA); aff'd on different grounds, 41.
[40] *Williams & Humbert Ltd.* v. *W. & H. Trade Marks (Jersey) Ltd.* [1986] AC 368.
[40a] *Soc. Eram Shipping Co. Ltd.* v *Compagnie Internationale de Navigation* [2001] CA Civ. 1317, 7 Aug. 2001, not yet reported.

matter of right; and the *situs* rule will therefore apply to this. Article 12 of
the Rome Convention, dealing as it does with voluntary assignments, is
irrelevant to the issue.

TRUSTS

The private international law of trusts is substantially contained in the
Hague Convention on the Recognition of Trusts, given force in England
by the Recognition of Trusts Act 1987.[41] From the perspective of English
law, however, the Convention has much more to do with the identification
of the governing law than with the recognition of foreign trusts. The
Convention defines a trust as the legal relationship, created (*inter vivos* or
on death) voluntarily and evidenced in writing, when the settlor places
assets under the control of a trustee for the benefit of a beneficiary or for a
specified purpose.[42] However, the Act extends this Convention definition
to encompass trusts of property arising under the law of any part of the
United Kingdom, and to trusts created by judicial decision;[43] and applies
it to trusts falling within its definition whatever the date of their creation.[44] Its application to implied, resulting, and constructive trusts is
therefore clear. Accordingly, the implied or constructive trust arising
from the joint purchase of property will fall squarely within the scope of
the Act; but where a constructive trust is sought against or imposed upon
a defendant found answerable to an equitable claim, the relevant choice of
law rules are probably those examined in the context of equitable
obligations.[45]

A trust is governed by the law chosen by the settlor; in default of such a
demonstrable choice it is governed by the law with which it is most
closely connected.[46] In identifying the latter regard is to be had to the
place of administration of the trust, the *situs* of the assets of the trust,
the place of residence of the trustee, and the objects of the trust and the
places where they are to be fulfilled. The governing law regulates the
trust, its construction, effect, and administration;[47] but gives way to
mandatory and conflicts rules of the *lex fori*, and to public policy.[48]

---

[41] Dicey & Morris, above n. 3, chap. 29.   [42] Art. 2.
[43] Recognition of Trusts Act 1987, s. 1(2).   [44] Art. 22.   [45] Chap. 7 above.
[46] Arts. 6, 7. Note that it is the connection to a law, and not to a country, which is the
determining factor.
[47] Art. 8.   [48] Art. 18.

THE EFFECT OF MARRIAGE ON PROPERTY RIGHTS

The impact of marriage on property rights is only a fragment of a larger picture.[49] Where a marriage is annulled or dissolved, many systems of law allow the court to make orders in relation to the property of the spouses which override rights created or existing prior to or independently of the marriage;[50] and where a marriage is terminated by death, many systems proceed by use of rules of succession, perhaps modified by limiting the testamentary freedom of a deceased. Others, more commonly civilian systems, employ the institution of a matrimonial property regime, often but not always community of property, to deal with the property rights of the quick and the dead. Our concern at this point is with the effect which marriage has on the property rights of spouses.

Where the parties on their marriage make a matrimonial contract the proper law of that contract governs its creation, validity, interpretation, and effect.[51] Such contracts are excluded from the Rome Convention, but the choice of law principles of the common law are not substantially different: the proper law may be chosen. In the absence of choice it will be that with which the marriage has its closest and most real connection, the matrimonial domicile:[52] there was a historical preference for this law being that of the husband's domicile, but this has been indefensible at least since the abolition of the wife's dependent domicile in 1974. The capacity of a person to make a marriage contract is governed by his or her domicile at the date of marriage.[53] It is consistent with principle that once a matrimonial contract has been made, a change in matrimonial domicile cannot alter its content and the rights created under it;[54] but there is nothing in principle, or probably in law, to prevent the spouses varying their contract by agreement. Where the parties do not make a matrimonial contract it was once thought that the foundation of the proprietary relationship was different, and a distinct set of answers was applicable. It was proposed that the law by reference to which they married (the law with which the marriage had its closest connection; the matrimonial domicile) applied to determine the proprietary consequences of marriage,[55] but that this original regime did not

[49] Dicey & Morris, above n. 3, chap. 28.
[50] e.g., Matrimonial Causes Act 1973, s. 24(1)(c).
[51] *Re Fitzgerald* [1904] 1 Ch. 573 (CA).
[52] *Duke of Marlborough* v. *Att.-Gen.* [1945] Ch. 78 (CA). The connection is to a law, not to a country.
[53] *Re Cooke's Trusts* (1887) 56 LT 737; *Cooper* v. *Cooper* (1888) 13 App. Cas. 88.
[54] *De Nicols* v. *Curlier* [1900] AC 21.   [55] *Re Egerton's Will Trusts* [1956] Ch. 593.

necessarily survive a change of spousal domicile. The better view[56] is, however, that on marriage the spouses simply accept the scheme which is imposed by the law of the matrimonial domicile, and which may be a system of community of property, or separation of property, or some other variant. Whether or not this is conceptualized as a tacit contract or default provision is an irrelevance: it continues to apply after a change in personal domicile, and for the same reasons, as where there is an express contract.

A seeming problem may arise when two systems of provision come into contact and become entangled. If spouses marry into a system of community, when one dies the community rules will determine what portion of the marital property accrues to the survivor, and what falls into the estate of the deceased. But if the deceased dies domiciled in a country where separation of property, and particular provision for inheritance, is the basis of the law, that law may give the survivor a claim to a portion of the estate of the deceased, with the result that, in principle at least, the survivor takes more than either system would have provided. A practical solution would be for characterization to lead to the result that only one of these schemes applies, but all the while it is seen that there are two, sequential, issues—what did the deceased own when he died? Who succeeds to the estate of the deceased?—each having its own choice of law rule, this will be hard to achieve. And in any case, can one really be certain that this generosity to the survivor was not what the parties sought to bring about?

THE EFFECT OF DEATH ON PROPERTY RIGHTS

When someone dies and the question arises of the ownership of his or her property, it is necessary to separate two issues, each having its own rules for choice of law.[57] The first stage is the administration of the estate of the deceased: the interim process during which the assets are identified and collected, the proven debts paid in the order of their priority, and the balance of the estate calculated. If the deceased was subject to a regime of community of property, the effect of this on his estate will be calculated at this stage of administration. During this period, legal systems differ on the question of who owns the property: in some, the property vests immediately in those who will ultimately take it, but in England it vests in those charged with the administration of the estate. The second stage is

---

[56] P. Goldberg, 'The Assignment of Property on Marriage' (1970) 19 *ICLQ* 557.
[57] Dicey & Morris, above n. 3, chap. 26.

the substantive devolution of the estate: once the administration is complete, a further set of rules determines who actually takes which property. Substantive devolution sub-divides into three kinds: testate succession, where devolution is governed by a will left by the deceased and proved in the administration; intestate succession, where the deceased left no valid will or a will which left some of his estate ungifted, where the law steps in to allocate the property according to a formula which usually incorporates a descending scale of relationship; and *bona vacantia* where, because there is no succession (because there is no will and according to the rules on intestacy there is no relative to whom the property will pass by operation of law), the property is regarded as truly ownerless and will be taken by the state as a matter of last resort.

THE ADMINISTRATION OF ESTATES

The administration of estates is the process by which the estate of a deceased person is organized and settled prior to its distribution to those to whom the assets will pass by way of succession. As a matter of English law, it requires an order of the court to empower a person to deal with the assets of a deceased, whether by proving a will in order to appoint a named and willing executor or by obtaining a grant of letters of administration.[58] Though the court may make a grant of representation of any deceased, only rarely will it do so if there is no property of the deceased in England. The making of a grant confirms or vests the property of the deceased in the grantee. Where the deceased died domiciled in a foreign country, the court will usually make a grant to the person who, under the law of the domicile, has been or is entitled to be appointed to administer the estate.[59] The representative may take all steps to get in all property, wherever situated, of the deceased. The substance of the administration is governed by the law of the country under which the grant of representation was made.[60] As a matter of English law, in the paying of the deceased's debts foreign creditors and English creditors are treated alike; the admissibility of and priority between claims is governed by English law as *lex fori*.

A foreign grant of representation has, in principle, no effect in England: the person appointed must obtain an English grant.[61] This stands in curious contrast to the fact that the status of a foreign-appointed trustee

[58] *New York Breweries Co.* v. *Att.-Gen.* [1899] AC 62.
[59] Supreme Court Act 1981, s. 25(1).
[60] *Re Kloebe* (1884) 28 Ch. D 175; *Re Lorillard* [1922] 2 Ch. 638 (CA).
[61] *New York Breweries Co.* v. *Att.-Gen.* [1899] AC 62.

in bankruptcy is recognized without the need for further order. It has been said that this is the best way to secure the interests of English creditors, but this cannot explain the difference in treatment between different types of representation.

SUBSTANTIVE DEVOLUTION OF PROPERTY

Except where its rules lead to the conclusion that there was no valid will and no relative of the deceased to take on the intestacy, it is the law of succession which determines who takes the property of a deceased who may have died with or without leaving a will.[62] When disputes about succession arise, if a duly appointed representative is before the court, an English court has jurisdiction to determine a question of succession.[63] A foreign court is regarded as having jurisdiction to determine succession to the property, wherever situated, of a deceased dying domiciled in that country, and its decision will be recognized in England;[64] it also has jurisdiction to determine succession to all property within its territorial jurisdiction, regardless of the domicile of the deceased. The potential overlapping of decisions will require the principles of estoppel by *res judicata* to regulate it.

Where the deceased died having left a will, any question of his testamentary capacity is governed by his domicile at the date of making the will,[65] and the capacity of a legatee to take is conferred by the law of either his own or the testator's domicile.[66] The formal validity of the will is satisfied if it is formally valid according to the law of the place when and where it was executed, or the law of the place (at the time of either execution or death) where the deceased died domiciled or habitually resident, or of which he was a national.[67] The same laws govern the formal validity of a will revoking an earlier will.[68] Wills of immoveables are formally valid if they conform to the *lex situs*.[69] The material validity of a will is governed by the law of the testator's domicile at death,[70] except for immoveables, where this is governed by the *lex situs*.[71] It follows that if it is argued that the testator was limited as regards the fraction of his estate

---

[62] Dicey & Morris, above n. 3, chap. 27.
[63] *Re Lorillard* [1922] 2 Ch. 638 (CA).
[64] *Re Trufort* (1887) 36 Ch. D 600; *Ewing v. Orr-Ewing* (1883) 9 App. Cas. 34; *Ewing v. Orr-Ewing* (1885) 10 App. Cas. 5.
[65] *Re Fuld's Estate (No 3)* [1968] P 675.
[66] *Re Hellmann's Will* (1866) LR 2 Eq. 363.
[67] Wills Act 1963, s. 1.   [68] Ibid., s. 2(1)(c).   [69] Ibid., s. 2(1)(c).
[70] *Whicker v. Hume* (1858) 7 HLC 124; *Re Groos* [1915] Ch. 572; *Re Ross* [1930] 1 Ch. 377.
[71] *Nelson v. Bridport* (1846) 8 Beav. 547; *Freke v. Carbery* (1873) LR 16 Eq. 461.

over which he had testamentary freedom, as is the case in systems which provide a statutory portion for spouses and children, this question will be treated as one of the material validity of the will. But the interpretation of the will is governed by the law of the domicile at the date of making the will.[72] The validity of an act of revocation is governed by the domicile of the testator at the date of revocation.[73] So the question whether subsequent marriage, or the tearing up or burning of a will, serves to revoke an earlier will is determined by the *lex domicilii* of the testator at the date of the marriage or other event.

Where the deceased dies without leaving a valid will or fails to will a part of his estate, the intestate succession is governed by the domiciliary law of the deceased at the date his death, except that succession to immoveables is governed by the *lex situs*.[74] It is inherent in the nature of intestate succession that it means the taking of property, by operation of law, but by a relative of the deceased who did not make a will.

Where there is no will and no person to take by way of intestate succession, the property still has to pass. In this case the principles can no longer be those of succession, for there is no-one to succeed to it. Instead, a state will assume title to local ownerless property as *bona vacantia*, and the question of which state is governed in all cases by the *lex situs* of the property. An illusory problem arises when the application of the law of the domicile would vest the property of an intestate deceased in the state of his domicile, it being provided that the state is the 'final heir' of a deceased. It has been said that in this context it is necessary to characterize the rule of law relied on by the claiming state to determine whether it is a succession rule or a rule about *bona vacantia*, and that this is a matter of ascertaining the substance of the foreign rule rather than being persuaded by its form.[75] This is misguided. Quite apart from the fact that the process of characterization is directed at issues as distinct from rules of law, the law requires a characterization line to be drawn to separate intestate succession from the devolution of *bona vacantia*, to which a different choice of law rule, the *lex situs*, applies. The court must first decide whether the issue concerns property which is owned by way of succession, or is ownerless for failure of succession: only in the latter case does an issue arise of its devolution as *bona vacantia*. Thus understood, there is no need to characterize rules rather than issues. The misunderstanding

---

[72] *Ewing v. Orr-Ewing* (1883) 9 App. Cas. 34.
[73] *In bonis Reid* (1866) LR 1 P & D 74.
[74] *Balfour v. Scott* (1793) 6 Bro. PC 550.
[75] *Re Maldonado's Estate* [1954] P 233 (CA).

arises where the process of taking property upon death is seen in every case as succession. Once it is accepted that the true characterization category is the devolution of property on death, which in turn subdivides into three possibilities, each with its own choice of law rule, there is no real difficulty.

9

Family Law

ADULTS

Family law, and the private international law of marriage in particular, is the one area in which the *lex domicilii*, the law of the domicile, is pre-eminent. Not every issue is answered by recourse to it, nor has statutory reform or the intrusion of public policy left its hegemony untouched. But family law is largely about status; status is generally determined by the personal law; and as a matter of English conflict of laws, the personal law is the *lex domicilii*, the law of the domicile. It should not be supposed, though, that this means that there will be international agreement on the status of an individual. For although most systems agree that status is a matter for the personal law, there is no agreement about which law—domicile, nationality, law of the religious group, etc.—actually is the personal law; and even as between countries which use the *lex domicilii* as the personal law, there are differences in its definition. In the context of family law, the reference to *law* usually indicates the whole law, including the rules of the conflict of laws, which would be applied by a judge hearing the case in his own court: the principle of *renvoi* is relevant to those family law cases in which it is pleaded and proved.[1]

The plan of this chapter is to examine adult relations: marriage, matrimonial causes, and financial provision, and to undertake a brief summary of the highly complex law relating to children.

MARRIAGE

The validity or invalidity of marriage requires a preliminary distinction to be drawn between formal validity, capacity to marry, and other impediments to marriage.[2] The first is concerned with the ceremony and its components, the second with whether the person is in law entitled to marry, or entitled to marry the other, and the third with a miscellany of

[1] P. 15 above.
[2] Dicey & Morris, *The Conflict of Laws* (13th edn., Sweet & Maxwell, London, 2000), chap. 17.

issues of validity which are not within the scope of the other two. The advantage of this division is that it reflects the possible and legitimate interest of a number of countries in the validity of marriage, but seeks to limit that interest to those particular matters with which they are most closely concerned. On the other hand, reference to a number of laws may be complex, and may be thought to increase the likelihood of the marriage being invalidated by one law among several; and if this were valid as a criticism, it might be preferable to have marriage governed by a single law, say that with which the marriage is most closely connected. It is generally assumed that this should not be the law of the place of celebration, though this is not without significant support in the laws of the United States. On the other hand, such a rule, by focusing on the marriage as if it were a self-contained contract as opposed to a step in a chain of status-determining events, would weaken or destroy the idea of status as an enduring concept.

From time to time it is said that English law makes a presumption of the validity of marriage.[3] All this appears to mean is that where there is room for any flexibility in the rules for choice of law, and the parties believe that they have gone through a valid ceremony of marriage, any doubt should be resolved in favour of validity. This cannot be taken to mean that marriage is a higher and more developed state of existence, but reflects the sensible fact that where there has been a wedding ceremony, and reliance has been placed on its validity, there needs to be good reason to surprise the parties and any interested third parties by regarding it as having been invalid all along.

Once an issue has been characterized, and the relevant choice of law rule invoked, it must be decided what precise question is to be formulated for answer by reference to the chosen law. Suppose facts are characterized as raising an issue of formal validity, and that this requires reference to a foreign law which, in the particular case, governs formal validity. The question to be referred to the foreign law for answer will be either 'is this marriage formally valid despite . . .' or 'is this marriage valid despite . . .', the difference being whether the characterization which led to the choice of law remains as a constraint on the formulation of the question. It was proposed above[4] that it does not: that where the English court may be trying to decide the case as the foreign judge would, there is no sense in pre-empting the foreign law on the first stage of the analysis which it would have to undertake.

---

[3] e.g. *Radwan v. Radwan (No 2)* [1973] Fam. 35.   [4] At p. 18.

Formal validity of marriage

The formal requirements of a marriage ceremony and the effects of non-compliance are governed by the law of the place of celebration of the marriage, the *lex loci celebrationis*.[5] The question whether there is need for a public, civil, or religious ceremony,[6] whether particular words need to be read or spoken in the course of the ceremony, whether the ceremony must be held in the particular building or in none, whether a priest need be present, whether it is necessary for either party to be present in person or by proxy,[7] or whether it is necessary for the parents or other third parties to give their consent,[8] are all characterized as issues of formal validity. They are all governed by the *lex loci celebrationis*, and the consequences in terms of nullity or otherwise are determined by it as well. If the marriage would be invalid by the domestic law of the place of celebration, but would be valid by reference to the law to which a judge at the *locus celebrationis* would look if he were dealing with the issue, the marriage will be formally validated via the principles of *renvoi*.[9] Though theoretically possible, it is extremely unlikely that the reverse proposition would invalidate a marriage, because all systems regard compliance with local forms as sufficient.

There is an exception to the proposition that a marriage is formally valid only if it complied with the *lex loci celebrationis*. In two cases a marriage will be formally valid by having complied with the rudimentary formal requirements of the English common law as this stood prior to 1753. This extraordinary proposition—that a completely foreign marriage may be formally valid if it complied with the requirements of a law prior to its alteration by statute nearly 250 years ago—is only a little less startling if it is remembered that this is in fact a reference to the canon law which prevailed across much of Europe, and in England until 1753. The requirements of the pre-1753 common law involve no more than the public declaration of intention to marry in the presence of witnesses with no need for a priest,[10] which comes close to saying that there are no formal requirements at all. This suffices to establish formal validity

[5] *Simonin* v. *Mallac* (1860) 2 Sw. & Tr. 67; *Berthiaume* v. *Dastous* [1930] AC 79 (PC).
[6] *Taczanowska* v. *Taczanowski* [1957] P 301 (CA).
[7] *Apt* v. *Apt* [1948] P 83 (CA); *McCabe* v. *McCabe* [1994] 1 FLR 257 (CA).
[8] *Simonin* v. *Mallac* (1860) 2 Sw. & Tr. 67; *Ogden* v. *Ogden* [1908] P 46 (CA) (both parental consent); cf *Sottomayor* v. *De Barros (No 1)* (1877) 2 PD 81 (CA) (papal consent, though this may instead be a question of personal capacity).
[9] *Taczanowska* v. *Taczanowski* [1957] P 301 (CA).
[10] *Wolfenden* v. *Wolfenden* [1946] P 61; *Penhas* v. *Tan Soo Eng* [1953] AC 304 (PC).

where it was impossible for the parties to comply with local forms, or where the place of celebration was under belligerent occupation and the parties belonged to or were associated with those occupying forces.[11] Impossibility may arise if two persons wish to marry in a place where civil order has broken down, or where there is no human population; but it is less clear whether it applies if the parties have ethical objections to the form—say that only religious marriage is permitted—of local marriage ceremony. It is hard to see why parties should be able to opt out of the local law, especially now that international travel is not difficult. But if the parties do not come within the local formality criteria for marriage, it is hard to deny that marriage is impossible for them. As regards belligerent occupation, it would be revolting to common sense to require Polish or Jewish persons who sought to marry while serving in forces in belligerent occupation of Germany or Italy in 1945, or in groups associated with them, to comply with the formal requirements of those laws, even if the marriage would not be technically impossible. The existence of this exception reflects the triumph of pragmatism over dogmatism. Statutory provision is made for members of H.M. forces to marry while serving abroad, and for consular marriages.[12]

Capacity of persons to marry

Each party is required to have capacity to marry the other according to the law of his or her ante-nuptial domicile, the *lex domicilii*.[13] The reason is said to be that whether someone is prepared for matrimony is determined by the society in which he or she has grown up. Some authorities suggest that the law of the intended matrimonial home might be a more appropriate test, but none has so decided, and the inherent uncertainty of such a test makes it difficult to support, at least when the question arises prospectively.[14] But it must be admitted that there is much to be said for the view that the law of the society in which the spouses are going to live has the closest interest in whether they have capacity to live as husband and wife. The characterization category of capacity includes the age of marital capacity[15] and the prohibited degrees of relationship.[16] But the

---

[11] *Taczanowska* v. *Taczanowski* [1957] P 301 (CA); *Preston* v. *Preston* [1963] P 411 (CA).
[12] Foreign Marriage Act 1892, ss. 22 (as amended) and 1, respectively.
[13] *Brook* v. *Brook* (1861) 9 HLC 193; *Sottomayor* v. *De Barros (No 2)* (1879) 5 PD 94.
[14] For its use retrospectively see *Radwan* v. *Radwan* [1973] Fam. 35.
[15] The Marriage Act 1949, s. 2, applies to any marriage in England, and requires that neither party be under 16.
[16] *Brook* v. *Brook* (1861) 9 HLC 193.

distinct issue of the effect of a previous marriage arguably dissolved or annulled by decree is examined below, as is the treatment of same-sex marriage.

The concurrent role of the *lex loci celebrationis* in the regulation of capacity is complex. One should first consider whether it is necessary to comply with the capacity rules of the *lex loci* as well as with those of the personal laws. If the marriage takes place in England it is probable that the parties must also satisfy the capacity requirements of English law,[17] at least if the issue arises prior to the celebration of the marriage, in the form of judicial review of a registrar's refusal to license the marriage. So if the registrar refuses to permit the marriage of two foreign-domiciled persons, one of whom is under 16, he will not be ordered to marry them even though each has domiciliary capacity. But if the marriage has taken place in England, the parties having had capacity by their personal laws, and subject to what is said about marriages celebrated overseas, it is hard to see the interest of English law in then regarding it as invalid. If they marry overseas, the dominant, though questionable, view is that the parties do not need capacity under the *lex loci* in addition to satisfying their personal laws, even though one case did assume that such capacity was required.[18] But there is a respectable argument that capacity by the *lex loci*, whether English or overseas, ought to be required. It is unconvincing to maintain that the law of the place is uniquely concerned with formal validity, and completely unconcerned with capacity. Moreover, if the law under which the celebrant is vested with authority considers that, on account of the parties' lack of capacity to marry, his purported act of marriage was a nullity, it is hard to see why English law should disagree. If it is correct to regard marriage as something which is done by a marriage officer, rather than by the parties themselves, the law which defines the officer's powers appears to be acutely interested in the question whether he has altered the capacity of the parties, even though reference to an additional law will tend to increase the invalidity of marriages.

By contrast with the possibility that the *lex loci* may invalidate a marriage, otherwise valid, for lack of capacity, it may also validate a marriage even though one of the parties lacks domiciliary capacity. If the marriage takes place in England, one party being domiciled in England, it suffices for the other to have capacity according to English domestic law, even

---

[17] There is no judicial authority to this effect, however.
[18] *Breen v. Breen* [1964] P 144.

though he or she lacks capacity under the domiciliary law.[19] This is a controversial principle, justified on the unconvincing basis that injustice would otherwise be done to an English domiciliary. Its weakness is magnified when it is observed that the foreign incapacities which the court indicated it was prepared to override were opposed to English public policy—prohibitions on inter-racial marriage, the need for the Pope to consent—and which could have been better accommodated under that exceptional rule. Tellingly, the rule has no counterpart for a marriage taking place overseas in the domicile of one of the parties.

Other impediments to marriage

There remain a number of other factors which may lead to the invalidity of marriage, but which it is not helpful to see as raising issues of personal capacity, and which are not the subject of a uniform choice of law rule. They are grouped together for convenience. First, each party must consent to marry the other. Any argument that there was no consent, whether this is said to follow from mistake, fraud, concealment, or duress, will be governed by the *lex domicilii* of the party said not to have consented, as if this were a question of personal capacity.[20] Secondly, it is rational, though not clearly established by law, that physical impediments such as inability or refusal to consummate the marriage by sexual intercourse are referable to the law of the allegedly incapable party,[21] although contrary views are not untenable: it may be argued that if the willing-and-able party has no capacity to marry a refuser, that party's law should apply instead. But as absence of consent and refusal both render a marriage voidable rather than void, there is room for the further alternative view that the case should be seen to be closer to divorce, and on that basis the appropriate choice of law would be the *lex fori*.

Thirdly, there are special rules which apply to the validity of polygamous marriages in so far as the polygamy is alleged to be an impediment. For the purpose of the rule, it is first necessary to identify a marriage as polygamous. This will be the case[22] if two conditions are met: it is celebrated in polygamous form[23] and the husband's *lex domicilii* gives him

[19] *Sottomayor v. De Barros (No 2)* (1879) 5 PD 94; *Ogden v. Ogden* [1908] P 46 (CA) (alternative ratio).
[20] *Szechter v. Szechter* [1971] P 286, but cf *Vervaeke v. Smith* [1983] 1 AC 145.
[21] *Ponticelli v. Ponticelli* [1958] P 204.
[22] Subject to the Private International Law (Miscellaneous Provisions) Act 1995, s. 5, a marriage is polygamous if actually or potentially so.
[23] *Lee v. Lau* [1967] P 14.

personal capacity for polygamy.[24] The first condition means that a marriage celebrated in England is inevitably monogamous but, if celebrated overseas, the nature of the marriage will depend on the nature of the ceremony. The second condition needs no further explanation, save that if the husband loses his personal capacity for polygamy, the nature of the marriage will change to monogamy.[25] When the matter was regulated by the common law, the second condition meant that a marriage celebrated overseas by an English domiciled man was not polygamous, for he lacked personal capacity for polygamy. But if celebrated by a English-domiciled woman it could be polygamous (as the husband may have personal capacity for polygamy), and it would on that account be invalid if her capacity to enter it was governed by English law as her *lex domicilii*. But it is now provided that if a potentially polygamous marriage is actually monogamous, an English woman does not lack capacity to enter it; the domiciliary incapacity is restricted to actually polygamous marriages. Moreover, while a woman domiciled in a country which permits polygamy may contract a polygamous marriage, and an Englishwoman has no personal capacity for actual polygamy,[26] it has been held, in a decision ostensibly designed to uphold the validity of a marriage which had endured for twenty years, that her personal capacity to contract a polygamous marriage is actually governed by the law of the intended matrimonial home.[27]

Fourthly, if a previous marriage has been dissolved or annulled by a decree recognized by English law otherwise than under Council Regulation (EC) 1347/2000,[28] the subsequent remarriage of either party is not invalidated by the refusal of some other system of law to recognize the decree.[29] So if a Maltese domiciliary is divorced by a decree recognized by the Family Law Act 1986 but denied recognition under Maltese law, the remarriage will be valid even though Maltese law, as the law of the domicile, would regard the first marriage as undissolved and the second marriage as bigamous and void: this result is brought about by legislation, and the deduction that a divorce is not really being recognized in accordance with Parliament's instruction if it still leaves the spouse incapable of marriage. In this it reverses the understanding of the common law

[24] *Hussain* v. *Hussain* [1983] Fam. 26 (CA).
[25] *Ali* v. *Ali* [1968] P 564; *Parkasho* v. *Singh* [1968] P 223.
[26] Private International Law (Miscellaneous Provisions) Act 1995, s. 5.
[27] *Radwan* v. *Radwan (No 2)* [1973] Fam. 35.
[28] [2000] OJ L160/19, discussed below, at p. 235.
[29] Family Law Act 1986, s. 50.

which, though allowing the recognition of a divorce to break the bonds of matrimony, accepted that capacity to remarry was a distinct issue having a different choice of law. The inverse position, where the *lex domicilii* recognizes the validity of a decree which English legislation does not, is not provided for. But if the *lex domicilii* regards an individual as capable of remarriage it is hard to see the rational interest of English law in contradicting it just because English law would not recognize the decree.[30] On the other hand, the wording of the Family Law Act 1986, section 45, may stand in the way of this result, on the ground that to accept the remarriage as valid is to grant constructive recognition to the divorce; and section 45 states that a divorce may not be recognized except in accordance with the Act.

But where recognition of the decree is mandated by Chapter III of Council Regulation (EC) 1347/2000,[31] the provisions of the Family Law Act 1986 do not apply[32] and the impact of the decree on the parties' capacity to remarry is more uncertain. As the Regulation governs the dissolution of matrimonial ties, and makes no claim to affect related issues,[33] it may not mean that a spouse whose personal law refuses to recognize the decree is free to remarry. The choice is to regard the issue as governed by the law of the state which granted the decree and to give it the effect it had under that law;[34] discerning the answer from the text of the Regulation; reverting to the common law;[35] or pretending that the Family Law Act 1986, section 50, had not been made inapplicable to such cases.[36]

Fifthly, English courts have not yet had to decide whether any special rule applies to marriages celebrated between persons of the same sex. Though this form of marriage is denied to English domiciliaries,[37] this statutory provision cannot be applied when neither party is English and the marriage was not celebrated in England.[38] Given that an overseas polygamous marriage was accepted as valid and lawful over a century ago,

---

[30] *Schwebel* v. *Ungar* (1963) 42 DLR (2d) 622 (Ont. CA) supports the application of the *lex domicilii* over the non-recognition of the *lex fori*.
[31] [2000] OJ L160/19; and see SI 2001/310.
[32] SI 2001/310, reg. 9, amending the Family Law Act 1986, Pt. III.
[33] Recital 10.
[34] Cf Case 145/86 *Hoffmann* v. *Krieg* [1988] ECR 645.
[35] Giving primacy to the personal law: *Schwebel* v. *Ungar* (1963) 42 DLR (2d) 622 (Ont. CA).
[36] Despite the wording of SI 2001/310, reg. 9.
[37] Matrimonial Causes Act 1973, s. 11(c). It is permitted under the laws of Denmark and the Netherlands.
[38] Cf *Pugh* v. *Pugh* [1951] P 482 on the reach of the Marriage Act 1949 (held not to apply to foreign marriages between foreigners).

despite the fact that English domiciliaries had and have[39] no capacity for it, and given that the marriage of uncle and niece, valid under the respective personal laws, was not held to offend against English public policy,[40] there is no rational reason to regard same-sex marriage as being the concern of laws other than the *lex domicilii* and the law of the place of celebration. Of course, if the *lex loci celebrationis* does not define the union as marriage it is most unlikely[41] that an English court would disagree.[42] But if the *lex loci* does define the union as marriage,[43] and the parties have personal capacity to enter it, it is no business of English law to override this conclusion. Though it is the discriminatory policy of English domestic law to deny the possibility of such marriage, the contamination of private international law by ecclesiastical bigotry would be a shaming act which the European Convention on Human Rights, if nothing else, should serve to prevent.

Sixthly, public policy may intervene at the point when a rule of the *lex causae*, even after making allowance for different cultural and social traditions, offends the English conception of marriage and freedom to marry. For example, if the personal law of one of the parties denies marital capacity to a person on grounds which are capricious, penal, or discriminatory,[44] such an impediment will be ignored. And if the personal laws were to confer marital capacity at the age of five, or allow marriage to a dead person, it is possible that public policy would deny recognition. But English law draws the limits of public policy tightly, with the result that marriages which are considerably different from the English domestic law model may be recognized.

MATRIMONIAL CAUSES

The private international law of matrimonial causes[45] has to juggle a number of laws which may all have some interest in the issues which arise. The laws which determine the initial validity of marriage may not be those which apply on its annulment or dissolution; the laws which

[39] At least where the marriage is actually polygamous.
[40] *Cheni* v. *Cheni* [1965] P 85.
[41] It is not impossible that English law could take a different view: cf *Lee* v. *Lau* [1967] P 14 on the characterization of a marriage as polygamous, where the *lex loci*'s classification was not followed.
[42] It will presumably still take effect as giving rise to contractual rights.
[43] Civil unions under French law are not regarded as marriages.
[44] *Scott* v. *Att.-Gen.* (1886) 11 PD 128; cf *Sottomayor* v. *De Barros (No 2)* (1879) 5 PD 94.
[45] The rules also cover judicial separation, but the infrequency of this form of decree justifies its omission from a book of this size.

determine the effectiveness of an annulment or dissolution may not, as has been seen, be the ones which determine the power to remarry. There are two parties who, by the time matters come to court, may have separated and have separate domiciles and residences; there will be laws which had, laws which have, and laws which will have, a connection to the facts and to the parties themselves. There may be third parties with personal laws which also have an interest in being taken into account. Decrees of nullity and divorce may be obtained by civil proceedings which may or may not also be judicial, but also by reference to religious law. A local policy of being disposed to grant recognition to divorces may clash with a foreign law's policy of not doing so; and all in all there is plenty of scope for a conflict of laws. Perhaps because of this, the role of the *lex fori* is more prominent than one might expect it to be in the field of status; and the rules on jurisdiction are complex.

Outside the context of choice of law, the law does not draw a sharp distinction between divorce and annulment, for though the two forms of decree are quite distinct, the law is complicated enough without having separate sets of rules for jurisdiction, choice of law, and recognition. Accordingly, they may be considered together as matrimonial causes.

Having been kept at bay until recently, the European Union has finally got its hoof in the door by the adoption of Council Regulation (EC) 1347/2000,[46] which governs the jurisdiction of Member States to grant matrimonial decrees and provides for the recognition and enforcement of decrees granted in other Member States. The internal market[47] is secure at last. It follows that the law on jurisdiction to grant, and recognition of, decrees needs to be divided into two parts.

Obtaining decrees from an English court

The jurisdiction of an English court to grant a decree of divorce, legal separation, or annulment is governed in the first instance by Council Regulation (EC) 1347/2000[48] and depends on the respondent spouse.[49] If the respondent is habitually resident in a Member State[50] or is a national of a Member State other than the United Kingdom or Ireland, or

[46] [2000] OJ L160/19.

[47] See Recital 2.

[48] [2000] OJ L160/19. Consequential amendments to statutes are made by SI 2001/310.

[49] In this respect the structure of the law is close to that of Council Reg. (EC) 44/2001 [2000] OJ L12/1, dealing with jurisdiction in civil and commercial matters, in which the domicile of the defendant is of principal concern.

[50] A state of the European Union excluding Denmark: Art. 1(3).

is domiciled[51] in England, Scotland, Northern Ireland, or Ireland, jurisdiction may be taken only in accordance with Articles 2 to 6 of the Regulation.[52] Accordingly the court has jurisdiction if both spouses are domiciled in England.[53] Alternatively, it has jurisdiction if England is where the spouses are habitually resident; or where they were last habitually resident, in so far as one of them still resides there; or where the respondent is habitually resident; or where (in the event of a joint application) either of the spouses is habitually resident; or where the applicant is, and for a year immediately before the application was made was, habitually resident; or where the applicant, who is domiciled in England, was habitually resident for six months immediately prior to the application.[54] If none of these provisions gives jurisdiction to the court, there is no jurisdictional basis for an application; where they give jurisdiction to the English courts and those of another Member State, Article 11 provides for a first-seised rule to settle any problem of *lis alibi pendens*.

If the respondent is not so resident, domiciled, or a national, Article 8 of the Regulation provides that 'residual' jurisdiction is a matter for national law to determine.[55] In England this will require that either party to the marriage was domiciled in England on the date the proceedings were begun;[56] jurisdiction over proceedings for nullity is substantially the same,[57] save that a decree of nullity may also be granted if one party has died but at death was domiciled, or had for a year been habitually resident, in England.[58] But proceedings may also be brought in a foreign court. In relation to parallel proceedings, if the other court is that of another Member State, Article 11 will apply a first-seised rule to deny the jurisdiction of the second court, but the Regulation otherwise takes no account of principles of *forum conveniens*. Subject to that overriding rule an English court has a statutory[59] power to stay proceedings. Accordingly,

---

[51] As a matter of the law of the UK: Art. 41(b).   [52] Art. 7.

[53] Art. 2(1)(b). The corresponding rule for the other Member States except Ireland is framed in terms of nationality rather than domicile. 'Domicile' has its common law meaning: Art. 4(2); and England is treated as if it were a Member State by reason of Art. 41.

[54] Art. 2(1)(a).

[55] Art. 8.

[56] Domicile and Matrimonial Proceedings Act 1973, s. 5(2) as amended by SI 2001/310, reg. 3(4).

[57] Domicile and Matrimonial Proceedings Act 1973, s. 5(3) as amended by SI 2001/310, reg. 3(5).

[58] Ibid.

[59] Domicile and Matrimonial Proceedings Act 1973, Sch. 1, para. 9, as amended by SI 2001/310, reg. 4. Whether a court may stay its proceedings if jurisdiction is founded on Art. 2 of the Reg. but the natural forum in a non-member state is uncertain: cf *Re Harrods (Buenos Aires) Ltd.* [1992] Ch. 72 (CA).

where jurisdiction is taken under Article 8, a stay may be obligatory given prior divorce proceedings in another part of the United Kingdom,[60] and is discretionary in all other cases. Though this statutory power is distinct from the inherent power to stay on grounds of *forum non conveniens*, any distinction between the two is more technical than substantial. It follows that if the foreign court is clearly and distinctly more appropriate than England for the resolution of the dispute, the fact that the petitioner will be disadvantaged by having to proceed in the foreign jurisdiction will not ward off a stay if substantial justice may be obtained there.[61] There is no[62] hard and fast rule that a stay should be granted if the foreign proceedings were begun first, but there will be a strong disinclination to allow later-begun proceedings to continue in a way which simply duplicates earlier ones.

On a petition for divorce, an English court applies English domestic law without exception. There has been no significant questioning of the rightness of this. Whenever there are proposals to alter the grounds upon which a divorce may be obtained, there is public debate and often sharp disagreement. In this sensitive context it would not be acceptable for some divorces to be granted on grounds insufficient in English domestic law, or for a petitioner to be denied a divorce though satisfying the criteria of English law. The general application of English law to everyone, equally and indiscriminately, is inevitable. For decrees of nullity, the applicable law will be deduced from the grounds of invalidity examined in relation to the original validity of marriage: allegations of personal incapacity will be governed by the *lex domicilii*, and so on. If the marriage is plainly void, as distinct from being voidable or dissoluble, there is no need to obtain a decree to this effect, though it will usually be prudent to do so. Where the alleged defect relied on is one which is in substance unknown, either precisely or by analogy, to English law, no reported authority exists to confer the power to annul the marriage.[63] Presumably such cases will be very rare indeed, and the chances must be that to grant a decree on such grounds would offend English public policy.

Recognition of judgments

There are three main statutory schemes for the recognition of foreign

---

[60] Domicile and Matrimonial Proceedings Act 1973, Sch. 1, para. 8.

[61] *De Dampierre v. De Dampierre* [1988] AC 92.

[62] By contrast, the High Court of Australia does appear to have such a view: *Henry v. Henry* (1996) 185 CLR 571.

[63] Cf *Vervaeke v. Smith* [1983] 1 AC 145.

judgments given in matrimonial causes. The principal distinction is the source of the judgment. A decree from Scotland, Northern Ireland, the Channel Islands, or the Isle of Man will be recognized on the same basis as an English decree, that is, that it was granted by a court.[64] A decree from a Member State bound by Council Regulation (EC) 1347/2000 will be governed by that regime;[65] otherwise recognition is governed by the Family Law Act 1986, Part III.

Council Regulation (EC) 1347/2000

The law on recognition of matrimonial decrees from Member States is contained in Chapter III of the Regulation. It is closely modelled on the corresponding provisions of Council Regulation (EC) 44/2001 on jurisdiction and judgments in civil and commercial matters, and the discussion here is, therefore, abbreviated. But the effect is to align civil, commercial, and matrimonial judgments for the purposes of recognition: this is a radical departure from the tradition of English law, which had kept them well apart. Recognition under Chapter III will apply to decrees obtained from a court in a Member State given in proceedings which were instituted after 1 March 2001, save that in the case of proceedings pre-dating commencement, recognition may be granted if jurisdiction was founded on rules corresponding to those of Chapter II.[66] Any divorce, legal separation, or annulment pronounced by a court[67] in a Member State is to be recognized without any procedure or formality.[68] Non-recognition is permitted[69] if recognition is manifestly contrary to public policy; if the judgment was given in default of appearance and there was no due and timely service, unless the respondent has unequivocally accepted the judgment; if the judgment is irreconcilable with a local judgment in proceedings between the same parties; or if it is irreconcilable with an earlier judgment from a non-member state in proceedings between the same parties which qualified for recognition. But the

---

[64] Family Law Act 1986, s. 44.
[65] [2000] OJ L160/19. Subject to the proceedings having been instituted after 1 March 2001, or having been founded on jurisdictional rules which correspond to those in the Reg.: Art. 42.
[66] Art. 42.
[67] Which includes all authorities with jurisdiction in these matters, so that non-judicial decrees are treated as if they were judicial decrees: Art. 1(2). By way of derogation, it appears from Recital 10 that 'purely religious procedures' are excluded from the scope of the Reg., and decrees granted by such bodies are therefore recognized, if at all, under the Family Law Act 1986.
[68] Art. 14.
[69] Art. 15, on which see Art. 34 of Council Reg. (EC) 44/2001 [2001] OJ L12/1.

jurisdiction of the adjudicating court may not be reviewed or subjected to the test of public policy;[70] recognition may not be withheld on the basis that the recognizing court would not itself have granted the decree;[71] and the substance of the judgment may not be reviewed.[72] Curiously, perhaps, recognition is said not to affect the property consequences of the marriage, maintenance obligations, or other ancillary measures,[73] though it is difficult to see how these can remain wholly unaffected. As was pointed out above, it is not said whether it is implicit in the obligation to recognize a decree that the parties to the former marriage have restored to them their capacity to marry, even if the personal law of one of them would refuse to acknowledge it. Recital 10 would suggest that recognition extends only to the dissolution of matrimonial ties, but there is English authority for the proposition that a decree can hardly be said to have been recognized if it does not carry with it the freedom to remarry.[74] The procedure for enforcement, where this is required as a separate legal effect, is set out in Articles 21 to 35, which also correspond to the provisions of Council Regulation (EC) 44/2001. Pre-existing conventions with non-member states continue to have effect.

Family Law Act 1986, Part III

Regulation 1347/2000 proceeds by fixing on the court[75] which granted the decree. This makes it easy to determine whether the decree is one to which the Regulation applies. The Family Law Act 1986[76] also draws a fundamental distinction according to where the decree was obtained: they are either divorces obtained in the British islands[77] or are overseas divorces. This would be sensible if divorces were always obtained in a single country, as will be seen, the untidy reality invariably does not conform to that template. Nevertheless, the point of departure is that divorces or annulments obtained in England must be obtained by means

---

[70] Art. 17. [71] Art. 18. [72] Art. 19.

[73] Recital 10 to the Reg.

[74] *Lawrence* v. *Lawrence* [1985] Fam. 106 (CA); Family Law Act 1986, s. 50. But s. 50 does not apply to decrees recognized under the Reg.: Family Law Act 1986, s. 45(2) as inserted by SI 2001/310, reg. 9.

[75] Which has a widened definition: [2000] OJ L160/19, Art. 1(2).

[76] The legislation draws no distinction between divorces and annulments, and the term 'decrees' is used to encompass both. But for convenience of explanation, we will use the term 'divorce' to include divorce and nullity.

[77] This expression includes England, Scotland, Northern Ireland, the Channel Islands, and the Isle of Man (decrees from Ireland fall under the Reg.). Nevertheless, for convenience we will refer to English and overseas divorces.

of judicial proceedings, otherwise they are of no effect.[78] 'Overseas divorces', which means divorces obtained in a country outside the British islands, will be recognized, according to section 45(1), only in accordance with sections 46 to 49; and according to section 46 it is necessary to decide whether they were obtained by means of proceedings (whether judicial or otherwise) or not.[79] The separate treatment of divorces obtained without proceedings requires the drawing of a peculiarly useless line of division. Were a distinction necessary, separate treatment of civil-judicial, and religious-non-judicial, divorces would have reflected the rather different procedures and assumptions underpinning each category of case. But this was not done and, for the recognition of foreign divorces, all now turns on whether the divorce was obtained by proceedings.

But the scheme put in place by sections 44 and 45(1) proceeds on the unspoken assumption that every divorce or annulment is obtained in a single country. Problems arise when a decree is obtained by means of proceedings whose components touch more countries than one. In relation to decrees presented for recognition as overseas divorces, the leading cases[80] were both ones where part of the procedure leading to the divorce—in each case a divorce obtained outside court and under religious law—had taken place in England. In holding that this precluded recognition of the decree, the court did not limit its reasoning to a case where part of the procedure had taken place in England. Instead, it deduced from the statutory definition of an overseas divorce that to be recognized as such, all the elements required for it to be obtained must be located in one foreign country. So a Jewish religious divorce obtained by the formal writing and delivery of a bill of divorce, or a modified Islamic divorce obtained by the writing of the words of repudiation and sending them to the wife and to a statutory body, will be denied recognition if any of the elements—it will often be the sending or service of a document— was geographically separated from the others; and it appears to be irrelevant that the divorce would be recognized as effective in each of the countries in which parts of it happened. Why English law should deny recognition to a divorce which is regarded as effective by the laws of all those countries which had a factual connection with it on this ground is beyond rational explanation.

Daft as this undoubtedly is, it produces three further consequences of

---

[78] Family Law Act 1986 (hereafter 'the 1986 Act'), s. 44. [79] Ibid., s. 46.
[80] *Berkovits* v. *Grinberg* [1995] Fam. 142, effectively following *R.* v. *Secretary of State for the Home Department, ex p. Fatima* [1986] AC 527 (a case on earlier legislation).

baffling absurdity. The first is that such a trans-national divorce, being excluded from the definition of an overseas divorce, is not one which section 45(1) requires to be recognized under the 1986 Act or not at all: this is true only for overseas divorces, which means those obtained in a country. No provision of the Act specifically proscribes the recognition of divorces which are not, in this particular sense, overseas divorces. As all other statutory schemes for recognition have been repealed, it appears to follow that such decrees fall to be recognized under the rules of the common law thought to have been abolished in 1971.[81] The second is that a divorce obtained from a Canadian court cannot be recognized as an overseas divorce if any of the procedural elements—such as the service of the petition on the respondent—took place outside Canada: it will no longer be a divorce obtained in Canada and it will no longer fall under section 45. The third is that where service of an English petition is made outside England, the divorce will, by parity of reasoning, not be seen as a divorce obtained in England, with the restrictions which the law places on such divorces. The result is quite impossible, but it follows from the legislative insistence that divorces can be categorized according to where they were obtained, and the judicial insistence that this means all elements must be concentrated in the one place. As a cautionary tale against legislation, the conflict of laws offers none more startling than this.

If the decree was obtained in a single country outside the British islands, the rules governing its recognition depend on whether it was obtained by judicial or other proceedings.[82] Judicial proceedings are not hard to identify as such, but 'other proceedings' require the involvement of an agency of or recognized by the state, having a role which is more than merely probative.[83] Quite why this was considered to be a line worth drawing is a mystery,[84] and it requires some intricate analysis of religious and foreign law. A religious divorce conforming to the (Pakistani) Muslim Family Law Ordinance 1961 is obtained by proceedings,[85] because the

---

[81] The Recognition of Divorces and Legal Separations Act 1971, which abolished them, was itself repealed by the Family Law Act 1986. The rules recognized a divorce if granted by a court which had a real and substantial connection to the case.

[82] 1986 Act, s. 54(1).

[83] *Chaudhary* v. *Chaudhary* [1985] Fam. 19 (CA).

[84] Indeed, it may not have been intended as a line at all: its appearance in the Recognition of Divorces and Legal Separations Act 1971 may have been intended to clarify that *all* divorces, whether judicial or not, were within the Act. Only after it had been held that 'judicial or other proceedings' were not inclusive, but served to exclude some forms of divorce, did the idea take root that there was a line to be drawn, and this understanding, or maybe misunderstanding, was subsequently incorporated into the 1986 Act.

[85] *Quazi* v. *Quazi* [1980] AC 744.

statutory requirement to notify the Chairman of the Union Council and the imposition of a statutory timetable amount to proceedings; likewise a Lebanese Muslim divorce which required registration in the Sharia court after being pronounced by the husband.[86] The same was held, but on rather less convincing grounds, in the case of a Jewish divorce: it was obtained by proceedings because, it seems, of the elaborate ceremonial involved.[87] But a traditional Muslim divorce, effected by unilateral words of repudiation,[88] is not obtained by means of proceedings.[89]

If the decree was obtained by proceedings and is to be recognized, it must be obtained where either[90] party was domiciled, according either to English law or to the law of the place of the obtaining,[91] or was habitually resident, or was a national. The decree must be effective under that law to dissolve the marriage.[92] Where domicile or habitual residence is relied on as the jurisdictional connection, the decree must be effective in the relevant law district, such as Nevada as distinct from the United States; but in the case of nationality, it must be effective throughout the entire national territory,[93] a fact which may raise issues of constitutional law. Recognition of the decree may be denied[94] on grounds of lack of notice or of the right to be heard, or if the matter is already *res judicata*. It may also be denied on grounds of public policy, and the operation of that policy may vary according to whether the marriage or the spouses had a significant connection to England.[95] Though the grounds upon which the decree was obtained are not specified as a ground of objection, they will, in an extreme case, be relevant, such as where a marriage is judicially[96] annulled for racial reasons. Indeed, some may also think that the very idea of recognizing a religious divorce in which one spouse has no right to be consulted, never mind be represented and heard, is so offensively discriminatory that legal tolerance stops well short of accepting it.

If the decree was obtained without proceedings, its recognition requires that it be obtained where both parties were domiciled when it was obtained, or where one was domiciled, with the country of domicile

---

[86] *El Fadl* v. *El Fadl* [2000] 1 FLR 175.   [87] *Berkovits* v. *Grinberg* [1995] Fam. 142.
[88] 'Talaq, talaq, talaq' ('I divorce you').
[89] *Chaudhary* v. *Chaudhary* [1985] Fam. 19 (CA).
[90] Husband or wife, petitioner or respondent.
[91] 1986 Act, s. 46(5).
[92] Ibid., s. 46(1); though not necessarily to re-attribute marital capacity: s. 50.
[93] Ibid., s. 49(3)(a).   [94] Ibid., s. 51.
[95] Cf *Chaudhary* v. *Chaudhary* [1985] Fam. 19 (CA).
[96] If a marriage is held to be dissolved by operation of law when one of the parties changes religion, this should not be seen as a case of divorce.

of the other party recognizing the decree. But it will be denied recognition in any event if either party had been habitually resident in the United Kingdom throughout the year prior to its being obtained.[97] The statutory grounds of non-recognition include those which may be raised against decrees obtained by proceedings but, in a final spasm of legislative caprice, recognition may also be denied if there is no official document certifying the effectiveness of the decree under the law of the foreign country.[98]

Financial provision and maintenance

The jurisdictional rules are particularly complex; and several bases need to be distinguished. The complexity reflects the fact that there are many reasons why an English court should be able to make such orders, and they comprise an untidy list, rather than proceeding from a concise statement of principle. English courts may make an order for financial provision on or before granting a decree of divorce, nullity, or judicial separation.[99] Subject to the jurisdictional rules of Council Regulation (EC) 44/2001,[100] they also have jurisdiction to make an order for financial provision after a foreign decree recognized in England if either party was domiciled in England when the divorce was obtained or when applying for leave to proceed, or if either party was habitually resident in England for the year preceding either of those dates, or if either has a beneficial interest in a dwelling house (once the matrimonial home) at the date of the application for leave to proceed.[101] A court may make an order for financial provision on the ground of failure to provide reasonable maintenance if either party is domiciled in England on the date of the application, or has been habitually resident for the year preceding that date, or if the respondent is present in England on that date.[102] A magistrates' court has jurisdiction to make a maintenance order if the respondent is resident in England,[103] or in a foreign country to which the Maintenance Orders (Facilities for Enforcement) Act 1920 extends,[104] or is resident in a country to which Part I of the Maintenance Orders (Reciprocal Enforcement)

---

[97] Family Law Act 1986, s. 46(2).

[98] Ibid., s. 51(4), a requirement read minimally in *Wicken* v. *Wicken* [1999] Fam. 224.

[99] Matrimonial Causes Act 1973, ss. 22, 23 (as amended).

[100] Council Reg. (EC) 1347/2000 [2000] OJ L160/19, has no application to financial provision: Recital 10.

[101] Matrimonial and Family Proceedings Act 1984, ss. 12, 15, 27.

[102] Matrimonial Causes Act 1973, s. 27 (as amended).

[103] *Forsyth* v. *Forsyth* [1948] P 125 (CA).

[104] Domestic Proceedings and Magistrates' Courts Act 1978, s. 30(3)(a).

Act 1972 extends,[105] or in accordance with Part II of the same Act.[106] English courts may vary an order if each of the parties is domiciled or resident in England.[107] English courts may make the orders against anyone over whom personal jurisdiction is conferred by the rules of Council Regulation (EC) 44/2001 or the Brussels or Lugano Convention.[108] Choice of law is, by contrast, straightforward: English courts apply English law to claims for financial provision.[109]

So far as concerns foreign orders, a foreign divorce, even if recognized in England, does not automatically terminate an English maintenance order.[110] A foreign maintenance order which is final and conclusive may be recognized and enforced in England at common law and under statute:[111] it is, after all, a judgment *in personam*. The provisions for recognition are largely reciprocal with the grounds of jurisdiction exercised by English courts; those from Member States to which Council Regulation (EC) 44/2001 applies and from contracting states to the Brussels and Lugano Conventions may be enforced under the provisions of those instruments.

CHILDREN

The law of children is principally concerned with guardianship and custody, which includes child abduction. Much has been accomplished by international convention, perhaps because the area is too delicate to be left to individual laws and national courts.

If a court is exercising jurisdiction under Council Regulation (EC) 1347/2000[112] in proceedings for divorce, legal separation, or annulment, it may also have jurisdiction over a matter of parental responsibility: the Regulation does not confer any parental responsibility jurisdiction on a court which is not exercising matrimonial jurisdiction. Nor does the Regulation make its provisions for jurisdiction in matters of parental responsibility exclusive. If the child is the child of both parents and habitually resident in the Member State whose courts are seised, that

---

[105] Maintenance Orders (Reciprocal Enforcement) Act 1972, s. 3 (as amended).
[106] Ibid., ss. 27A–28B.
[107] Matrimonial Causes Act 1973, s. 35 (as amended).
[108] Chap. 2 above.   [109] *Sealey* v. *Callan* [1953] P 135 (CA).
[110] *Macaulay* v. *Macaulay* [1991] 1 WLR 179.
[111] Maintenance Orders Act 1950, Pt. II, Maintenance Orders (Facilities for Enforcement) Act 1920, Maintenance Orders (Reciprocal Enforcement) Act 1972, Civil Jurisdiction and Judgments Act 1982, Council Reg. (EC) 44/2001 [2001] OJ L12/1.
[112] [2000] OJ L160/19.

court has jurisdiction.[113] If it is not so habitually resident, the court will still have jurisdiction if the child is habitually resident in a Member State, at least one of the spouses has parental responsibility, and the jurisdiction has been accepted by the spouses and is in the best interests of the child.[114] Jurisdiction ceases once the matrimonial proceedings have terminated in dismissal or a final decree, or on final judgment in the responsibilty proceedings. But this jurisdiction is not to conflict with Article 3 of the Hague Convention on International Child Abduction 1980.[115] For the purposes of recognition of foreign orders, Article 13 includes a judgment relating to parental responsibility within the definition of a 'judgment', and this will therefore be recognized under Chapter III of the Regulation, subject to the same minimal objections[116] as may be advanced in the case of a matrimonial decree recognized under Chapter III.

In cases falling outside the scope of the Regulation, the law lies outside the Regulation. So far as concerns orders for guardianship and custody, the English courts have jurisdiction to make an order otherwise than as regards care, education, and contact where the child is a British national or is present within the jurisdiction of the court.[117] Orders for contact, residence, or specific issues may be made in matrimonial proceedings;[118] also if the child is habitually resident in England or is present in England and not habitually resident in Scotland or Northern Ireland[119] (and on such basis, an order for care, education, or contact may also be made; this is also permitted if the child is present and the immediate exercise of the power is necessary for the protection of the child[120]). But if the matter of the proceedings has already been determined by a foreign court the English court may decline to act;[121] and if proceedings are pending in a foreign court the English court has a discretion to stay its own if it is appropriate to do so.[122] Where they have jurisdiction the courts apply English law.[123] So far as concerns foreign orders, a guardianship order made by a court of a country of which the child was a national or in which it was present will usually be recognized in England;[124] but the power of the guardian will extend no further than the powers of a foreign parent. A

---

[113] Art. 3(1).   [114] Art. 3(2).   [115] Art. 4.
[116] Plus two more: that it was given without the child having been heard in violation of fundamental principles of English procedure and that it infringes a person's parental responsibility if it was given without that person having had a right to be heard.
[117] *Re P (G.E.) (An Infant)* [1965] Ch. 568 (CA).
[118] Family Law Act 1986, ss. 1, 2 (as amended).
[119] Ibid., s. 2(2) (as amended).   [120] Ibid., s. 1(1)(d) (as amended).
[121] Ibid., s. 5 (as amended).   [122] Ibid.   [123] *J v. C* [1970] AC 668.
[124] *Re P (G.E.)(An Infant)* [1965] Ch. 568 (CA).

foreign custody order does not prevent an English court making such order as it thinks fit in relation to the welfare of the child.[125]

The private international law on child abduction is now largely derived from international convention.[126] As a matter of common law, the power to order the return of a child who has been abducted is a particular example of orders generally made in the interests of the welfare of the child.[127] But this was superseded by the Luxembourg Convention on Recognition and Enforcement of Decisions Concerning Custody of Children 1980,[128] and the Hague Convention on the Civil Aspects of Child Abduction 1980.[129] The point of departure for these instruments is that a child who has wrongfully[130] been removed, or who is being wrongfully retained, outside the jurisdiction of the court of his or her habitual residence should be restored to custody[131] in the country of its habitual residence,[132] whether or not a prior court order has been made, for this will be the place in which it is most appropriate that decisions are made. The Conventions prescribe defences to the claim for restoration, such as acquiescence in the removal, but the inclination of the English courts is to read them restrictively. By contrast, in relation to non-Convention countries, the courts will accord greater weight to their assessment of the welfare of the child, but subject to that will generally follow the principles of the Convention. But if the law of the country of habitual residence does apply the welfare principle in matters of children law, the return of the child is likely to be ordered.[133]

In relation to adoption, a court has jurisdiction to make an order if at least one of the applicants is domiciled in a part of the United Kingdom and the child is in England when the application is made;[134] and in deciding whether to make the order it will apply English law.[135] Foreign

---

[125] *McKee* v. *McKee* [1951] AC 352 (PC).   [126] Dicey & Morris, above n. 3, Rule 96.

[127] *J* v. *C* [1970] AC 668 (PC).

[128] Child Abduction and Custody Act 1985, Sch. 2.

[129] Ibid., Sch. 1.

[130] That is, in breach of custody rights attributed to a person, institution, or other body under the law of the state of habitual residence and which were actually exercised, or would have been exercised but for the removal: Art. 3 of the Hague Convention.

[131] Which may be of a person or, in appropriate cases, a court: *Re H (Child Abduction: Rights of Custody)* [2000] 2 WLR 337 (HL).

[132] *Re J (a Minor)(Abduction: Custody Rights)* [1990] 2 AC 562; *Re F (a Minor) (Abduction: Custody Rights)* [1991] Fam. 25 (CA).

[133] *D* v. *D (Child Abduction)* [1994] 1 FLR 137 (CA); *Re P (a Minor)(Abduction: Non-Convention Country)* [1997] Fam. 45 (CA); *Osman* v. *Elisha* [2000] Fam. 62 (CA).

[134] Adoption Act 1976, ss. 14, 15, 62.

[135] *Re B (S)(An Infant)* [1968] Ch. 204.

adoptions may be recognized under the Adoption Act 1976[136] or under the common law if the adopted child was domiciled in the foreign country at the time of the adoption.[137] As legitimacy and legitimation are now mercifully insignificant in English law, their place in the conflict of laws need not be examined.

[136] Adoption Act 1976, ss. 38, 72.   [137] *Re Marshall* [1957] Ch. 507 (CA).

10

Corporations and Insolvency

It has been the tradition of English private international law to yoke the treatment of corporations and the laws of insolvency, presumably as corporate insolvency generates more conflicts litigation than individual bankruptcy does. That aside, there was no other reason to treat them together: the respective rules on jurisdiction and on choice of law were unrelated. However, the new EU Regulation on bankruptcy and insolvency applies to corporate insolvency as well as to individual bankruptcy, and this provides a practical reason to adhere to tradition. We will look first at the private international law of corporations, and then at the law of insolvency.

CORPORATIONS

CORPORATIONS AND THE LAW

A corporation is an artificial creation, a legal person. The question whether, and with what powers, a body corporate has been created is determined by the law under which its creation took place, the *lex incorporationis*. Likewise, the question who is empowered to act on its behalf is a matter for the *lex incorporationis*, even though the consequences in law of an act which an officer or organ was not entitled to do may also be referred to another law.[1] The question whether an individual is liable for the acts of a corporation is also governed by the *lex incorporationis*; and, in principle, all issues having to do with the internal government and management of a corporation are for that law.[2] It is undeniable that this may offer an incentive to incorporate under a law which offers advantages to

---

[1] *Janred v. ENIT* [1989] 2 All ER 444 (CA).
[2] *Risdon Iron and Locomotive Works* v. *Furness* [1906] 1 KB 49 (CA); *Bonanza Creek Gold Mining Co.* v. *R.* [1916] 1 AC 566 (PC); *Lazard Bros.* v. *Midland Bank* [1933] AC 289; *National Bank of Greece and Athens SA* v. *Metliss* [1958] AC 509; *Carl Zeiss Stiftung* v. *Rayner & Keeler Ltd. (No 2)* [1967] 1 AC 853; *J. H. Rayner (Mincing Lane) Ltd.* v. *Department of Trade and Industry* [1990] 2 AC 418.

those who may wish to create a corporation with wide powers but restricted liabilities, or with no significant risk of allowing liability to affect individual officers or corporators. This is, though, little more than a consequence of the doctrine of corporate personality. Though it is sometimes suggested that the place of incorporation should not be decisive, and that the law of the place of management and control should assume a more prominent role;[3] or that the doctrine of separate corporate personality really needs to be countered by an analysis based on the economic realities of life and the need to assert effective control over multi-national enterprises,[4] these arguments have tended to be directed at jurisdiction over companies rather than at the hegemony of the *lex incorporationis* as the determinant of legal personality and power.

Recognition and dissolution of foreign corporations

English law recognizes the creation of corporations, and the conferment of legal personality upon them, under the *lex incorporationis*.[5] The recognition of corporations has been extended to those which are created under the ordinances of a non-state, such as Taiwan, or the *soi-disant* 'Turkish Republic of Northern Cyprus'.[6] Moreover, although English law does not recognize the legal personality of an international organization in the absence of domestic legislation to confer such status, where a foreign law has conferred such personality under its law, the resultant legal person will be recognized in England.[7] So the Arab Monetary Fund, an international organization of states of which the United Kingdom is not a member, had been given legal personality under the law of the United Arab Emirates, and was accordingly recognized as a person under English law. What would have happened if it had been given personality under the laws of more states than one raises questions to which no easy answers exist.

But what the law creates the same law can also destroy, so the question whether a corporation has been dissolved is likewise one for the *lex incorporationis*[8] alone. The validity of a dissolution may raise difficult

---

[3] J. Drury, 'The Regulation and Recognition of Foreign Corporations: Response to the "Delaware Syndrome"' [1998] *CLJ* 165.

[4] P. Muchlinski, 'Corporations in International Litigation: Problems of Jurisdiction and the United Kingdom Asbestos Cases' (2001) 50 *ICLQ* 1.

[5] See the cases cited in n. 2 above.

[6] Foreign Corporations Act 1991, s. 1.

[7] *Arab Monetary Fund v. Hashim (No 3)* [1991] 2 AC 114; *Westland Helicopters Ltd. v. Arab Organisation for Industrialisation* [1995] QB 282.

[8] *Lazard Bros. v. Midland Bank* [1933] AC 289; *Russian and English Bank v. Baring Bros.* [1932] 1 Ch. 435 (and if there is a branch in England it cannot sue after the corporation has been dissolved; it should be wound up).

questions when the law under which the corporation was created ceases to exist and in its geographical place a new law arises. But corporations created under the law of Russia were recognized as being dissolved under the law of the Soviet Union, and, later the same century, *vice versa*.[9] A combination of the rules for creation and dissolution means that the amalgamation of corporations, the recognition of the new corporation, and whether it assumes the rights and liabilities of the dissolved corporation(s), are in principle all questions for the *lex incorporationis*,[10] though the issue whether this process discharges liabilities incurred by the old corporation is a distinct and contractual one, governed by the law applicable to those obligations.[11] A court will endeavour to give effect to a case of corporate succession, and will do what it can to ensure that it is effective in English private international law.[12] But corporate reconstruction can be untidy, and a court may reach the view in a particular case that the process is not a true succession or amalgamation notwithstanding the language used by the foreign legislator.[13]

Domicile of corporations

As a matter of common law, a corporation is domiciled at the place of its incorporation.[14] This, for example, means that its capacities[15] are governed by its *lex incorporationis*, and the general principle that legal capacity is governed by the law of the domicile is preserved. In other contexts, however, a statutory domicile may be conferred. In the context of jurisdiction under Council Regulation (EC) 44/2001, a corporation is domiciled where it has its statutory seat or has its central administration or has its principal place of business.[16] It is obvious that this cannot be

---

[9] *The Kommunar (No 2)* [1997] 1 Lloyd's Rep. 8.

[10] *National Bank of Greece and Athens SA* v. *Metliss* [1958] AC 509; if the two corporations are incorporated in different countries it is probable that the *lex incorporationis* of each must recognize the amalgamation. See also *Adams* v. *National Bank of Greece and Athens SA* [1961] AC 255 for cases where there may not be a true and complete succession to the rights and liabilities of the former companies.

[11] *Adams* v. *National Bank of Greece and Athens SA* [1961] AC 255.

[12] *Toprak Enerji Sanayi SA* v. *Sale Tilney Technology plc* [1994] 1 WLR 840; *Eurosteel* v. *Stinnes* [2000] 1 All ER (Comm.) 964; *Astra SA Insurance and Reinsurance Co.* v. *Sphere Drake Insurance Ltd.* [2000] 2 Lloyd's Rep. 550.

[13] *The Kommunar (No 2)* [1997] 1 Lloyd's Rep. 8.

[14] *Gasque* v. *Inland Revenue Commissioners* [1940] KB 80.

[15] To some extent this will also determine its liability to pay taxes.

[16] See Art. 60. For the purposes of the UK, 'statutory seat' means the registered office or, where there is no such office anywhere, the place of incorporation or, where there is no such place anywhere, the place under the law of which the formation took place: Art. 60(2). The Regulation is at [2001] OJ L12/1.

seen as 'the' domicile which determines corporate capacity, for a corporation may, under this slightly inelegant provision, have three domiciles for jurisdictional purposes.

Jurisdiction over corporations

Just as with individual defendants, a corporation can be sued in England when process can be served on it. In one respect, service on a corporation is more complex than service on individual defendants, for there can be no personal service on an artificial person. But the changes to the methods of service ushered in by the Civil Procedure Rules have simplified matters considerably. It is now necessary to distinguish service pursuant to statute from service under the Civil Procedure Rules, but once this is done and the differences noted, it may be that there will rarely be a need to rely on the statute to effect service on a company.[17]

Statutory service on a company distinguishes between companies registered in England under the Companies Acts and unregistered companies. English companies may be served at their registered offices,[18] though if in liquidation service is effected on the liquidator and only with the permission of the court.[19] If the company is not incorporated in Great Britain it is an unregistered company; but it is also an 'oversea company' if it establishes a place of business within the jurisdiction.[20] Establishment of such a place of business imposes an obligation upon the oversea company to file certain particulars with the Registrar of Companies, which include provisions for the service of process. In fact, two parallel systems regulate statutory service on overseas companies. A limited company incorporated outside the United Kingdom or Gibraltar with a branch[21] in Great Britain must deliver to the Registrar the names of those authorized to accept service in respect of the business of the branch: this means that the business of the branch must be part of, but need not be substantially all of, the subject of the claim.[22] If these particulars are not supplied or those nominated refuse to accept service, service may be effected at any place of business established by the company in Great Britain.[23]

---

[17] *Sea Assets Ltd.* v. *PT Garuda International* [2000] 4 All ER 371.

[18] Companies Act 1985, s. 725. In addition, personal service may be made by leaving process with a person holding a senior position: CPR 6.4(4).

[19] Insolvency Act 1986, s. 130(2). If in administration, not without the consent of the administrators or the leave of the court: ibid., s. 11(3)(d).

[20] Companies Act 1985, s. 744.   [21] Ibid., s. 690A.

[22] Ibid., s. 694A; *Saab* v. *Saudi American Bank* [1999] 1 WLR 1861 (CA).

[23] Companies Act 1985, s. 694A(3).

Companies having a place of business but not such a branch[24] may be served by service on the individuals whose names were provided to the Registrar, but if this is not possible, process may be served at any place of business established within the jurisdiction.[25] In this context a place of business connotes somewhere fixed and definite and from which the business of the company is carried on. A general guide to whether the company carries on business at such a place is to ask whether it can make contracts there. If there is such a place of business, jurisdictional competence is not limited to the activities of the place of business.[26] But if there is no place of business there is no basis for service within the jurisdiction under the Companies Acts[27] in the absence of an agreement to accept service or otherwise submit. Where the company is domiciled in a Member State for the purposes of Council Regulation (EC) 44/2001, or in a contracting state to the Brussels or Lugano Convention, Article 22(2) gives exclusive jurisdiction to the courts of the seat of the corporation in proceedings having as their object the validity of the constitution, the nullity or dissolution of companies or decisions of their organs.[28]

As indicated above, in addition to statutory service under the Companies Acts, a company, including an overseas company,[29] may be served in accordance with Part 6 of the Civil Procedure Rules, at any place within the jurisdiction where it carries on its activities, or at any place of business within the jurisdiction. Service is effected by leaving the document with a person holding a senior position[30] within the company. In practice this will avoid some of the interpretive difficulties which arise under the statutory scheme, and will not require it to be shown that the claim arises, in any degree, out of the local activity of the company.[31]

Contracts made by corporations

The principal issue when dealing with contracts made by corporations is one of capacity: of the corporation to make the contract at all and of the

---

[24] Ibid., s. 691.   [25] Ibid., s. 695.

[26] *Okura & Co. Ltd.* v. *Forsbacka Jernverks AB* [1914] 1 KB 715; cf *Adams* v. *Cape Industries plc* [1990] Ch. 433 (CA).

[27] *The Theodohos* [1977] 2 Lloyd's Rep. 428.

[28] [2001] OJ L12/1 and Chap. 2 above. The seat is, for this purpose, defined by national law and not Art. 60.

[29] Service under CPR Pt. 6 is permitted on overseas companies as an alternative to statutory service: CPR 6.2(2).

[30] CPR r. 6.4(4); for the definition of 'senior position', see the Practice Direction—Service, para. 6.2(2).

[31] *Saab* v. *Saudi American Bank* [1999] 1 WLR 1861 (CA); *Sea Assets Ltd.* v. *P. T. Garuda International* [2000] 4 All ER 371.

organ or officer to bind it. As the private international law of agency is apparently incapable of reform by convention, the questions are mainly dealt with under common law choice of law rules. If the corporation had capacity under the *lex incorporationis* and the *lex contractus* to enter into the contract, no problems arise. But where it is alleged that it did not, the contract will be *ultra vires* the corporation. Even so, it may in a proper case be estopped by its own conduct from relying on its own incapacity,[32] though it is unclear whether the applicable estoppel principles will be those of the *lex fori* or of the *lex contractus*.[33] Where the corporation had capacity to enter the contract, but the person purporting to act on its behalf did not have authority to so act, the question whether the contract made between the agent and the third party binds or may be relied on by the company is a difficult one, though it may well be a matter for the *lex contractus* of that contract which was created.[34] The case law is difficult. It seems right that where an agent acts on behalf of a principal, a third party is generally entitled to assume that the agent has such power and authority as he would have under the law which governs the contract which they make. It is true that where the agent is the representative of a company, a third party will or should be aware that the *lex incorporationis* may place limits upon the extent to which a company can be bound, but this deemed awareness applies more obviously to the legal capacities of the company than to the powers which it has chosen to vest in a particular officer. It follows that there is no reason to make a special rule for contracts made by corporate agents who acted outside their authority: the extent to which the company is bound and entitled should be a matter for the law of the contract made between the agent and the third party. If a corporation has been dissolved and amalgamated with, or to create, another, the question whether dissolution terminates the contract as a source of obligation is a matter for the *lex contractus*. So although the amalgamation may provide for the vesting of all liabilities in the new corporation, it cannot discharge those liabilities, then or later, unless it is also the law applicable to them.[35]

---

[32] *Janred v. ENIT* [1989] 2 All ER 444 (CA).

[33] If there would be estoppel under the one but not the other, there is a conflict of laws; principle suggests that the *lex fori* should defer to the *lex contractus*.

[34] *Chatenay v. Brazilian Submarine Telegraph Co.* [1891] 1 QB 279; *Maspons v. Mildred* (1882) 9 QBD 530 (CA); *Ruby SS Corporation v. Commercial Union Assurance Co. Ltd.* (1933) 150 LT 38 (CA).

[35] *Adams v. National Bank of Greece and Athens SA* [1961] AC 255.

WINDING UP OF COMPANIES

It is necessary to distinguish between solvent and insolvent companies when dealing with winding up.[36]

Solvent companies

English courts may wind up a company registered in England.[37] But a solvent company may not be wound up if it has a seat only in a Member State bound by Council Regulation (EC) 44/2001 or in a contracting state to the Brussels or Lugano Convention.[38]

Insolvent companies

The law on the winding up of insolvent companies has been made more complex as a result of Council Regulation (EC) 1346/2000 on insolvency proceedings,[39] which is in force from 31 May 2002. As a result, it is necessary to look at the old and the new law, not least because the new law is not exclusive in its scope.

The Regulation will not apply to proceedings which predate its entry into force, or to cases in which the matter is excluded from its scope. Where that is the case, the law allows an English court to wind up a company registered in England.[40] Less expected, perhaps, is the fact that the court may wind up an unregistered company so long as it has a sufficient connection with the jurisdiction, it is insolvent, and it is not otherwise inappropriate to make the order.[41] A 'sufficient connection' will exist if there are persons in England who could benefit from a winding-up order and there is enough connection with England to justify making the order.[42] Most unexpected of all is that an insolvent company which has been dissolved under its *lex incorporationis* may be revived for the purpose of being wound up.[43] As Parliament can make any provision it cares to, this is not an impossible surprise. But it represents a small

[36] See I. Fletcher, *Insolvency in Private International Law* (OUP, Oxford, 1999).
[37] Insolvency Act 1986, s. 117.
[38] Art 22(2) of the Council Reg. [2001] OJ L12/1; Art. 16(2) of the Brussels and Lugano Conventions.
[39] [2000] OJ L160/1.
[40] Insolvency Act 1986, s. 117.
[41] Ibid., ss. 220, 221; *Re A Company (No 00359 of 1987)* [1988] Ch. 210; *Re Paramount Airways Ltd.* [1993] Ch. 223 (CA).
[42] *Re A Company (No 00359 of 1987)* [1988] Ch. 210; *Re A Company (No 003102 of 1991), ex p. Nyckeln Finance Co. Ltd.* [1991] BCLC 539; *Stocznia Gdanska SA v. Latreefers Inc., The Times, 15 March 2000.*
[43] Insolvency Act 1986, s. 225.

victory for pragmatism over the principle that dissolution is the exclusive concern of the *lex incorporationis*. Upon making the order, the assets of the company subject to the order are bound by a trust for the benefit of those interested in the winding-up. The liquidator is under an obligation to get in all the assets to which the company appears to be entitled, and is obliged to use them to discharge English and foreign liabilities. If there is also a foreign liquidation he is obliged to seek to secure equal treatment for all claimants, not just for English creditors.[44] Many provisions of the Insolvency Act 1986 dealing with orders which may be made in the course of liquidation are unhelpfully silent about what their international scope is intended to be, but they will probably be interpreted as requiring a sufficient connection with England,[45] which is not much more helpful.

So far as concerns a foreign winding-up, a liquidator appointed under the *lex incorporationis* is recognized by English private international law,[46] but there appears to be no authority on the recognition of a liquidator appointed under the law of a third country. The courts of the United Kingdom have a statutory obligation to assist each other in a winding-up;[47] in relation to countries outside the United Kingdom the Secretary of State may designate states whose courts (but not liquidators acting on their own authority[48]) may request co-operation from an English court;[49] the court will assist unless there is some good reason for not doing so.[50]

By contrast, in insolvencies to which Council Regulation (EC) 1346/2000 applies, this instrument prescribes the jurisdiction of the courts of Member States[51] in relation to the opening of insolvency proceedings; the choice of law for the insolvency proceedings; and the recognition of judgments from other Member States ordering the opening, conduct, and closure of such proceedings. Its purpose is to bring order to an area which was excluded from the jurisdictional scheme of the Brussels Convention, and in which the co-ordination of the judicial function has been particularly problematic. In a similar development, the UNCITRAL has produced a model law on cross-border insolvency, and the Insolvency

---

[44] *Re Bank of Credit and Commerce International SA* [1992] BCLC 570.

[45] *Re Paramount Airways Ltd.* [1993] Ch. 223 (CA); cf *Re Seagull Manufacturing Co. Ltd. (No 2)* [1994] Ch. 91 (notice under the Company Directors Disqualification Act 1986).

[46] *Bank of Ethiopia* v. *National Bank of Egypt and Ligouri* [1937] Ch. 513.

[47] Insolvency Act 1986, s. 426(4).

[48] *Re Bank of Credit and Commerce International SA (No 9)* [1994] 3 All ER 764.

[49] Insolvency Act 1986, s. 426(4), (11); Co-operation of Insolvency Courts (Designation of Relevant Countries and Territories) Order 1986, SI 1986/2123.

[50] *Hughes* v. *Hannover Ruckversicherungs AG* [1997] 1 BCLC 497 (CA).

[51] The members of the European Union excluding Denmark: [2000] OJ L160/1, Recital 33.

Act 2000[52] permits the Secretary of State to make regulations[53] for the purpose of implementing this model law in English law.

The material scope of the Regulation is that it applies to collective insolvency proceedings which involve the complete or partial divestment of a debtor and the appointment of a liquidator,[54] whether the debtor is an individual or a corporate body. Its personal scope extends to debtors wherever domiciled, but it is restricted to cases in which 'the centre of a debtor's main interests' is located in a Member State. It excludes insurance undertakings and credit institutions.[55]

The overall aim is, within the community of Member States, to give the lead role to a single court, and to relegate to a subordinate role proceedings in all other courts. Accordingly, 'main proceedings' may be opened only in the Member State in which the centre of a debtor's main interests is situated.[56] 'Secondary' or 'territorial' proceedings may be opened in any Member State in which the debtor has an 'establishment;'[57] though their effect is confined to assets situated[58] in the Member State in which the secondary or territorial proceedings are opened; they may be opened before main proceedings are.[59] The law which is generally applicable to insolvency proceedings and their effects is the *lex fori*,[60] which governs most issues,[61] but exceptions are made for a list of other matters for which this would not be the appropriate choice of law.[62] An order from a court in a Member State opening insolvency proceedings must be recognized, from the time it becomes effective, in all other Member States, and be given the same effect as it has in the state of origin.[63] Judgments relating to the conduct and closure of insolvency proceedings will be recognized in all other Member States,[64] and their enforcement is to take place under the Regulation on jurisdiction and judgments in civil and commercial matters.[65] A liquidator appointed in the main proceedings will be recognized in all other Member States,[66] and he will be accorded

---

[52] S. 14(1). [53] None has yet been made.
[54] Including a trustee or an administrative receiver appointed under a floating charge: Art. 1(1).
[55] Art. 1(2).
[56] In the case of a company, this is rebuttably presumed to be the place of the registered office.
[57] Any place of operations where the debtor carries out a non-transitory economic activity with human means and goods.
[58] Defined in Art. 2(g).
[59] They are then known as territorial proceedings.
[60] Art. 4. [61] Art. 4. [62] Arts. 5–15.
[63] Arts. 10 and 17. [64] Art. 25. [65] [2001] OJ L160/1.
[66] Art. 18(1).

the powers which he has under the law of the state of his appointment. If there are secondary proceedings in another Member State, his powers are limited in relation to those assets; but the various liquidators are under an obligation to share information and to co-operate with each other.[67]

BANKRUPTCY

COUNCIL REGULATION (EC) 1346/2000

The Regulation applies its regime of jurisdiction, choice of law, and recognition and enforcement of judgments to bankruptcy as well as to corporate insolvencies. Accordingly, the summary of its provisions given above is equally applicable to bankruptcies, and for this reason those provisions are not repeated here. The account which follows is therefore of the law as it applies to bankruptcies to which the Regulation does not apply,[68] which principally means cases where the centre of the debtor's main interests is outside the territory of the Member States or cases which predate the coming into force of the Regulation.

JURISDICTION

The English courts have jurisdiction to declare bankrupt any debtor who is domiciled or present in England on the day of presentation of the petition.[69] They also have jurisdiction if he was ordinarily resident, or had a place of residence, or carried on business (or was a member of a partnership firm which carried on business) in England at any time within the three years prior to the presentation of the petition.[70] A debtor who has subjected himself to a voluntary arrangement submits to the jurisdiction by doing so.[71] In deciding whether to exercise their discretion to make the order the courts will consider the location of assets, any foreign bankruptcy, and other issues of general convenience.[72] The bankrupt may be examined by order of the court, but the private examination of any other person is probably limited to those who are present within the jurisdiction to be served with the summons requesting their attendance.[73]

---

[67] Art. 31. [68] See Fletcher, above n. 36. [69] Insolvency Act 1986, s. 265.
[70] Ibid. [71] Ibid., s. 264.
[72] *Re Behrends* (1865) 12 LT 149; *Re Robinson, ex p. Robinson* (1883) 22 Ch. D 816 (CA).
[73] Cf *Re Seagull Manufacturing Co. Ltd.* [1993] Ch. 345 (CA).

CHOICE OF LAW

An English court applies English law to the bankruptcy.[74] The making of the order operates as a statutory assignment of all the debtor's property, wherever situated, to his trustee;[75] the bankrupt may be ordered to assist the trustee in recovering property outside the control of the court. A creditor subject to the personal jurisdiction of the court may be restrained from taking proceedings overseas, in order to safeguard the principle of equal division.[76] Foreign debts must be shown to be good by the law under which they arise, but the court will use its own rules to secure, as best it may, equality between creditors of the same class.[77] The power of the court to set aside an antecedent transaction is not subject to express limitation, but the defendant against whom reversal of the transaction is sought must be (or by service out with leave of the court, be made) subject to the jurisdiction of the court, and the test is whether it is just and convenient in all the circumstances of the case to make the order.[78]

DISCHARGE

An English discharge operates in relation to all the debts provable in the bankruptcy, irrespective of the law which governed the debt,[79] and a discharge under the law which governed the debt will be effective in England.[80]

FOREIGN BANKRUPTCIES

A foreign bankruptcy will be recognized if the debtor was domiciled[81] in or submitted[82] to the jurisdiction of the court; and the bankruptcy will vest English moveables (but not land) in the assignee if this is the effect it has under the foreign law.[83] The result may be that the debtor no longer has property in England, and this will tell strongly against making an English order. A discharge from a foreign bankruptcy is effective in

---

[74] *Re Kloebe* (1884) 28 Ch. D 175; *Re Doetsch* [1896] 2 Ch. 836.
[75] Insolvency Act 1986, ss. 283, 306, 436.
[76] *Barclays Bank plc* v. *Homan* [1993] BCLC 680 (CA).
[77] *Re Scheibler* (1874) 9 Ch. App. 722.
[78] *Re Paramount Airways Ltd.* [1993] Ch. 223 (CA).
[79] Insolvency Act 1986, s. 281.
[80] *Gibbs and Sons* v. *Soc. Industrielle et Commerciale des Métaux* (1890) 25 QBD 399 (CA).
[81] *Re Hayward* [1897] 1 Ch. 905.
[82] *Re Anderson* [1911] 1 KB 896.
[83] *Re Craig* (1916) 86 LJ Ch. 62.

England only if it is effective under the law which governed the debt.[84] A court may not question the bankruptcy jurisdiction of a Scottish or Northern Irish court; and the effect of such an order extends to all property in England, not excluding land.[85]

---

[84] *Gibbs and Sons v. Soc. Industrielle et Commerciale des Métaux* (1890) 25 QBD 399 (CA).
[85] Insolvency Act 1986, s. 426.

Index

connecting factor, as 22
corporation, of 60–1, 247
Council Regulation 44/2001, provisions
of 60–1
dependency, of 26
lex domicilii 22
non-country, in 23
origin, of 24
reform of law, proposals for 26
resident, presence as 25
statutory definition 26
territory with changed boundaries, in 23
trust, of 61

Employment contract
choice of law, modification of 165
Council Regulation 44/2001 66–8,
121
Equitable obligations
basis of 191
choice of law
anti-suit injunctions 202
assimilationist approach 200–1
characterization categories 201
conclusion 203
foreign law, role of 202
forum-centric approach 201–3
lex delicti 200
English causes of action 200–1
jurisdiction 203–4
lex fori, applicable as part of 201
tort, analogous to 200
Equity
conflict of laws, within 192, 199
fraud, enforcement of acts against 201–2
good faith, standards of 201–2
obligations *see* **Equitable obligations**
remedies 192, 200
European Free Trade Area
Lugano Convention 52–3
European law
harmonization 2
Evidence
admissibility as procedural issue 34
foreign tax authority, taking for 42
Exemption clauses
English law, application of 4
Extradition
liability for crime, enforcement of 43

Family law
children, concerning *see* **Children**
lex domicili, pre-eminence of 223

marriage *see* **Marriage**
matrimonial causes *see* **Matrimonial
causes**
Foreign law
applicability, pleading 4
application, meaning 7–8
content and effect, determining 5
default of proof of content 6
English judge, application by 3–8
expert evidence of 5–7
expert, question for 18
report on 7
same as English law, taken to be 6
Forum (non) conveniens
Council Regulation 44/2001, provisions
of 85–8
English development of 94–5
foreign court, effect of contract to sue in
97–9
issues of 86
litigation about place of litigation,
leading to 95
natural forum, proof of 96
stay of proceedings
application for 94–9
on grounds of 87–8
test of 95–6
unjust to order stay, effect of 96–7
Fraud
contract procured by 171–2
enforcement of acts against 201–2
judgment procured by, refusal of
recognition 139–42
Freight
Council Regulation 44/2001,
jurisdiction under 78

Gifts
contractual obligations 154

Human rights
provisions, effect on public policy
44

Injunction
anti-suit
contractual right not to be sued in
foreign court, based on 110
Council Regulation 44/2001, impact
of 88–9, 111
discretion to grant 108–11
England as natural forum, where
108–9

judgment contrary to, refusal of
    recognition 142
marriage laws repugnant to 45–6
marriage, in relation to 231
overriding effect, statutes with 46–7
recognition of judgment contrary to 123
restraint of trade, as to 45
sufficient connection to England,
    requirement of 45–6
third countries, of 47

Recognition and enforcement of
    foreign judgments
Brussels Convention, under 117
categories of 114
common law, at
    enforcement 144–5
    recognition 132–44 *see also*
        recognition at common law *below*
    rules of 131–2
    scheme of 132
Council Regulation 44/2001, under *see*
    Council Regulation 44/2001
Denmark, from 131
effects derived from judgment, and 115
enforcement
    application for 128
    colonial and Commonwealth
        territories 146
    common law, at 144–5
    Foreign Judgments (Reciprocal
        Enforcement) Act, under 146
    proceedings for 115–16
    registration for 129
    statutory registration, by 145–6
Gibraltar, from 131
Iceland, from 131
Northern Ireland, from 131
Norway, from 131
partial success, effect of 116
Poland, from 131
recognition
    common law, at 132–44 *see also*
        recognition at common law *below*
    primary concern, as 116
    purposes of 115
recognition at common law
    appearance to contest jurisdiction
        134–5
    arbitration agreement, effect of
        violation 139
    choice of court agreement, effect of
        violation 139

corporate defendant, presence of 137–8
default judgments 133
defences to 138–43
    effect of 143
    enforcement action, paving way for
        143
    final and conclusive judgment, of 132–3
    forum non coveniens, foreign court
        being 137
    fraud, effect of 139–42
    interlocutory matters 133
    international jurisdiction 133–8
    issue estoppel, effect of 135
    local jurisdiction, effect of absence of
        139
    natural or substantial justice, want of
        142
    presence or residence within
        jurisdiction, defendant with 136–8
    public policy, offending against 142
    res judicata in England, effect of 142
    submission to jurisdiction 134–6
requirement of 114
res judicata 115
Scotland, from 131
Switzerland, from 131
Renvoi
aim of 16–17
application of 18
arguments in favour of 16–17
criticism of 15
expert, interpretation of law by 18
foreign court theory 15
foreign legal system, rules of 16
hostility to 18
personal status, application to area of 20
principle, operation of 14
subordination of English choice of law
    rules to foreign 16–17
title to property, application to 20
Residence
domicile of choice, establishing 25
habitual 26–7
more than one place, in 27
Restitution
reform of rules 31
service of process outside the
    jurisdiction, order for 104
Restitutionary claims
choice of law
    characterization for 193
    contribution claims 198–9
    place of enrichment, of 195–6